Worship Celebrations for Youth

John Brown

D1403959

Judson Press ® Valley Forge

WORSHIP CELEBRATIONS FOR YOUTH

Copyright © 1980
Judson Press, Valley Forge, PA 19481

Library of Congress Cataloging in Publication Data

Brown, John, 1934—
    Worship celebrations for youth.

    Includes bibliographical references.
    1. Worship programs.   I. Title.
BV29.B74   264   79-20738
ISBN 0-8170-0866-7

The name JUDSON PRESS is registered as a trademark
in the U.S. Patent Office.
Printed in the U.S.A. ⊕

Contents

Celebrating with This Book

The modern-day church has rediscovered worship as a celebration, although the Mass, the main worship service of Christianity for centuries, has traditionally been spoken of as a celebration. Worship is an occasion to rejoice, to be glad, to give thanks for what God is doing for us through Christ. Think of the meanings of some of the expressions of our faith. The gospel means Good News! Blessed means happy, joyous! And worship should be as joyful as a birthday party or a wedding reception! We celebrate the Good News that Christ has come to free us from the bondage of sin and give us the assurance that we are God's children. Why settle for crumbs from his table when he has prepared a feast in our honor? He told us to call God our Father! Shout for joy and celebrate!

Throughout this book, worship is referred to as a celebration. Even in the times when we think deep and probing thoughts, the concepts of God the Father and Christ our Redeemer should make us feel merry in spite of ourselves.

These experiences of devotion and worship are organized in such a way as to make them highly usable for every youth group and in a variety of settings. Your group may be small. This gives all the more opportunity for group members to take more active part and leadership. You may have a larger group. The material can be divided up among more people.

This material is not intended to be used as is. The various parts within each service should be adapted to meet the needs of your own group and locality. There is nothing more deadly in youth worship than for people to read "canned" parts without expression and meaning. Add to each service your own thoughts and creativity. Say things in your own words. Do your thing! The "bottom line" is: Don't use it as it is; just tell it like it is.

Be selective in the use of this material. Combine parts and portions from various chapters to suit your own themes, needs, and occasions. Add your own material, edit, write in, cut out, fill in, make the material your own.

Some chapters are geared to holiday themes, but within these chapters you will find material suitable to other themes. Some chapters are organized according to themes. Also use parts from these chapters as holiday worship resources.

There is variety in this material. Some of it can be thought of as quite traditional. Other parts may be too far-out for your group. Try, experiment, adjust, modify, create.

For the supplemental material, duplicate tear-out pages are provided so that each participant can have his or her own copy from which to read.

Scripture readings are a vital part of each chapter. We suggest that you use the *Good News Bible,* since the book was written with this version in mind. However, use a version with which you are comfortable.

Along with a Bible, you have all the resources you need. This book can be taken to camps and conferences, hiking and camping. It also is very usable in churches, individual homes, and any other place your group meets.

Let's celebrate!

For Everything There Is a Season

A Celebration for the New Year

This experience of worship is planned with a New Year theme in mind, but with very slight modification it can be used for any occasion when the theme is "renewal." It will stimulate personal and individual thinking to consider past experiences, both negative and positive, as they influence our futures. The experience also provides for renewal and rededication.

Preparation

It is usually more effective in group worship to have the group seated in a circle because a greater sense of individual participation is created. When we sit, row on row, facing "front," we sometimes think of ourselves as spectators rather than participants. As a focal point, in the center place a calendar from the year just ending and one for the new year. Also have a notebook in prominence opened to clean, empty pages.

Throughout the worship experience, play records of the popular songs of the past year. Also have someone read aloud the headings and first paragraphs of selected news articles from this past year's newspapers. You may be able to locate only the very recent issues, but these will serve the purpose. The music and reading will help to set a mood and stimulate our memories of the past year. These things are to be done softly, barely audibly, so as not to detract greatly from the rest of the content.

The Experience

Song: "Turn! Turn! Turn!" ("To Everything There Is a Season.") The words and music are by Pete Seeger and are an adaptation from Ecclesiastes 3:1-8. Someone in the group may be able to play and sing this song accompanied by piano or guitar. The song has been recorded by various groups, but one place it can be found is on Columbia Records, Stereo 9416, "Pete Seeger's Greatest Hits." An alternative to using this Scripture set to music is to read the passage from Ecclesiastes from a modern translation of the Bible.

Reading: See Supplement A. To be delivered slowly, allowing time for personal thought.

Feelings: Individual reflections on the successes and failures of the past (Supplement A).

Thoughts: A meditation (Supplement A).

Scripture: Matthew 6:25-34.

A Song: "Sweet Surrender." This song by John Denver complements the passage from Matthew. The group may know it or at least the refrain. It would be more effective to have it sung by a person from the group, joined by the entire group. It can be found on RCA CPL 2-0764 Stereo, "An Evening with John Denver," and on other recordings (Supplement A). (Or use a hymn which is familiar to your group.)

Reflection: Guided prayer (Supplement A).

A Celebration: A time of personal interaction (Supplement A).

For Everything There Is a Season

Reading

When I look ahead to a new year, I think
It's like flashing down a white hill on a sled
    or skis.
I'm the first to take the plunge,
    to brave the steep, to mark the slope.
No one has ever been on that snow before.
It's white and clear, without trail marks.
I have only my past experiences and skills to
    guide me.
They are not all good, nor all bad,
    but they help me know the way.
I have learned from the unpleasant things,
    while the pleasant events in life give me
    courage and confidence.
It's like starting a brand new chapter in my
    life.

Feelings

Ask people in the group to think for a few minutes, silently, about what comes to their minds as the most difficult time or experience of their lives. These could range from the loss of a loved one to some difficulty or trouble at school or elsewhere. Then ask them to think of the best time in their lives—what gave them the happiest, most fulfilling feelings.

Now ask the participants to share their thoughts with the group. Request that they concentrate on how they felt inside during each experience and how they feel now as they look back in retrospect. Take as long as necessary for this portion of the group experience. There may be pauses and perhaps a long wait at the beginning until someone feels like sharing his or her thoughts.

Thoughts: (A meditation)

Who we've been helps shape who we will become. Where we've been influences where we're going. Our past hopes and dreams are the inspiration for future accomplishments. Everyone we know helps to mold our thoughts and actions. Even our unhappy experiences teach us something which influences our futures. The happy times give us confidence that life has its positive, good side.

For everything there is a season. Not only do we have "up" and "down" days, but there is a kind of life-long principle of biorhythms. Inevitably we will face times of failure, sorrow, embarrassment, disappointment, frustration, futility. But life's lessons teach us that sooner or later these times will pass, and we will walk in the warmth of sunlight once again.

When everything is going really right, enjoy it fully, knowing that darker days are bound to come our way. No one is exempt. But trust in life and in the Father's good care, for he cares for us.

A Song

"Sweet Surrender"—this song, written by John Denver, seems to parallel Matthew 6 to such an extent that one wonders if this Scripture passage, in fact, inspired its writing. The words speak of surrender to life, which, if rightly understood, is practically the same as surrendering to God, the author and giver of life.

Reflection

This is a time of reflection and prayer. (Pause for about a minute after each question.)

How do the memories of our personal successes and our failures serve to help us in the future? Think about it. Pray about it. (*Pause*)

What were our greatest moments of defeat and victory during the past twelve months? (*Pause*)

What are our hopes and goals for this coming year? (*Pause*)

What hymn lyrics or Scripture verses come easily to our minds as we look ahead? (*Pause*)

What concerns, burdens, or worries do we carry? (*Pause*)

What areas of our lives are we determined to improve in the months to come? (*Pause*)

Are we willing to entrust all these things to the Father, knowing that he really cares? (*Pause*)

A Celebration

Close the experience by giving instructions similar to these: "Each of you should find one other person in the group and tell that person how much you appreciate him or her. Then share with that person something of your own concerns or hopes for the year ahead."

SUPPLEMENT A

For Everything There Is a Season

Reading

When I look ahead to a new year, I think
It's like flashing down a white hill on a sled
    or skis.
I'm the first to take the plunge,
    to brave the steep, to mark the slope.
No one has ever been on that snow before.
It's white and clear, without trail marks.
I have only my past experiences and skills to
    guide me.
They are not all good, nor all bad,
    but they help me know the way.
I have learned from the unpleasant things,
    while the pleasant events in life give me
    courage and confidence.
It's like starting a brand new chapter in my
    life.

Feelings

Ask people in the group to think for a few minutes, silently, about what comes to their minds as the most difficult time or experience of their lives. These could range from the loss of a loved one to some difficulty or trouble at school or elsewhere. Then ask them to think of the best time in their lives—what gave them the happiest, most fulfilling feelings.

Now ask the participants to share their thoughts with the group. Request that they concentrate on how they felt inside during each experience and how they feel now as they look back in retrospect. Take as long as necessary for this portion of the group experience. There may be pauses and perhaps a long wait at the beginning until someone feels like sharing his or her thoughts.

Thoughts: (A meditation)

Who we've been helps shape who we will become. Where we've been influences where we're going. Our past hopes and dreams are the inspiration for future accomplishments. Everyone we know helps to mold our thoughts and actions. Even our unhappy experiences teach us something which influences our futures. The happy times give us confidence that life has its positive, good side.

For everything there is a season. Not only do we have "up" and "down" days, but there is a kind of life-long principle of biorhythms. Inevitably we will face times of failure, sorrow, embarrassment, disappointment, frustration, futility. But life's lessons teach us that sooner or later these times will pass, and we will walk in the warmth of sunlight once again.

When everything is going really right, enjoy it fully, knowing that darker days are bound to come our way. No one is exempt. But trust in life and in the Father's good care, for he cares for us.

A Song

"Sweet Surrender"—this song, written by John Denver, seems to parallel Matthew 6 to such an extent that one wonders if this Scripture passage, in fact, inspired its writing. The words speak of surrender to life, which, if rightly understood, is practically the same as surrendering to God, the author and giver of life.

Reflection

This is a time of reflection and prayer. (Pause for about a minute after each question.)

How do the memories of our personal successes and our failures serve to help us in the future? Think about it. Pray about it. (*Pause*)

What were our greatest moments of defeat and victory during the past twelve months? (*Pause*)

What are our hopes and goals for this coming year? (*Pause*)

What hymn lyrics or Scripture verses come easily to our minds as we look ahead? (*Pause*)

What concerns, burdens, or worries do we carry? (*Pause*)

What areas of our lives are we determined to improve in the months to come? (*Pause*)

Are we willing to entrust all these things to the Father, knowing that he really cares? (*Pause*)

A Celebration

Close the experience by giving instructions similar to these: "Each of you should find one other person in the group and tell that person how much you appreciate him or her. Then share with that person something of your own concerns or hopes for the year ahead."

SUPPLEMENT A

For Everything There Is a Season

Reading

When I look ahead to a new year, I think
It's like flashing down a white hill on a sled
   or skis.
I'm the first to take the plunge,
   to brave the steep, to mark the slope.
No one has ever been on that snow before.
It's white and clear, without trail marks.
I have only my past experiences and skills to
   guide me.
They are not all good, nor all bad,
   but they help me know the way.
I have learned from the unpleasant things,
   while the pleasant events in life give me
   courage and confidence.
It's like starting a brand new chapter in my
   life.

Feelings

Ask people in the group to think for a few minutes, silently, about what comes to their minds as the most difficult time or experience of their lives. These could range from the loss of a loved one to some difficulty or trouble at school or elsewhere. Then ask them to think of the best time in their lives—what gave them the happiest, most fulfilling feelings.

Now ask the participants to share their thoughts with the group. Request that they concentrate on how they felt inside during each experience and how they feel now as they look back in retrospect. Take as long as necessary for this portion of the group experience. There may be pauses and perhaps a long wait at the beginning until someone feels like sharing his or her thoughts.

Thoughts: (A meditation)

Who we've been helps shape who we will become. Where we've been influences where we're going. Our past hopes and dreams are the inspiration for future accomplishments. Everyone we know helps to mold our thoughts and actions. Even our unhappy experiences teach us something which influences our futures. The happy times give us confidence that life has its positive, good side.

For everything there is a season. Not only do we have "up" and "down" days, but there is a kind of life-long principle of biorhythms. Inevitably we will face times of failure, sorrow, embarrassment, disappointment, frustration, futility. But life's lessons teach us that sooner or later these times will pass, and we will walk in the warmth of sunlight once again.

When everything is going really right, enjoy it fully, knowing that darker days are bound to come our way. No one is exempt. But trust in life and in the Father's good care, for he cares for us.

A Song

"Sweet Surrender"—this song, written by John Denver, seems to parallel Matthew 6 to such an extent that one wonders if this Scripture passage, in fact, inspired its writing. The words speak of surrender to life, which, if rightly understood, is practically the same as surrendering to God, the author and giver of life.

Reflection

This is a time of reflection and prayer. (Pause for about a minute after each question.)

How do the memories of our personal successes and our failures serve to help us in the future? Think about it. Pray about it. (*Pause*)

What were our greatest moments of defeat and victory during the past twelve months? (*Pause*)

What are our hopes and goals for this coming year? (*Pause*)

What hymn lyrics or Scripture verses come easily to our minds as we look ahead? (*Pause*)

What concerns, burdens, or worries do we carry? (*Pause*)

What areas of our lives are we determined to improve in the months to come? (*Pause*)

Are we willing to entrust all these things to the Father, knowing that he really cares? (*Pause*)

A Celebration

Close the experience by giving instructions similar to these: "Each of you should find one other person in the group and tell that person how much you appreciate him or her. Then share with that person something of your own concerns or hopes for the year ahead."

For Everything There Is a Season

Reading

When I look ahead to a new year, I think
It's like flashing down a white hill on a sled
  or skis.
I'm the first to take the plunge,
  to brave the steep, to mark the slope.
No one has ever been on that snow before.
It's white and clear, without trail marks.
I have only my past experiences and skills to
  guide me.
They are not all good, nor all bad,
  but they help me know the way.
I have learned from the unpleasant things,
  while the pleasant events in life give me
  courage and confidence.
It's like starting a brand new chapter in my
  life.

Feelings

Ask people in the group to think for a few minutes, silently, about what comes to their minds as the most difficult time or experience of their lives. These could range from the loss of a loved one to some difficulty or trouble at school or elsewhere. Then ask them to think of the best time in their lives—what gave them the happiest, most fulfilling feelings.

Now ask the participants to share their thoughts with the group. Request that they concentrate on how they felt inside during each experience and how they feel now as they look back in retrospect. Take as long as necessary for this portion of the group experience. There may be pauses and perhaps a long wait at the beginning until someone feels like sharing his or her thoughts.

Thoughts: (A meditation)

Who we've been helps shape who we will become. Where we've been influences where we're going. Our past hopes and dreams are the inspiration for future accomplishments. Everyone we know helps to mold our thoughts and actions. Even our unhappy experiences teach us something which influences our futures. The happy times give us confidence that life has its positive, good side.

For everything there is a season. Not only do we have "up" and "down" days, but there is a kind of life-long principle of biorhythms. Inevitably we will face times of failure, sorrow, embarrassment, disappointment, frustration, futility. But life's lessons teach us that sooner or later these times will pass, and we will walk in the warmth of sunlight once again.

When everything is going really right, enjoy it fully, knowing that darker days are bound to come our way. No one is exempt. But trust in life and in the Father's good care, for he cares for us.

A Song

"Sweet Surrender"—this song, written by John Denver, seems to parallel Matthew 6 to such an extent that one wonders if this Scripture passage, in fact, inspired its writing. The words speak of surrender to life, which, if rightly understood, is practically the same as surrendering to God, the author and giver of life.

Reflection

This is a time of reflection and prayer. (Pause for about a minute after each question.)

How do the memories of our personal successes and our failures serve to help us in the future? Think about it. Pray about it. (*Pause*)

What were our greatest moments of defeat and victory during the past twelve months? (*Pause*)

What are our hopes and goals for this coming year? (*Pause*)

What hymn lyrics or Scripture verses come easily to our minds as we look ahead? (*Pause*)

What concerns, burdens, or worries do we carry? (*Pause*)

What areas of our lives are we determined to improve in the months to come? (*Pause*)

Are we willing to entrust all these things to the Father, knowing that he really cares? (*Pause*)

A Celebration

Close the experience by giving instructions similar to these: "Each of you should find one other person in the group and tell that person how much you appreciate him or her. Then share with that person something of your own concerns or hopes for the year ahead."

For Everything There Is a Season

Reading

When I look ahead to a new year, I think
It's like flashing down a white hill on a sled
   or skis.
I'm the first to take the plunge,
   to brave the steep, to mark the slope.
No one has ever been on that snow before.
It's white and clear, without trail marks.
I have only my past experiences and skills to
   guide me.
They are not all good, nor all bad,
   but they help me know the way.
I have learned from the unpleasant things,
   while the pleasant events in life give me
   courage and confidence.
It's like starting a brand new chapter in my
   life.

Feelings

Ask people in the group to think for a few minutes, silently, about what comes to their minds as the most difficult time or experience of their lives. These could range from the loss of a loved one to some difficulty or trouble at school or elsewhere. Then ask them to think of the best time in their lives—what gave them the happiest, most fulfilling feelings.

Now ask the participants to share their thoughts with the group. Request that they concentrate on how they felt inside during each experience and how they feel now as they look back in retrospect. Take as long as necessary for this portion of the group experience. There may be pauses and perhaps a long wait at the beginning until someone feels like sharing his or her thoughts.

Thoughts: (A meditation)

Who we've been helps shape who we will become. Where we've been influences where we're going. Our past hopes and dreams are the inspiration for future accomplishments. Everyone we know helps to mold our thoughts and actions. Even our unhappy experiences teach us something which influences our futures. The happy times give us confidence that life has its positive, good side.

For everything there is a season. Not only do we have "up" and "down" days, but there is a kind of life-long principle of biorhythms. Inevitably we will face times of failure, sorrow, embarrassment, disappointment, frustration, futility. But life's lessons teach us that sooner or later these times will pass, and we will walk in the warmth of sunlight once again.

When everything is going really right, enjoy it fully, knowing that darker days are bound to come our way. No one is exempt. But trust in life and in the Father's good care, for he cares for us.

A Song

"Sweet Surrender"—this song, written by John Denver, seems to parallel Matthew 6 to such an extent that one wonders if this Scripture passage, in fact, inspired its writing. The words speak of surrender to life, which, if rightly understood, is practically the same as surrendering to God, the author and giver of life.

Reflection

This is a time of reflection and prayer. (Pause for about a minute after each question.)

How do the memories of our personal successes and our failures serve to help us in the future? Think about it. Pray about it. (*Pause*)

What were our greatest moments of defeat and victory during the past twelve months? (*Pause*)

What are our hopes and goals for this coming year? (*Pause*)

What hymn lyrics or Scripture verses come easily to our minds as we look ahead? (*Pause*)

What concerns, burdens, or worries do we carry? (*Pause*)

What areas of our lives are we determined to improve in the months to come? (*Pause*)

Are we willing to entrust all these things to the Father, knowing that he really cares? (*Pause*)

A Celebration

Close the experience by giving instructions similar to these: "Each of you should find one other person in the group and tell that person how much you appreciate him or her. Then share with that person something of your own concerns or hopes for the year ahead."

P.S. I Love You

A Celebration for Valentine's Day or Sweetest Day

Valentine's Day long has been a popular holiday, and Sweetest Day has been growing in popularity. These are special times when we think about romantic love. When we were in grade school, we often sent valentine cards to every person in our class and hoped we would receive some cards in return. As we grew older, we began to think in terms of that very special person. We used Valentine's Day to make our feelings known and hoped with all our hearts that the feeling was mutual. This is a special day for expressing love. In this devotional experience we will be reflecting on many expressions and types of love, and we will focus on the love of God, the author of love itself.

Preparation

This worship experience could be part of a larger celebration of Valentine's Day. It could be an occasion for a group party with worship as its culmination. We are celebrating love, and as with all celebrations, a festive atmosphere is in order. Have favors, hearts, and flowers if you wish. In recent times, many people have been afraid or ashamed of becoming sentimental. It has not been the "in" thing. But what harm is there in a little romantic sentimentality? It cannot harm us. It may even do us some good. (See "Celebration of Love" at the close of Supplement A to get an idea of how we can express our feelings.)

The experience will progress through an exploration of the meaning of Valentine's Day and an examination of the various kinds of love, to the reading of Scripture passages which speak of God's love toward us and the response we should make toward him.

Your group might consider arranging your meeting place in circular seating and creating a mobile out of coat hangers and strings, suspended from the ceiling directly in the center of the circle. Suspended from the mobile could be magazine cutouts pasted on cardboard backing. Select different items which may speak to your group of a variety of expressions of love and friendship. These might include anything from pictures of mothers and fathers caring for children to people embracing or showing love and caring. Those with special parts in the service need not come "front and center" but can participate from where they are seated within the group.

The Experience

Hymn: "Love Divine, All Loves Excelling."
Meditation: This section gives background and sets the tone for what is to follow (Supplement A).
Thoughts and Feelings: Supplement A.
Scripture Reading: 1 Corinthians 13.
A Song: Select a popular song which has the theme of love. Play it as a recording or have someone in your group sing it, accompanied by guitar or piano.
Scripture Reading: John 3:16-17.
Hymn: "Immortal Love, Forever Full."
Reading: "How Do I Love Thee?" by Elizabeth Barrett Browning (Supplement A).
Celebrating Love: A time of personal interaction (Supplement A).
Prayer: Supplement A.

P.S. I Love You

Meditation

VOICE: Very little really is known about Saint Valentine, and modern Valentine customs have little to do with him. All we have are some ancient legends which may be based on historical fact. Behind every legend or tradition there is usually historical fact or a significant personality.

There was a person named Valentine who was martyred under the Roman emperor Claudius II on February 14, A.D. 270, and it is this date of his martyrdom which we celebrate as Valentine's Day.

Tradition has it that Saint Valentine had the power to settle lovers' quarrels, and he has become known as the patron saint of lovers. We do know that his love for God was strong enough that he was willing to lay down his life for the kingdom of Christ. At the very least, we must respect and admire him for that.

But legends, stories, and traditions which are significant concerning Saint Valentine have evolved over the years. One fanciful writer (unknown) has imagined that Saint Valentine was a brother in a monastic order who felt keenly that he was without talent. Brother Angelo was an artist. Brother Vittorio was gifted with an excellent singing voice. Brother Anselmo was a doctor; Brother Johannes, a skilled scribe, and Brother Paul, a teacher. Valentine longed to do useful things, but all he seemed to manage was to care for a small garden. The story goes that he used to grow flowers, tie them into little bundles, and drop them over the monastery wall to children below. He gave his flowers and garden produce away on every appropriate occasion. He learned the birthday of each child in the village and would hang some small gift he had made himself on the door of the birthday child. It seemed that the only thing he had to share was love. And he became known as the patron saint of love!

VOICE: Another version of Valentine's life and death is that Saint Valentine was a priest in Rome in the early years when Christianity was in its infancy. Claudius the Cruel was the Roman emperor, and he issued an edict that the young men of the Roman Empire were not to marry. His idea was that if young people were not involved with love and marriage, the young men would be more willing to join the Roman armies and become dedicated men of battle.

But Valentine acted in civil disobedience and, as a priest, performed marriages for many young sweethearts. For displeasing Claudius, he was condemned to death and put in prison. Many people of Rome knew and loved Valentine and would pick flowers, attach notes of cheer and encouragement, and toss them through the barred windows of Valentine's prison cell.

While awaiting execution, Valentine became friends with the jailer's daughter, who was blind. He prayed for her, and she received her sight. Before his death, Valentine wrote her a farewell letter signed "From your Valentine."

VOICE: A variety of signs and symbols have been associated with Valentine's Day.

Ribbons, laces, and frills became popular when knights of the Middle Ages rode into battle, carrying a scarf or ribbon given them by their "lady fair" as a good-luck charm.

Cupid was one of the gods of the ancient world. He was the son of Venus, the goddess of love. He is depicted as a cherub-type youth with a mischievous smile. His favorite sport was to go around and shoot young couples through the heart with mystical arrows which caused them to fall in love.

The rose is the most popular flower in the entire world, and it has stood over the years as the symbol of love. By changing the letters in "rose" around, you come up with "Eros," the Greek goddess of love.

Tradition has it that turtledoves and lovebirds choose their mates on February 14, and that is why the dove has become associated with Valentine's Day. We know from Scripture that the dove is the Christian symbol of peace, love, and the Holy Spirit.

Hearts broken, pierced, united in love, and alive with joy have been a favorite fun part of Valentine's Day. Many cultures through the centuries have believed that the heart was the seat of the soul, the center of human emotion, the location of love.[1]

[1] Parts of this have been adapted from Frances Cavanah and Lucile Pannell, comps., *Holiday Round Up* (Philadelphia: Macrae Smith Company, 1950).

VOICE: We are known by how much we love and by how much we are loved.

Thoughts and Feelings

VOICE: Love is a girl and a boy smiling at each other or holding hands.

VOICE: Love is one person reaching out to another.

VOICE: Love is being frustrated because you are too embarrassed or because you don't know how to say, "I love you."

VOICE: Love is a mother gently caring for her child—

VOICE: A father talking to his kids—

VOICE: Mothers and fathers helping each other to grow, develop, mature.

VOICE: Love is two lives helping each other to become the best person each is capable of becoming, allowing each other to be the "me" inside that each likes best to be.

VOICE: Love can be one-sided. Love given but not returned is a tragic thing, a painful thing—

VOICE: One person using another in the name of love—

VOICE: Trying to gain economic or political advantage, fame or fortune, or personal gratification.

VOICE: This is a mockery of love.

VOICE: There is love between husbands and wives, parents and children, boy friends and girl friends.

VOICE: There is love of country, love of a worthy cause, love of school or social organization.

VOICE: There is love of life.

VOICE: There is love of things—money, possessions—hardly a worthy love.

VOICE: There is love in true friendship, in sharing and supporting.

VOICE: But the highest love is God's love for us as we see it displayed in the personality of Jesus Christ.

VOICE: And having seen, we are compelled to love him in return.

Reading

Following is one of the all-time classic poems expressing romantic love. It is entitled "How Do I Love Thee?" and was written many years ago by Elizabeth Barrett Browning.

> How do I love thee? Let me count the ways.
> I love thee to the depth and breadth and
>   height
> My soul can reach, when feeling out of sight
> For the ends of Being and ideal Grace.
> I love thee to the level of every day's
> Most quiet need, by sun and candle-light.
> I love thee freely, as men strive for Right;
> I love thee purely, as they turn from Praise.
> I love thee with the passion put to use
> In my old griefs, and with my childhood's
>   faith.
> I love thee with a love I seemed to lose
> With my lost saints,—I love thee with the
>   breath,
> Smiles, tears, of all my life!—and, if God
>   choose,
> I shall but love thee better after death.

Celebration of Love

Find someone in the group and give that person a hug. Then tell him or her to pass it on. There is no finer expression of our feelings for one another than this physical way of saying, "I like you. I love you." The hug and the kiss have been symbols of this all over the world since biblical times. Our culture is unique in that we sometimes feel embarrassed to express our love in this outward, emotional way.

Prayer

O Lord, we love you because you first loved us. You are the author of love. You are the essence of love. And the only way we have of showing our love to you is by loving one another. "No one has ever seen God, but if we love one another, God lives in union with us, and his love is made perfect in us. . . . The command that Christ has given us is this: whoever loves God must love his brother also" (1 John 4:12, 21). Amen.

P.S. I Love You

Meditation

VOICE: Very little really is known about Saint Valentine, and modern Valentine customs have little to do with him. All we have are some ancient legends which may be based on historical fact. Behind every legend or tradition there is usually historical fact or a significant personality.

There was a person named Valentine who was martyred under the Roman emperor Claudius II on February 14, A.D. 270, and it is this date of his martyrdom which we celebrate as Valentine's Day.

Tradition has it that Saint Valentine had the power to settle lovers' quarrels, and he has become known as the patron saint of lovers. We do know that his love for God was strong enough that he was willing to lay down his life for the kingdom of Christ. At the very least, we must respect and admire him for that.

But legends, stories, and traditions which are significant concerning Saint Valentine have evolved over the years. One fanciful writer (unknown) has imagined that Saint Valentine was a brother in a monastic order who felt keenly that he was without talent. Brother Angelo was an artist. Brother Vittorio was gifted with an excellent singing voice. Brother Anselmo was a doctor; Brother Johannes, a skilled scribe, and Brother Paul, a teacher. Valentine longed to do useful things, but all he seemed to manage was to care for a small garden. The story goes that he used to grow flowers, tie them into little bundles, and drop them over the monastery wall to children below. He gave his flowers and garden produce away on every appropriate occasion. He learned the birthday of each child in the village and would hang some small gift he had made himself on the door of the birthday child. It seemed that the only thing he had to share was love. And he became known as the patron saint of love!

VOICE: Another version of Valentine's life and death is that Saint Valentine was a priest in Rome in the early years when Christianity was in its infancy. Claudius the Cruel was the Roman emperor, and he issued an edict that the young men of the Roman Empire were not to marry. His idea was that if young people were not involved with love and marriage, the young men would be more willing to join the Roman armies and become dedicated men of battle.

But Valentine acted in civil disobedience and, as a priest, performed marriages for many young sweethearts. For displeasing Claudius, he was condemned to death and put in prison. Many people of Rome knew and loved Valentine and would pick flowers, attach notes of cheer and encouragement, and toss them through the barred windows of Valentine's prison cell.

While awaiting execution, Valentine became friends with the jailer's daughter, who was blind. He prayed for her, and she received her sight. Before his death, Valentine wrote her a farewell letter signed "From your Valentine."

VOICE: A variety of signs and symbols have been associated with Valentine's Day.

Ribbons, laces, and frills became popular when knights of the Middle Ages rode into battle, carrying a scarf or ribbon given them by their "lady fair" as a good-luck charm.

Cupid was one of the gods of the ancient world. He was the son of Venus, the goddess of love. He is depicted as a cherub-type youth with a mischievous smile. His favorite sport was to go around and shoot young couples through the heart with mystical arrows which caused them to fall in love.

The rose is the most popular flower in the entire world, and it has stood over the years as the symbol of love. By changing the letters in "rose" around, you come up with "Eros," the Greek goddess of love.

Tradition has it that turtledoves and lovebirds choose their mates on February 14, and that is why the dove has become associated with Valentine's Day. We know from Scripture that the dove is the Christian symbol of peace, love, and the Holy Spirit.

Hearts broken, pierced, united in love, and alive with joy have been a favorite fun part of Valentine's Day. Many cultures through the centuries have believed that the heart was the seat of the soul, the center of human emotion, the location of love.[1]

---

[1] Parts of this have been adapted from Frances Cavanah and Lucile Pannell, comps., *Holiday Round Up* (Philadelphia: Macrae Smith Company, 1950).

VOICE: We are known by how much we love and by how much we are loved.

Thoughts and Feelings

VOICE: Love is a girl and a boy smiling at each other or holding hands.

VOICE: Love is one person reaching out to another.

VOICE: Love is being frustrated because you are too embarrassed or because you don't know how to say, "I love you."

VOICE: Love is a mother gently caring for her child—

VOICE: A father talking to his kids—

VOICE: Mothers and fathers helping each other to grow, develop, mature.

VOICE: Love is two lives helping each other to become the best person each is capable of becoming, allowing each other to be the "me" inside that each likes best to be.

VOICE: Love can be one-sided. Love given but not returned is a tragic thing, a painful thing—

VOICE: One person using another in the name of love—

VOICE: Trying to gain economic or political advantage, fame or fortune, or personal gratification.

VOICE: This is a mockery of love.

VOICE: There is love between husbands and wives, parents and children, boy friends and girl friends.

VOICE: There is love of country, love of a worthy cause, love of school or social organization.

VOICE: There is love of life.

VOICE: There is love of things—money, possessions—hardly a worthy love.

VOICE: There is love in true friendship, in sharing and supporting.

VOICE: But the highest love is God's love for us as we see it displayed in the personality of Jesus Christ.

VOICE: And having seen, we are compelled to love him in return.

Reading

Following is one of the all-time classic poems expressing romantic love. It is entitled "How Do I Love Thee?" and was written many years ago by Elizabeth Barrett Browning.

How do I love thee? Let me count the ways.
I love thee to the depth and breadth and
    height
My soul can reach, when feeling out of sight
For the ends of Being and ideal Grace.
I love thee to the level of every day's
Most quiet need, by sun and candle-light.
I love thee freely, as men strive for Right;
I love thee purely, as they turn from Praise.
I love thee with the passion put to use
In my old griefs, and with my childhood's
    faith.
I love thee with a love I seemed to lose
With my lost saints,—I love thee with the
    breath,
Smiles, tears, of all my life!—and, if God
    choose,
I shall but love thee better after death.

Celebration of Love

Find someone in the group and give that person a hug. Then tell him or her to pass it on. There is no finer expression of our feelings for one another than this physical way of saying, "I like you. I love you." The hug and the kiss have been symbols of this all over the world since biblical times. Our culture is unique in that we sometimes feel embarrassed to express our love in this outward, emotional way.

Prayer

O Lord, we love you because you first loved us. You are the author of love. You are the essence of love. And the only way we have of showing our love to you is by loving one another. "No one has ever seen God, but if we love one another, God lives in union with us, and his love is made perfect in us. . . . The command that Christ has given us is this: whoever loves God must love his brother also" (1 John 4:12, 21). Amen.

P.S. I Love You

Meditation

VOICE: Very little really is known about Saint Valentine, and modern Valentine customs have little to do with him. All we have are some ancient legends which may be based on historical fact. Behind every legend or tradition there is usually historical fact or a significant personality.

There was a person named Valentine who was martyred under the Roman emperor Claudius II on February 14, A.D. 270, and it is this date of his martyrdom which we celebrate as Valentine's Day.

Tradition has it that Saint Valentine had the power to settle lovers' quarrels, and he has become known as the patron saint of lovers. We do know that his love for God was strong enough that he was willing to lay down his life for the kingdom of Christ. At the very least, we must respect and admire him for that.

But legends, stories, and traditions which are significant concerning Saint Valentine have evolved over the years. One fanciful writer (unknown) has imagined that Saint Valentine was a brother in a monastic order who felt keenly that he was without talent. Brother Angelo was an artist. Brother Vittorio was gifted with an excellent singing voice. Brother Anselmo was a doctor; Brother Johannes, a skilled scribe, and Brother Paul, a teacher. Valentine longed to do useful things, but all he seemed to manage was to care for a small garden. The story goes that he used to grow flowers, tie them into little bundles, and drop them over the monastery wall to children below. He gave his flowers and garden produce away on every appropriate occasion. He learned the birthday of each child in the village and would hang some small gift he had made himself on the door of the birthday child. It seemed that the only thing he had to share was love. And he became known as the patron saint of love!

VOICE: Another version of Valentine's life and death is that Saint Valentine was a priest in Rome in the early years when Christianity was in its infancy. Claudius the Cruel was the Roman emperor, and he issued an edict that the young men of the Roman Empire were not to marry. His idea was that if young people were not involved with love and marriage, the young men would be more willing to join the Roman armies and become dedicated men of battle.

But Valentine acted in civil disobedience and, as a priest, performed marriages for many young sweethearts. For displeasing Claudius, he was condemned to death and put in prison. Many people of Rome knew and loved Valentine and would pick flowers, attach notes of cheer and encouragement, and toss them through the barred windows of Valentine's prison cell.

While awaiting execution, Valentine became friends with the jailer's daughter, who was blind. He prayed for her, and she received her sight. Before his death, Valentine wrote her a farewell letter signed "From your Valentine."

VOICE: A variety of signs and symbols have been associated with Valentine's Day.

Ribbons, laces, and frills became popular when knights of the Middle Ages rode into battle, carrying a scarf or ribbon given them by their "lady fair" as a good-luck charm.

Cupid was one of the gods of the ancient world. He was the son of Venus, the goddess of love. He is depicted as a cherub-type youth with a mischievous smile. His favorite sport was to go around and shoot young couples through the heart with mystical arrows which caused them to fall in love.

The rose is the most popular flower in the entire world, and it has stood over the years as the symbol of love. By changing the letters in "rose" around, you come up with "Eros," the Greek goddess of love.

Tradition has it that turtledoves and lovebirds choose their mates on February 14, and that is why the dove has become associated with Valentine's Day. We know from Scripture that the dove is the Christian symbol of peace, love, and the Holy Spirit.

Hearts broken, pierced, united in love, and alive with joy have been a favorite fun part of Valentine's Day. Many cultures through the centuries have believed that the heart was the seat of the soul, the center of human emotion, the location of love.[1]

[1]Parts of this have been adapted from Frances Cavanah and Lucile Pannell, comps., *Holiday Round Up* (Philadelphia: Macrae Smith Company, 1950).

VOICE: We are known by how much we love and by how much we are loved.

Thoughts and Feelings

VOICE: Love is a girl and a boy smiling at each other or holding hands.

VOICE: Love is one person reaching out to another.

VOICE: Love is being frustrated because you are too embarrassed or because you don't know how to say, "I love you."

VOICE: Love is a mother gently caring for her child—

VOICE: A father talking to his kids—

VOICE: Mothers and fathers helping each other to grow, develop, mature.

VOICE: Love is two lives helping each other to become the best person each is capable of becoming, allowing each other to be the "me" inside that each likes best to be.

VOICE: Love can be one-sided. Love given but not returned is a tragic thing, a painful thing—

VOICE: One person using another in the name of love—

VOICE: Trying to gain economic or political advantage, fame or fortune, or personal gratification.

VOICE: This is a mockery of love.

VOICE: There is love between husbands and wives, parents and children, boy friends and girl friends.

VOICE: There is love of country, love of a worthy cause, love of school or social organization.

VOICE: There is love of life.

VOICE: There is love of things—money, possessions—hardly a worthy love.

VOICE: There is love in true friendship, in sharing and supporting.

VOICE: But the highest love is God's love for us as we see it displayed in the personality of Jesus Christ.

VOICE: And having seen, we are compelled to love him in return.

Reading

Following is one of the all-time classic poems expressing romantic love. It is entitled "How Do I Love Thee?" and was written many years ago by Elizabeth Barrett Browning.

How do I love thee? Let me count the ways.
I love thee to the depth and breadth and height
My soul can reach, when feeling out of sight
For the ends of Being and ideal Grace.
I love thee to the level of every day's
Most quiet need, by sun and candle-light.
I love thee freely, as men strive for Right;
I love thee purely, as they turn from Praise.
I love thee with the passion put to use
In my old griefs, and with my childhood's faith.
I love thee with a love I seemed to lose
With my lost saints,—I love thee with the breath,
Smiles, tears, of all my life!—and, if God choose,
I shall but love thee better after death.

Celebration of Love

Find someone in the group and give that person a hug. Then tell him or her to pass it on. There is no finer expression of our feelings for one another than this physical way of saying, "I like you. I love you." The hug and the kiss have been symbols of this all over the world since biblical times. Our culture is unique in that we sometimes feel embarrassed to express our love in this outward, emotional way.

Prayer

O Lord, we love you because you first loved us. You are the author of love. You are the essence of love. And the only way we have of showing our love to you is by loving one another. "No one has ever seen God, but if we love one another, God lives in union with us, and his love is made perfect in us. . . . The command that Christ has given us is this: whoever loves God must love his brother also" (1 John 4:12, 21). Amen.

P.S. I Love You

Meditation

VOICE: Very little really is known about Saint Valentine, and modern Valentine customs have little to do with him. All we have are some ancient legends which may be based on historical fact. Behind every legend or tradition there is usually historical fact or a significant personality.

There was a person named Valentine who was martyred under the Roman emperor Claudius II on February 14, A.D. 270, and it is this date of his martyrdom which we celebrate as Valentine's Day.

Tradition has it that Saint Valentine had the power to settle lovers' quarrels, and he has become known as the patron saint of lovers. We do know that his love for God was strong enough that he was willing to lay down his life for the kingdom of Christ. At the very least, we must respect and admire him for that.

But legends, stories, and traditions which are significant concerning Saint Valentine have evolved over the years. One fanciful writer (unknown) has imagined that Saint Valentine was a brother in a monastic order who felt keenly that he was without talent. Brother Angelo was an artist. Brother Vittorio was gifted with an excellent singing voice. Brother Anselmo was a doctor; Brother Johannes, a skilled scribe, and Brother Paul, a teacher. Valentine longed to do useful things, but all he seemed to manage was to care for a small garden. The story goes that he used to grow flowers, tie them into little bundles, and drop them over the monastery wall to children below. He gave his flowers and garden produce away on every appropriate occasion. He learned the birthday of each child in the village and would hang some small gift he had made himself on the door of the birthday child. It seemed that the only thing he had to share was love. And he became known as the patron saint of love!

VOICE: Another version of Valentine's life and death is that Saint Valentine was a priest in Rome in the early years when Christianity was in its infancy. Claudius the Cruel was the Roman emperor, and he issued an edict that the young men of the Roman Empire were not to marry. His idea was that if young people were not involved with love and marriage, the young men would be more willing to join the Roman armies and become dedicated men of battle.

But Valentine acted in civil disobedience and, as a priest, performed marriages for many young sweethearts. For displeasing Claudius, he was condemned to death and put in prison. Many people of Rome knew and loved Valentine and would pick flowers, attach notes of cheer and encouragement, and toss them through the barred windows of Valentine's prison cell.

While awaiting execution, Valentine became friends with the jailer's daughter, who was blind. He prayed for her, and she received her sight. Before his death, Valentine wrote her a farewell letter signed "From your Valentine."

VOICE: A variety of signs and symbols have been associated with Valentine's Day.

Ribbons, laces, and frills became popular when knights of the Middle Ages rode into battle, carrying a scarf or ribbon given them by their "lady fair" as a good-luck charm.

Cupid was one of the gods of the ancient world. He was the son of Venus, the goddess of love. He is depicted as a cherub-type youth with a mischievous smile. His favorite sport was to go around and shoot young couples through the heart with mystical arrows which caused them to fall in love.

The rose is the most popular flower in the entire world, and it has stood over the years as the symbol of love. By changing the letters in "rose" around, you come up with "Eros," the Greek goddess of love.

Tradition has it that turtledoves and lovebirds choose their mates on February 14, and that is why the dove has become associated with Valentine's Day. We know from Scripture that the dove is the Christian symbol of peace, love, and the Holy Spirit.

Hearts broken, pierced, united in love, and alive with joy have been a favorite fun part of Valentine's Day. Many cultures through the centuries have believed that the heart was the seat of the soul, the center of human emotion, the location of love.[1]

[1]Parts of this have been adapted from Frances Cavanah and Lucile Pannell, comps., *Holiday Round Up* (Philadelphia: Macrae Smith Company, 1950).

VOICE: We are known by how much we love and by how much we are loved.

Thoughts and Feelings

VOICE: Love is a girl and a boy smiling at each other or holding hands.

VOICE: Love is one person reaching out to another.

VOICE: Love is being frustrated because you are too embarrassed or because you don't know how to say, "I love you."

VOICE: Love is a mother gently caring for her child—

VOICE: A father talking to his kids—

VOICE: Mothers and fathers helping each other to grow, develop, mature.

VOICE: Love is two lives helping each other to become the best person each is capable of becoming, allowing each other to be the "me" inside that each likes best to be.

VOICE: Love can be one-sided. Love given but not returned is a tragic thing, a painful thing—

VOICE: One person using another in the name of love—

VOICE: Trying to gain economic or political advantage, fame or fortune, or personal gratification.

VOICE: This is a mockery of love.

VOICE: There is love between husbands and wives, parents and children, boy friends and girl friends.

VOICE: There is love of country, love of a worthy cause, love of school or social organization.

VOICE: There is love of life.

VOICE: There is love of things—money, possessions—hardly a worthy love.

VOICE: There is love in true friendship, in sharing and supporting.

VOICE: But the highest love is God's love for us as we see it displayed in the personality of Jesus Christ.

VOICE: And having seen, we are compelled to love him in return.

Reading

Following is one of the all-time classic poems expressing romantic love. It is entitled "How Do I Love Thee?" and was written many years ago by Elizabeth Barrett Browning.

How do I love thee? Let me count the ways.
I love thee to the depth and breadth and height
My soul can reach, when feeling out of sight
For the ends of Being and ideal Grace.
I love thee to the level of every day's
Most quiet need, by sun and candle-light.
I love thee freely, as men strive for Right;
I love thee purely, as they turn from Praise.
I love thee with the passion put to use
In my old griefs, and with my childhood's faith.
I love thee with a love I seemed to lose
With my lost saints,—I love thee with the breath,
Smiles, tears, of all my life!—and, if God choose,
I shall but love thee better after death.

Celebration of Love

Find someone in the group and give that person a hug. Then tell him or her to pass it on. There is no finer expression of our feelings for one another than this physical way of saying, "I like you. I love you." The hug and the kiss have been symbols of this all over the world since biblical times. Our culture is unique in that we sometimes feel embarrassed to express our love in this outward, emotional way.

Prayer

O Lord, we love you because you first loved us. You are the author of love. You are the essence of love. And the only way we have of showing our love to you is by loving one another. "No one has ever seen God, but if we love one another, God lives in union with us, and his love is made perfect in us. . . . The command that Christ has given us is this: whoever loves God must love his brother also" (1 John 4:12, 21). Amen.

P.S. I Love You

Meditation

VOICE: Very little really is known about Saint Valentine, and modern Valentine customs have little to do with him. All we have are some ancient legends which may be based on historical fact. Behind every legend or tradition there is usually historical fact or a significant personality.

There was a person named Valentine who was martyred under the Roman emperor Claudius II on February 14, A.D. 270, and it is this date of his martyrdom which we celebrate as Valentine's Day.

Tradition has it that Saint Valentine had the power to settle lovers' quarrels, and he has become known as the patron saint of lovers. We do know that his love for God was strong enough that he was willing to lay down his life for the kingdom of Christ. At the very least, we must respect and admire him for that.

But legends, stories, and traditions which are significant concerning Saint Valentine have evolved over the years. One fanciful writer (unknown) has imagined that Saint Valentine was a brother in a monastic order who felt keenly that he was without talent. Brother Angelo was an artist. Brother Vittorio was gifted with an excellent singing voice. Brother Anselmo was a doctor; Brother Johannes, a skilled scribe, and Brother Paul, a teacher. Valentine longed to do useful things, but all he seemed to manage was to care for a small garden. The story goes that he used to grow flowers, tie them into little bundles, and drop them over the monastery wall to children below. He gave his flowers and garden produce away on every appropriate occasion. He learned the birthday of each child in the village and would hang some small gift he had made himself on the door of the birthday child. It seemed that the only thing he had to share was love. And he became known as the patron saint of love!

VOICE: Another version of Valentine's life and death is that Saint Valentine was a priest in Rome in the early years when Christianity was in its infancy. Claudius the Cruel was the Roman emperor, and he issued an edict that the young men of the Roman Empire were not to marry. His idea was that if young people were not involved with love and marriage, the young men would be more willing to join the Roman armies and become dedicated men of battle.

But Valentine acted in civil disobedience and, as a priest, performed marriages for many young sweethearts. For displeasing Claudius, he was condemned to death and put in prison. Many people of Rome knew and loved Valentine and would pick flowers, attach notes of cheer and encouragement, and toss them through the barred windows of Valentine's prison cell.

While awaiting execution, Valentine became friends with the jailer's daughter, who was blind. He prayed for her, and she received her sight. Before his death, Valentine wrote her a farewell letter signed "From your Valentine."

VOICE: A variety of signs and symbols have been associated with Valentine's Day.

Ribbons, laces, and frills became popular when knights of the Middle Ages rode into battle, carrying a scarf or ribbon given them by their "lady fair" as a good-luck charm.

Cupid was one of the gods of the ancient world. He was the son of Venus, the goddess of love. He is depicted as a cherub-type youth with a mischievous smile. His favorite sport was to go around and shoot young couples through the heart with mystical arrows which caused them to fall in love.

The rose is the most popular flower in the entire world, and it has stood over the years as the symbol of love. By changing the letters in "rose" around, you come up with "Eros," the Greek goddess of love.

Tradition has it that turtledoves and lovebirds choose their mates on February 14, and that is why the dove has become associated with Valentine's Day. We know from Scripture that the dove is the Christian symbol of peace, love, and the Holy Spirit.

Hearts broken, pierced, united in love, and alive with joy have been a favorite fun part of Valentine's Day. Many cultures through the centuries have believed that the heart was the seat of the soul, the center of human emotion, the location of love.[1]

[1] Parts of this have been adapted from Frances Cavanah and Lucile Pannell, comps., *Holiday Round Up* (Philadelphia: Macrae Smith Company, 1950).

VOICE: We are known by how much we love and by how much we are loved.

Thoughts and Feelings

VOICE: Love is a girl and a boy smiling at each other or holding hands.

VOICE: Love is one person reaching out to another.

VOICE: Love is being frustrated because you are too embarrassed or because you don't know how to say, "I love you."

VOICE: Love is a mother gently caring for her child—

VOICE: A father talking to his kids—

VOICE: Mothers and fathers helping each other to grow, develop, mature.

VOICE: Love is two lives helping each other to become the best person each is capable of becoming, allowing each other to be the "me" inside that each likes best to be.

VOICE: Love can be one-sided. Love given but not returned is a tragic thing, a painful thing—

VOICE: One person using another in the name of love—

VOICE: Trying to gain economic or political advantage, fame or fortune, or personal gratification.

VOICE: This is a mockery of love.

VOICE: There is love between husbands and wives, parents and children, boy friends and girl friends.

VOICE: There is love of country, love of a worthy cause, love of school or social organization.

VOICE: There is love of life.

VOICE: There is love of things—money, possessions—hardly a worthy love.

VOICE: There is love in true friendship, in sharing and supporting.

VOICE: But the highest love is God's love for us as we see it displayed in the personality of Jesus Christ.

VOICE: And having seen, we are compelled to love him in return.

Reading

Following is one of the all-time classic poems expressing romantic love. It is entitled "How Do I Love Thee?" and was written many years ago by Elizabeth Barrett Browning.

How do I love thee? Let me count the ways.
I love thee to the depth and breadth and
    height
My soul can reach, when feeling out of sight
For the ends of Being and ideal Grace.
I love thee to the level of every day's
Most quiet need, by sun and candle-light.
I love thee freely, as men strive for Right;
I love thee purely, as they turn from Praise.
I love thee with the passion put to use
In my old griefs, and with my childhood's
    faith.
I love thee with a love I seemed to lose
With my lost saints,—I love thee with the
    breath,
Smiles, tears, of all my life!—and, if God
    choose,
I shall but love thee better after death.

Celebration of Love

Find someone in the group and give that person a hug. Then tell him or her to pass it on. There is no finer expression of our feelings for one another than this physical way of saying, "I like you. I love you." The hug and the kiss have been symbols of this all over the world since biblical times. Our culture is unique in that we sometimes feel embarrassed to express our love in this outward, emotional way.

Prayer

O Lord, we love you because you first loved us. You are the author of love. You are the essence of love. And the only way we have of showing our love to you is by loving one another. "No one has ever seen God, but if we love one another, God lives in union with us, and his love is made perfect in us. . . . The command that Christ has given us is this: whoever loves God must love his brother also" (1 John 4:12, 21). Amen.

P.S. I Love You

Meditation

VOICE: Very little really is known about Saint Valentine, and modern Valentine customs have little to do with him. All we have are some ancient legends which may be based on historical fact. Behind every legend or tradition there is usually historical fact or a significant personality.

There was a person named Valentine who was martyred under the Roman emperor Claudius II on February 14, A.D. 270, and it is this date of his martyrdom which we celebrate as Valentine's Day.

Tradition has it that Saint Valentine had the power to settle lovers' quarrels, and he has become known as the patron saint of lovers. We do know that his love for God was strong enough that he was willing to lay down his life for the kingdom of Christ. At the very least, we must respect and admire him for that.

But legends, stories, and traditions which are significant concerning Saint Valentine have evolved over the years. One fanciful writer (unknown) has imagined that Saint Valentine was a brother in a monastic order who felt keenly that he was without talent. Brother Angelo was an artist. Brother Vittorio was gifted with an excellent singing voice. Brother Anselmo was a doctor; Brother Johannes, a skilled scribe, and Brother Paul, a teacher. Valentine longed to do useful things, but all he seemed to manage was to care for a small garden. The story goes that he used to grow flowers, tie them into little bundles, and drop them over the monastery wall to children below. He gave his flowers and garden produce away on every appropriate occasion. He learned the birthday of each child in the village and would hang some small gift he had made himself on the door of the birthday child. It seemed that the only thing he had to share was love. And he became known as the patron saint of love!

VOICE: Another version of Valentine's life and death is that Saint Valentine was a priest in Rome in the early years when Christianity was in its infancy. Claudius the Cruel was the Roman emperor, and he issued an edict that the young men of the Roman Empire were not to marry. His idea was that if young people were not involved with love and marriage, the young men would be more willing to join the Roman armies and become dedicated men of battle.

But Valentine acted in civil disobedience and, as a priest, performed marriages for many young sweethearts. For displeasing Claudius, he was condemned to death and put in prison. Many people of Rome knew and loved Valentine and would pick flowers, attach notes of cheer and encouragement, and toss them through the barred windows of Valentine's prison cell.

While awaiting execution, Valentine became friends with the jailer's daughter, who was blind. He prayed for her, and she received her sight. Before his death, Valentine wrote her a farewell letter signed "From your Valentine."

VOICE: A variety of signs and symbols have been associated with Valentine's Day.

Ribbons, laces, and frills became popular when knights of the Middle Ages rode into battle, carrying a scarf or ribbon given them by their "lady fair" as a good-luck charm.

Cupid was one of the gods of the ancient world. He was the son of Venus, the goddess of love. He is depicted as a cherub-type youth with a mischievous smile. His favorite sport was to go around and shoot young couples through the heart with mystical arrows which caused them to fall in love.

The rose is the most popular flower in the entire world, and it has stood over the years as the symbol of love. By changing the letters in "rose" around, you come up with "Eros," the Greek goddess of love.

Tradition has it that turtledoves and lovebirds choose their mates on February 14, and that is why the dove has become associated with Valentine's Day. We know from Scripture that the dove is the Christian symbol of peace, love, and the Holy Spirit.

Hearts broken, pierced, united in love, and alive with joy have been a favorite fun part of Valentine's Day. Many cultures through the centuries have believed that the heart was the seat of the soul, the center of human emotion, the location of love.[1]

[1] Parts of this have been adapted from Frances Cavanah and Lucile Pannell, comps., *Holiday Round Up* (Philadelphia: Macrae Smith Company, 1950).

VOICE: We are known by how much we love and by how much we are loved.

Thoughts and Feelings

VOICE: Love is a girl and a boy smiling at each other or holding hands.

VOICE: Love is one person reaching out to another.

VOICE: Love is being frustrated because you are too embarrassed or because you don't know how to say, "I love you."

VOICE: Love is a mother gently caring for her child—

VOICE: A father talking to his kids—

VOICE: Mothers and fathers helping each other to grow, develop, mature.

VOICE: Love is two lives helping each other to become the best person each is capable of becoming, allowing each other to be the "me" inside that each likes best to be.

VOICE: Love can be one-sided. Love given but not returned is a tragic thing, a painful thing—

VOICE: One person using another in the name of love—

VOICE: Trying to gain economic or political advantage, fame or fortune, or personal gratification.

VOICE: This is a mockery of love.

VOICE: There is love between husbands and wives, parents and children, boy friends and girl friends.

VOICE: There is love of country, love of a worthy cause, love of school or social organization.

VOICE: There is love of life.

VOICE: There is love of things—money, possessions—hardly a worthy love.

VOICE: There is love in true friendship, in sharing and supporting.

VOICE: But the highest love is God's love for us as we see it displayed in the personality of Jesus Christ.

VOICE: And having seen, we are compelled to love him in return.

Reading

Following is one of the all-time classic poems expressing romantic love. It is entitled "How Do I Love Thee?" and was written many years ago by Elizabeth Barrett Browning.

How do I love thee? Let me count the ways.
I love thee to the depth and breadth and height
My soul can reach, when feeling out of sight
For the ends of Being and ideal Grace.
I love thee to the level of every day's
Most quiet need, by sun and candle-light.
I love thee freely, as men strive for Right;
I love thee purely, as they turn from Praise.
I love thee with the passion put to use
In my old griefs, and with my childhood's faith.
I love thee with a love I seemed to lose
With my lost saints,—I love thee with the breath,
Smiles, tears, of all my life!—and, if God choose,
I shall but love thee better after death.

Celebration of Love

Find someone in the group and give that person a hug. Then tell him or her to pass it on. There is no finer expression of our feelings for one another than this physical way of saying, "I like you. I love you." The hug and the kiss have been symbols of this all over the world since biblical times. Our culture is unique in that we sometimes feel embarrassed to express our love in this outward, emotional way.

Prayer

O Lord, we love you because you first loved us. You are the author of love. You are the essence of love. And the only way we have of showing our love to you is by loving one another. "No one has ever seen God, but if we love one another, God lives in union with us, and his love is made perfect in us. . . . The command that Christ has given us is this: whoever loves God must love his brother also" (1 John 4:12, 21). Amen.

Nature's Biorhythms

A Celebration for an Outdoor Vesper

As the world turns on its axis, we witness the changing of the seasons. There are gloomy, wet, cold days, but our experiences tell us that these are temporary. The sun will shine again, and we will enjoy warm, pleasing days. Nature becomes dormant for periods of time; yet we know there will be a rebirth in the spring. Volcanoes erupt in fiery spectacle, then subside and lay quiet for years. The universe is alive with changes.

We see a similarity between the cycles of nature and our personal lives. We experience troubled and depressing times—times we think will never pass. Yet life teaches us that the "down" times also pass and that pleasant, good days follow.

In this worship experience, we will reflect on the endless cycles of nature under the masterful direction of God the Creator, and we will have opportunity to examine the parallels between the movements of creation and our own lives.

Preparation

This experience may take place at camp, in a lodge or group meetinghouse, in a tent, along the banks of a stream or river, or in the open meadows. Circular seating on the floor or ground will help provide your group with a sense of closeness. If parts are to be read, be sure each person is familiar with the material. Better still, ask each person to familiarize himself or herself with the material so that the person can give the ideas and thoughts in his or her own words.

The Experience

Opening Thought: God, who created the grandeur of the universe, is dynamic, the master of change. He has created us in his image. Let us open our lives to him so that we may be ever changing, growing, progressing, more like him.

Hymn: "God Who Touches Earth with Beauty" (If the group meets outdoors where no hymnals are available, choose a song everyone knows by heart).

Scripture: Psalm 8.

Reflections: This part of the service can be done with several people speaking parts or by one person alone. Another alternative is to have two people alternating the voice parts in a kind of antiphonal reading (Supplement A).

Reading: "I Am a Seed" (Supplement A).

Prayer: Encourage each person to offer sentence prayers.

A Song: "The Flower Song" ("Where Have All the Flowers Gone?"). This song, known to most groups, expresses the concept of the cycle of change. When the song is completed, the first verse is repeated, thus completing the cycle.

Nature's Biorhythms

Reflections

VOICE: The universe is alive with action, teeming with life, dynamic, moving, as creation unfolds.

VOICE: The vastness of it all is beyond comprehension; it boggles our minds, for we are but a speck, dwarfed by time and space.

VOICE: A visitor to our galaxy probably would pass us right by because of our size. We are but a grain of sand on the beach.

VOICE: The universe moves with precision, each body in its appointed orbit. The universe is predictable—or so we think—but it also accommodates the unexpected. It is alive, ever moving, ever changing.

VOICE: We see on earth the precision of creation. The warmth and beauty of summer yields to the frosts of autumn. The leaves, once green, are caught up in the endless cycle of changes, turning yellow, orange, brown, red.

VOICE: And then they have to die so that nature can live again.

VOICE: Then comes the time we call the "dead of winter."

VOICE: The trees are bare in many parts of the world, and the ground is white with snow.

VOICE: How can life live again after death? It is impossible, unbelievable, that from this despair comes the breath of life. It is nature's rhythm and the Father's will.

VOICE: And the cycle continues as the earth swings on its elliptical course, nearer the sun again.

VOICE: Spring! Its coming is almost imperceptible. But the days grow longer by seconds and minutes. Temperatures moderate and rise, snow melts; the floods of spring are upon us, the rains of April, the blooms of May. Wild animals emerge from their haunts, caves, and hiding places.

VOICE: And look—they are not alone, for they have multiplied, reproduced, each after its own kind. And the cycle is completed.

VOICE: Nature's wheel has turned one revolution.

VOICE: Death is caught off guard.

VOICE: And life leaps forth, defying all logic, all obstacles, defeating all odds. It is nature's biorhythm.

VOICE: These rhythms of nature offer us some clues, parallels, parables, which help us understand the complexities of our personal feelings and circumstances.

VOICE: Though their progress is not so clear-cut, our lives seem to roll through rhythms of change something like the seasons.

VOICE: We are not always "up," not always "down." There are times when we experience a sort of wintertime of our spirits—

VOICE: When things go wrong. We are depressed, fearful, despondent. Gloom is all around us; no one can change us, comfort us. We feel alone, isolated, reluctant to face a new day, afraid even to hope.

VOICE: For some of us, things at times *really* go wrong. We face loss, tragedy, sorrow, grief, even death.

VOICE: Aren't these times like the "dead of winter"? Have you ever felt that the "me" inside, the "me" as I know me, is disappearing?

VOICE: Have you ever felt that you couldn't make it? That life has dealt you an unfair blow?

VOICE: Have you ever felt that you could make no sense out of your existence?

VOICE: You are not alone. All, to one degree or another, have experienced this "wintertime" of their souls, this storm of their spirits and of their emotions. But the lesson life teaches is that for every bad time, there is an opposite—though at times we cannot believe it, things will improve.

VOICE: What will the troubles of today mean a year from now, or ten years, or a hundred? It is a passing moment in the sea of time.

VOICE: For every cloud there is a silver lining. But for every silver lining, there is a cloud. It is Nature's way.

VOICE: But it's more than a silver lining, more than grasping at straws, more than whistling in the dark. It is life's rhythms.

VOICE: "Down" times don't last forever, but neither do the "ups." Enjoy the good times to their fullest, and don't worry about the bad. They, too, will come, and after that, some more good.

VOICE: The sun will break forth. Life is worth the living; we can be sure. When we are down—

VOICE: Meaning will return, problems will

be resolved or melt into the repository of forgotten pasts, and the joy of life will flood our spirits again.

Reading: "I Am a Seed"

I am a seed as small as a grain of sand. I will fall upon the earth, lie quietly for several weeks, then begin to change. As the sun warms the soil around me and the gentle rains and mists of night provide nurture, it will seem that "me" as I know me will disappear and disintegrate. But within my shell there is life. As the outer layer begins to break up, a tiny, hairlike sprout will appear, growing toward the sun. Then roots will form to grasp the earth and borrow from it the nutrients I need to grow.

The sprout will grow into a stalk, and leaves will form. Weeks later, a bud will form on the stalk. Changes will take place within the bud, and petals will burst forth, forming a flower. And at the base of the flower, concealed within the pod, will be new seeds.

Storms will come, and slashing rains will bow my stem to the ground as furrows of mud claw at my roots. But when the sun shines, I will perk up again and show new growth because of the experience. Then the droughts of late summer will once again come to challenge my very existence. But I will survive. Yes, *I will survive!*

"Me," as I knew me, will have changed from insignificance to a thing of beauty. People will admire me, never thinking of the tiny seed I once was. And I will forget the agonies of change, the storm clouds, the painfully dry times. For I will be the best "me" I know how to be—the "me" in me which is beautiful.

Nature's Biorhythms

Reflections

VOICE: The universe is alive with action, teeming with life, dynamic, moving, as creation unfolds.

VOICE: The vastness of it all is beyond comprehension; it boggles our minds, for we are but a speck, dwarfed by time and space.

VOICE: A visitor to our galaxy probably would pass us right by because of our size. We are but a grain of sand on the beach.

VOICE: The universe moves with precision, each body in its appointed orbit. The universe is predictable—or so we think—but it also accommodates the unexpected. It is alive, ever moving, ever changing.

VOICE: We see on earth the precision of creation. The warmth and beauty of summer yields to the frosts of autumn. The leaves, once green, are caught up in the endless cycle of changes, turning yellow, orange, brown, red.

VOICE: And then they have to die so that nature can live again.

VOICE: Then comes the time we call the "dead of winter."

VOICE: The trees are bare in many parts of the world, and the ground is white with snow.

VOICE: How can life live again after death? It is impossible, unbelievable, that from this despair comes the breath of life. It is nature's rhythm and the Father's will.

VOICE: And the cycle continues as the earth swings on its elliptical course, nearer the sun again.

VOICE: Spring! Its coming is almost imperceptible. But the days grow longer by seconds and minutes. Temperatures moderate and rise, snow melts; the floods of spring are upon us, the rains of April, the blooms of May. Wild animals emerge from their haunts, caves, and hiding places.

VOICE: And look—they are not alone, for they have multiplied, reproduced, each after its own kind. And the cycle is completed.

VOICE: Nature's wheel has turned one revolution.

VOICE: Death is caught off guard.

VOICE: And life leaps forth, defying all logic, all obstacles, defeating all odds. It is nature's biorhythm.

VOICE: These rhythms of nature offer us some clues, parallels, parables, which help us understand the complexities of our personal feelings and circumstances.

VOICE: Though their progress is not so clear-cut, our lives seem to roll through rhythms of change something like the seasons.

VOICE: We are not always "up," not always "down." There are times when we experience a sort of wintertime of our spirits—

VOICE: When things go wrong. We are depressed, fearful, despondent. Gloom is all around us; no one can change us, comfort us. We feel alone, isolated, reluctant to face a new day, afraid even to hope.

VOICE: For some of us, things at times *really* go wrong. We face loss, tragedy, sorrow, grief, even death.

VOICE: Aren't these times like the "dead of winter"? Have you ever felt that the "me" inside, the "me" as I know me, is disappearing?

VOICE: Have you ever felt that you couldn't make it? That life has dealt you an unfair blow?

VOICE: Have you ever felt that you could make no sense out of your existence?

VOICE: You are not alone. All, to one degree or another, have experienced this "wintertime" of their souls, this storm of their spirits and of their emotions. But the lesson life teaches is that for every bad time, there is an opposite—though at times we cannot believe it, things will improve.

VOICE: What will the troubles of today mean a year from now, or ten years, or a hundred? It is a passing moment in the sea of time.

VOICE: For every cloud there is a silver lining. But for every silver lining, there is a cloud. It is Nature's way.

VOICE: But it's more than a silver lining, more than grasping at straws, more than whistling in the dark. It is life's rhythms.

VOICE: "Down" times don't last forever, but neither do the "ups." Enjoy the good times to their fullest, and don't worry about the bad. They, too, will come, and after that, some more good.

VOICE: The sun will break forth. Life is worth the living; we can be sure. When we are down—

VOICE: Meaning will return, problems will

be resolved or melt into the repository of forgotten pasts, and the joy of life will flood our spirits again.

Reading: "I Am a Seed"

I am a seed as small as a grain of sand. I will fall upon the earth, lie quietly for several weeks, then begin to change. As the sun warms the soil around me and the gentle rains and mists of night provide nurture, it will seem that "me" as I know me will disappear and disintegrate. But within my shell there is life. As the outer layer begins to break up, a tiny, hairlike sprout will appear, growing toward the sun. Then roots will form to grasp the earth and borrow from it the nutrients I need to grow.

The sprout will grow into a staik, and leaves will form. Weeks later, a bud will form on the stalk. Changes will take place within the bud, and petals will burst forth, forming a flower. And at the base of the flower, concealed within the pod, will be new seeds.

Storms will come, and slashing rains will bow my stem to the ground as furrows of mud claw at my roots. But when the sun shines, I will perk up again and show new growth because of the experience. Then the droughts of late summer will once again come to challenge my very existence. But I will survive. Yes, *I will survive!*

"Me," as I knew me, will have changed from insignificance to a thing of beauty. People will admire me, never thinking of the tiny seed I once was. And I will forget the agonies of change, the storm clouds, the painfully dry times. For I will be the best "me" I know how to be—the "me" in me which is beautiful.

SUPPLEMENT A

Nature's Biorhythms

Reflections

VOICE: The universe is alive with action, teeming with life, dynamic, moving, as creation unfolds.

VOICE: The vastness of it all is beyond comprehension; it boggles our minds, for we are but a speck, dwarfed by time and space.

VOICE: A visitor to our galaxy probably would pass us right by because of our size. We are but a grain of sand on the beach.

VOICE: The universe moves with precision, each body in its appointed orbit. The universe is predictable—or so we think—but it also accommodates the unexpected. It is alive, ever moving, ever changing.

VOICE: We see on earth the precision of creation. The warmth and beauty of summer yields to the frosts of autumn. The leaves, once green, are caught up in the endless cycle of changes, turning yellow, orange, brown, red.

VOICE: And then they have to die so that nature can live again.

VOICE: Then comes the time we call the "dead of winter."

VOICE: The trees are bare in many parts of the world, and the ground is white with snow.

VOICE: How can life live again after death? It is impossible, unbelievable, that from this despair comes the breath of life. It is nature's rhythm and the Father's will.

VOICE: And the cycle continues as the earth swings on its elliptical course, nearer the sun again.

VOICE: Spring! Its coming is almost imperceptible. But the days grow longer by seconds and minutes. Temperatures moderate and rise, snow melts; the floods of spring are upon us, the rains of April, the blooms of May. Wild animals emerge from their haunts, caves, and hiding places.

VOICE: And look—they are not alone, for they have multiplied, reproduced, each after its own kind. And the cycle is completed.

VOICE: Nature's wheel has turned one revolution.

VOICE: Death is caught off guard.

VOICE: And life leaps forth, defying all logic, all obstacles, defeating all odds. It is nature's biorhythm.

VOICE: These rhythms of nature offer us some clues, parallels, parables, which help us understand the complexities of our personal feelings and circumstances.

VOICE: Though their progress is not so clear-cut, our lives seem to roll through rhythms of change something like the seasons.

VOICE: We are not always "up," not always "down." There are times when we experience a sort of wintertime of our spirits—

VOICE: When things go wrong. We are depressed, fearful, despondent. Gloom is all around us; no one can change us, comfort us. We feel alone, isolated, reluctant to face a new day, afraid even to hope.

VOICE: For some of us, things at times *really* go wrong. We face loss, tragedy, sorrow, grief, even death.

VOICE: Aren't these times like the "dead of winter"? Have you ever felt that the "me" inside, the "me" as I know me, is disappearing?

VOICE: Have you ever felt that you couldn't make it? That life has dealt you an unfair blow?

VOICE: Have you ever felt that you could make no sense out of your existence?

VOICE: You are not alone. All, to one degree or another, have experienced this "wintertime" of their souls, this storm of their spirits and of their emotions. But the lesson life teaches is that for every bad time, there is an opposite—though at times we cannot believe it, things will improve.

VOICE: What will the troubles of today mean a year from now, or ten years, or a hundred? It is a passing moment in the sea of time.

VOICE: For every cloud there is a silver lining. But for every silver lining, there is a cloud. It is Nature's way.

VOICE: But it's more than a silver lining, more than grasping at straws, more than whistling in the dark. It is life's rhythms.

VOICE: "Down" times don't last forever, but neither do the "ups." Enjoy the good times to their fullest, and don't worry about the bad. They, too, will come, and after that, some more good.

VOICE: The sun will break forth. Life is worth the living; we can be sure. When we are down—

VOICE: Meaning will return, problems will

be resolved or melt into the repository of forgotten pasts, and the joy of life will flood our spirits again.

Reading: "I Am a Seed"

I am a seed as small as a grain of sand. I will fall upon the earth, lie quietly for several weeks, then begin to change. As the sun warms the soil around me and the gentle rains and mists of night provide nurture, it will seem that "me" as I know me will disappear and disintegrate. But within my shell there is life. As the outer layer begins to break up, a tiny, hairlike sprout will appear, growing toward the sun. Then roots will form to grasp the earth and borrow from it the nutrients I need to grow.

The sprout will grow into a stalk, and leaves will form. Weeks later, a bud will form on the stalk. Changes will take place within the bud, and petals will burst forth, forming a flower. And at the base of the flower, concealed within the pod, will be new seeds.

Storms will come, and slashing rains will bow my stem to the ground as furrows of mud claw at my roots. But when the sun shines, I will perk up again and show new growth because of the experience. Then the droughts of late summer will once again come to challenge my very existence. But I will survive. Yes, *I will survive!*

"Me," as I knew me, will have changed from insignificance to a thing of beauty. People will admire me, never thinking of the tiny seed I once was. And I will forget the agonies of change, the storm clouds, the painfully dry times. For I will be the best "me" I know how to be—the "me" in me which is beautiful.

Nature's Biorhythms

Reflections

VOICE: The universe is alive with action, teeming with life, dynamic, moving, as creation unfolds.

VOICE: The vastness of it all is beyond comprehension; it boggles our minds, for we are but a speck, dwarfed by time and space.

VOICE: A visitor to our galaxy probably would pass us right by because of our size. We are but a grain of sand on the beach.

VOICE: The universe moves with precision, each body in its appointed orbit. The universe is predictable—or so we think—but it also accommodates the unexpected. It is alive, ever moving, ever changing.

VOICE: We see on earth the precision of creation. The warmth and beauty of summer yields to the frosts of autumn. The leaves, once green, are caught up in the endless cycle of changes, turning yellow, orange, brown, red.

VOICE: And then they have to die so that nature can live again.

VOICE: Then comes the time we call the "dead of winter."

VOICE: The trees are bare in many parts of the world, and the ground is white with snow.

VOICE: How can life live again after death? It is impossible, unbelievable, that from this despair comes the breath of life. It is nature's rhythm and the Father's will.

VOICE: And the cycle continues as the earth swings on its elliptical course, nearer the sun again.

VOICE: Spring! Its coming is almost imperceptible. But the days grow longer by seconds and minutes. Temperatures moderate and rise, snow melts; the floods of spring are upon us, the rains of April, the blooms of May. Wild animals emerge from their haunts, caves, and hiding places.

VOICE: And look—they are not alone, for they have multiplied, reproduced, each after its own kind. And the cycle is completed.

VOICE: Nature's wheel has turned one revolution.

VOICE: Death is caught off guard.

VOICE: And life leaps forth, defying all logic, all obstacles, defeating all odds. It is nature's biorhythm.

VOICE: These rhythms of nature offer us some clues, parallels, parables, which help us understand the complexities of our personal feelings and circumstances.

VOICE: Though their progress is not so clear-cut, our lives seem to roll through rhythms of change something like the seasons.

VOICE: We are not always "up," not always "down." There are times when we experience a sort of wintertime of our spirits—

VOICE: When things go wrong. We are depressed, fearful, despondent. Gloom is all around us; no one can change us, comfort us. We feel alone, isolated, reluctant to face a new day, afraid even to hope.

VOICE: For some of us, things at times *really* go wrong. We face loss, tragedy, sorrow, grief, even death.

VOICE: Aren't these times like the "dead of winter"? Have you ever felt that the "me" inside, the "me" as I know me, is disappearing?

VOICE: Have you ever felt that you couldn't make it? That life has dealt you an unfair blow?

VOICE: Have you ever felt that you could make no sense out of your existence?

VOICE: You are not alone. All, to one degree or another, have experienced this "wintertime" of their souls, this storm of their spirits and of their emotions. But the lesson life teaches is that for every bad time, there is an opposite—though at times we cannot believe it, things will improve.

VOICE: What will the troubles of today mean a year from now, or ten years, or a hundred? It is a passing moment in the sea of time.

VOICE: For every cloud there is a silver lining. But for every silver lining, there is a cloud. It is Nature's way.

VOICE: But it's more than a silver lining, more than grasping at straws, more than whistling in the dark. It is life's rhythms.

VOICE: "Down" times don't last forever, but neither do the "ups." Enjoy the good times to their fullest, and don't worry about the bad. They, too, will come, and after that, some more good.

VOICE: The sun will break forth. Life is worth the living; we can be sure. When we are down—

VOICE: Meaning will return, problems will

be resolved or melt into the repository of forgotten pasts, and the joy of life will flood our spirits again.

Reading: "I Am a Seed"

I am a seed as small as a grain of sand. I will fall upon the earth, lie quietly for several weeks, then begin to change. As the sun warms the soil around me and the gentle rains and mists of night provide nurture, it will seem that "me" as I know me will disappear and disintegrate. But within my shell there is life. As the outer layer begins to break up, a tiny, hairlike sprout will appear, growing toward the sun. Then roots will form to grasp the earth and borrow from it the nutrients I need to grow.

The sprout will grow into a stalk, and leaves will form. Weeks later, a bud will form on the stalk. Changes will take place within the bud, and petals will burst forth, forming a flower. And at the base of the flower, concealed within the pod, will be new seeds.

Storms will come, and slashing rains will bow my stem to the ground as furrows of mud claw at my roots. But when the sun shines, I will perk up again and show new growth because of the experience. Then the droughts of late summer will once again come to challenge my very existence. But I will survive. Yes, *I will survive!*

"Me," as I knew me, will have changed from insignificance to a thing of beauty. People will admire me, never thinking of the tiny seed I once was. And I will forget the agonies of change, the storm clouds, the painfully dry times. For I will be the best "me" I know how to be—the "me" in me which is beautiful.

Nature's Biorhythms

Reflections

VOICE: The universe is alive with action, teeming with life, dynamic, moving, as creation unfolds.

VOICE: The vastness of it all is beyond comprehension; it boggles our minds, for we are but a speck, dwarfed by time and space.

VOICE: A visitor to our galaxy probably would pass us right by because of our size. We are but a grain of sand on the beach.

VOICE: The universe moves with precision, each body in its appointed orbit. The universe is predictable—or so we think—but it also accommodates the unexpected. It is alive, ever moving, ever changing.

VOICE: We see on earth the precision of creation. The warmth and beauty of summer yields to the frosts of autumn. The leaves, once green, are caught up in the endless cycle of changes, turning yellow, orange, brown, red.

VOICE: And then they have to die so that nature can live again.

VOICE: Then comes the time we call the "dead of winter."

VOICE: The trees are bare in many parts of the world, and the ground is white with snow.

VOICE: How can life live again after death? It is impossible, unbelievable, that from this despair comes the breath of life. It is nature's rhythm and the Father's will.

VOICE: And the cycle continues as the earth swings on its elliptical course, nearer the sun again.

VOICE: Spring! Its coming is almost imperceptible. But the days grow longer by seconds and minutes. Temperatures moderate and rise, snow melts; the floods of spring are upon us, the rains of April, the blooms of May. Wild animals emerge from their haunts, caves, and hiding places.

VOICE: And look—they are not alone, for they have multiplied, reproduced, each after its own kind. And the cycle is completed.

VOICE: Nature's wheel has turned one revolution.

VOICE: Death is caught off guard.

VOICE: And life leaps forth, defying all logic, all obstacles, defeating all odds. It is nature's biorhythm.

VOICE: These rhythms of nature offer us some clues, parallels, parables, which help us understand the complexities of our personal feelings and circumstances.

VOICE: Though their progress is not so clear-cut, our lives seem to roll through rhythms of change something like the seasons.

VOICE: We are not always "up," not always "down." There are times when we experience a sort of wintertime of our spirits—

VOICE: When things go wrong. We are depressed, fearful, despondent. Gloom is all around us; no one can change us, comfort us. We feel alone, isolated, reluctant to face a new day, afraid even to hope.

VOICE: For some of us, things at times *really* go wrong. We face loss, tragedy, sorrow, grief, even death.

VOICE: Aren't these times like the "dead of winter"? Have you ever felt that the "me" inside, the "me" as I know me, is disappearing?

VOICE: Have you ever felt that you couldn't make it? That life has dealt you an unfair blow?

VOICE: Have you ever felt that you could make no sense out of your existence?

VOICE: You are not alone. All, to one degree or another, have experienced this "wintertime" of their souls, this storm of their spirits and of their emotions. But the lesson life teaches is that for every bad time, there is an opposite—though at times we cannot believe it, things will improve.

VOICE: What will the troubles of today mean a year from now, or ten years, or a hundred? It is a passing moment in the sea of time.

VOICE: For every cloud there is a silver lining. But for every silver lining, there is a cloud. It is Nature's way.

VOICE: But it's more than a silver lining, more than grasping at straws, more than whistling in the dark. It is life's rhythms.

VOICE: "Down" times don't last forever, but neither do the "ups." Enjoy the good times to their fullest, and don't worry about the bad. They, too, will come, and after that, some more good.

VOICE: The sun will break forth. Life is worth the living; we can be sure. When we are down—

VOICE: Meaning will return, problems will

be resolved or melt into the repository of forgotten pasts, and the joy of life will flood our spirits again.

Reading: "I Am a Seed"

I am a seed as small as a grain of sand. I will fall upon the earth, lie quietly for several weeks, then begin to change. As the sun warms the soil around me and the gentle rains and mists of night provide nurture, it will seem that "me" as I know me will disappear and disintegrate. But within my shell there is life. As the outer layer begins to break up, a tiny, hairlike sprout will appear, growing toward the sun. Then roots will form to grasp the earth and borrow from it the nutrients I need to grow.

The sprout will grow into a stalk, and leaves will form. Weeks later, a bud will form on the stalk. Changes will take place within the bud, and petals will burst forth, forming a flower. And at the base of the flower, concealed within the pod, will be new seeds.

Storms will come, and slashing rains will bow my stem to the ground as furrows of mud claw at my roots. But when the sun shines, I will perk up again and show new growth because of the experience. Then the droughts of late summer will once again come to challenge my very existence. But I will survive. Yes, *I will survive!*

"Me," as I knew me, will have changed from insignificance to a thing of beauty. People will admire me, never thinking of the tiny seed I once was. And I will forget the agonies of change, the storm clouds, the painfully dry times. For I will be the best "me" I know how to be—the "me" in me which is beautiful.

Enter the Gates with Praise

A Celebration for Lent

Palm Sunday and the events which surrounded it in Jesus' life are studies in contrast. The sentiments of the crowds ranged from jubilant acceptance to final rejection. The events appear to be a dramatic demonstration that people really do not know their own minds, that loyalty and allegiance are easily swayed. Within a few days the scene changed from one of joyful success to tragedy. This worship experience will help point up these facts as well as provide opportunity for dedication.

Preparation

In spite of the tragic death Jesus faced just a few days after entering Jerusalem, Palm Sunday and what has come to be known as the "triumphant entry" was a time of praise, worship, and adoration. This theme of praise and celebration will highlight the group experience. For this reason, use of Scripture readings and hymns of praise will be dominant. If palm branches are available, let each person in your group have one, for it is the palm branch which is the symbol of this day. When the moment of dedication comes, encourage each person to step forward and lay his or her palm branch on the floor, thus symbolizing that person's dedication. An even more dramatic effect would be to place articles of clothing—coats, jackets, or sweaters—on the floor, for the Scriptures tell us that this is what people did as an act of worship when Jesus entered Jerusalem.

The Experience

Beginning Thoughts: Psalm 24:7-10.
Hymn: "O Worship the King."
Scripture Reading: Luke 19:28-38.
Reflections: "The Visitor" with voice parts (Supplement A).
Scripture Reading: John 1:10-13.
Hymn of Dedication: "O Jesus, I Have Promised."

SUPPLEMENT A

5

Enter the Gates with Praise

Reflections: "The Visitor"

A VOICE: I happened to be standing on the sidewalk along the boulevard, just one person among a great crowd of people who lined the streets. I asked the person next to me why all these people were here, looking up the street as if to catch a glimpse of some amazing sight.

"Haven't you heard? It's the Visitor."

"What visitor?" I wanted to know.

"Where in the world have you been? It's been on TV and radio constantly since we started receiving the signals."

"What signals?" I asked. "What are you talking about?"

Then I learned that for some time, various communications centers around the world had been receiving messages from outer space. They were easily translated into human language, and their message was that a visitor was coming from another galaxy to bring news to the people on Earth. I don't know how I had missed the news. It didn't matter now anyway because I was in a perfect spot to see the Visitor.

What would the Visitor look like? Where did the Visitor come from, and why pick Earth for a special visit when there are so many millions of other planets much bigger than ours and probably far more interesting?

And what was the mysterious news?

I must confess that I was disappointed in the Visitor's looks because I was expecting someone totally different—more great and glorious—at least with two heads or green in color, I guess.

When the motorcade approached, people were waving flags and cheering wildly. This had never happened before—a visitor from outer space—and people were ecstatic with enthusiasm. I cheered, too, because this was a very special time—perhaps never to be repeated—and I was there to witness history being made.

The Visitor rode in an open car alongside the president. She looked just like any human, and except for the space uniform she wore, you couldn't have picked her out of the crowd.

Too bad what they did to her! What she came to tell us was something we already knew—that mankind was on a path to annihilation with the super weapons we've developed. That was the bad news. The good news was that there was hope—a way of solving our problems of politics and power—and she would help us by. . . .

I guess she never got that far. They decided to do away with her because she was supposed to be posing some kind of world threat, and she might cause panic because of her warnings. Then there was suspicion that she and her people would take over the world with their superior technology.

And people turned out on the day of her execution, too—the same shouting, shoving, cheering crowd—right downtown and big as life. I was there too.

ANOTHER VOICE: The Visitor was a kind of modern-day parallel of the kind of thing which took place two thousand years ago. It was not a perfect parallel as the details were quite different, but the idea was the same or similar. Someone came to bring us hope, but he also had disturbing things to say—things we knew deep down inside to be true about us and our world, things we didn't particularly like to hear. It has been true with most prophets and messengers throughout history—we never quite listen, and to protect ourselves (or so we think), we try to do away with the person and his or her message. In doing so, we think we have silenced the truth.

ANOTHER VOICE: God speaks through nature, through the prophets, through the Bible. But when he wanted us to sit up and take notice—to really see him—he did not send a visitor, an ambassador, or a representative. He came in person: the person of Christ.

ANOTHER VOICE: Let us worship God who visited us through Christ and who calls upon us daily through his Spirit. Let our hearts be true, and let us not betray him. We need not be one of the crowd. We can stand alone by his grace, even when others fail.

Hymn of Dedication

During the singing of this hymn, if you decide to lay down palm branches or other symbolic tokens of adoration, place them in the center of your worship circle or at the front of your meeting place.

55

SUPPLEMENT A

Enter the Gates with Praise

Reflections: "The Visitor"

A VOICE: I happened to be standing on the sidewalk along the boulevard, just one person among a great crowd of people who lined the streets. I asked the person next to me why all these people were here, looking up the street as if to catch a glimpse of some amazing sight.

"Haven't you heard? It's the Visitor."

"What visitor?" I wanted to know.

"Where in the world have you been? It's been on TV and radio constantly since we started receiving the signals."

"What signals?" I asked. "What are you talking about?"

Then I learned that for some time, various communications centers around the world had been receiving messages from outer space. They were easily translated into human language, and their message was that a visitor was coming from another galaxy to bring news to the people on Earth. I don't know how I had missed the news. It didn't matter now anyway because I was in a perfect spot to see the Visitor.

What would the Visitor look like? Where did the Visitor come from, and why pick Earth for a special visit when there are so many millions of other planets much bigger than ours and probably far more interesting?

And what was the mysterious news?

I must confess that I was disappointed in the Visitor's looks because I was expecting someone totally different—more great and glorious—at least with two heads or green in color, I guess.

When the motorcade approached, people were waving flags and cheering wildly. This had never happened before—a visitor from outer space—and people were ecstatic with enthusiasm. I cheered, too, because this was a very special time—perhaps never to be repeated—and I was there to witness history being made.

The Visitor rode in an open car alongside the president. She looked just like any human, and except for the space uniform she wore, you couldn't have picked her out of the crowd.

Too bad what they did to her! What she came to tell us was something we already knew—that mankind was on a path to annihilation with the super weapons we've developed. That was the bad news. The good news was that there was hope—a way of solving our problems of politics and power—and she would help us by. . . .

I guess she never got that far. They decided to do away with her because she was supposed to be posing some kind of world threat, and she might cause panic because of her warnings. Then there was suspicion that she and her people would take over the world with their superior technology.

And people turned out on the day of her execution, too—the same shouting, shoving, cheering crowd—right downtown and big as life. I was there too.

ANOTHER VOICE: The Visitor was a kind of modern-day parallel of the kind of thing which took place two thousand years ago. It was not a perfect parallel as the details were quite different, but the idea was the same or similar. Someone came to bring us hope, but he also had disturbing things to say—things we knew deep down inside to be true about us and our world, things we didn't particularly like to hear. It has been true with most prophets and messengers throughout history—we never quite listen, and to protect ourselves (or so we think), we try to do away with the person and his or her message. In doing so, we think we have silenced the truth.

ANOTHER VOICE: God speaks through nature, through the prophets, through the Bible. But when he wanted us to sit up and take notice—to really see him—he did not send a visitor, an ambassador, or a representative. He came in person: the person of Christ.

ANOTHER VOICE: Let us worship God who visited us through Christ and who calls upon us daily through his Spirit. Let our hearts be true, and let us not betray him. We need not be one of the crowd. We can stand alone by his grace, even when others fail.

Hymn of Dedication

During the singing of this hymn, if you decide to lay down palm branches or other symbolic tokens of adoration, place them in the center of your worship circle or at the front of your meeting place.

SUPPLEMENT A

Enter the Gates with Praise

Reflections: "The Visitor"

A VOICE: I happened to be standing on the sidewalk along the boulevard, just one person among a great crowd of people who lined the streets. I asked the person next to me why all these people were here, looking up the street as if to catch a glimpse of some amazing sight.

"Haven't you heard? It's the Visitor."

"What visitor?" I wanted to know.

"Where in the world have you been? It's been on TV and radio constantly since we started receiving the signals."

"What signals?" I asked. "What are you talking about?"

Then I learned that for some time, various communications centers around the world had been receiving messages from outer space. They were easily translated into human language, and their message was that a visitor was coming from another galaxy to bring news to the people on Earth. I don't know how I had missed the news. It didn't matter now anyway because I was in a perfect spot to see the Visitor.

What would the Visitor look like? Where did the Visitor come from, and why pick Earth for a special visit when there are so many millions of other planets much bigger than ours and probably far more interesting?

And what was the mysterious news?

I must confess that I was disappointed in the Visitor's looks because I was expecting someone totally different—more great and glorious—at least with two heads or green in color, I guess.

When the motorcade approached, people were waving flags and cheering wildly. This had never happened before—a visitor from outer space—and people were ecstatic with enthusiam. I cheered, too, because this was a very special time—perhaps never to be repeated—and I was there to witness history being made.

The Visitor rode in an open car alongside the president. She looked just like any human, and except for the space uniform she wore, you couldn't have picked her out of the crowd.

Too bad what they did to her! What she came to tell us was something we already knew—that mankind was on a path to annihilation with the super weapons we've developed. That was the bad news. The good news was that there was hope—a way of solving our problems of politics and power—and she would help us by. . . .

I guess she never got that far. They decided to do away with her because she was supposed to be posing some kind of world threat, and she might cause panic because of her warnings. Then there was suspicion that she and her people would take over the world with their superior technology.

And people turned out on the day of her execution, too—the same shouting, shoving, cheering crowd—right downtown and big as life. I was there too.

ANOTHER VOICE: The Visitor was a kind of modern-day parallel of the kind of thing which took place two thousand years ago. It was not a perfect parallel as the details were quite different, but the idea was the same or similar. Someone came to bring us hope, but he also had disturbing things to say—things we knew deep down inside to be true about us and our world, things we didn't particularly like to hear. It has been true with most prophets and messengers throughout history—we never quite listen, and to protect ourselves (or so we think), we try to do away with the person and his or her message. In doing so, we think we have silenced the truth.

ANOTHER VOICE: God speaks through nature, through the prophets, through the Bible. But when he wanted us to sit up and take notice—to really see him—he did not send a visitor, an ambassador, or a representative. He came in person: the person of Christ.

ANOTHER VOICE: Let us worship God who visited us through Christ and who calls upon us daily through his Spirit. Let our hearts be true, and let us not betray him. We need not be one of the crowd. We can stand alone by his grace, even when others fail.

Hymn of Dedication

During the singing of this hymn, if you decide to lay down palm branches or other symbolic tokens of adoration, place them in the center of your worship circle or at the front of your meeting place.

6

Good Grief

A Celebration for Lent or Good Friday

While the material in this chapter is geared to a specific day or season of the year, as is most of the material in this book, it need not be thought of as exclusively for that day but can be adapted to other themes and occasions. Use this material as a guide, a starting point, and blend with it your own ideas and creativity.

This chapter concentrates on the death of Christ as described in the Scriptures, the tragedy and meaning of the cross, and the expression of grief. There are readings throughout aimed at stimulating thinking. This season of the year has been traditionally a time of reflection on the passion of Christ and the meaning of the cross in modern times, and in our personal lives it should be prominent. Let this be a time of deep soul-searching.

Preparation

Create a crude cross to be used as a focal point in your worship experience. Some groups who have been able to plan months in advance have saved the trunk from the sanctuary Christmas tree, stripped it of all branches, and cut it in such a way as to fashion a cross out of it to be used during Lent. The idea is to link the birth of Christ to his death and resurrection in a meaningful way. It may not be possible for your group to carry out this idea. Any cross your group can make will serve the purpose of providing a focal point for worship. You might want to give the idea a contemporary touch by making the cross out of two-by-fours. Maybe some person in the group might be able to fashion a cross out of metal in your school's metal-working shop.

In the readings, make use of pauses to allow time for people to think through the ideas and concepts presented. Be sure that all readings are presented slowly and with meaning.

The Experience

Hymn: "In the Cross of Christ I Glory."
Scripture: Isaiah 53.
Grief: A reading from Supplement A.
Contrasts: A reading from Supplement A.
A Song: "Were You There?"
    "Let Me Be There."
    "Beneath the Cross of Jesus."
Reading: Voice parts (Supplement A).
Prayer: Provide one minute of silence for prayer. Encourage each group member to make his or her own needs and confessions known to God.

Good Grief

Grief

A Voice: We have been a death-denying society. Most deaths take place in the sterile, clinical, and sometimes impersonal isolation room or intensive care unit of a hospital. Professionals fix up the bodies of the dead and make them look as though they are merely sleeping. When someone is about to die, we are often whisked out of the room so that we can be spared seeing the end of life. Just when a person needs the comfort of another human being—at the hour of death—we usually leave him or her to face the final time alone.

But death is a part of life. It has been defined as the final stage of growth. And only in recent years has our society dared to acknowledge death, to study it, and to try to come to grips with the process of grief.

Jesus' death was untimely and unnatural. He did not die of disease or old age or by accident. He was executed at an age when life should have been full of promise, accomplishment, and hope. Instead, he was cut down, and life was cut short—but for a higher purpose.

We learn a lot about grief from the death of Jesus. On the way to Calvary, he said to the women who were mourning his coming death, "Weep for yourselves . . . ." When we mourn the loss of someone we love, we also are thinking about ourselves, for now we must face life without that person. But deeper still, when we see death, we not only feel for the person who has died, but we also feel for ourselves. We know that we, too, must face the end of our lives.

Jesus took care of some last bit of family business just before he died. He entrusted Mary, his mother, to the care of the disciple John. He was concerned for others even while facing his own death.

Reader: (John 19:25-27)

Voice: He was mindful of God, at first feeling God-forsaken, then trusting his very being to God's care. Most people are mindful of God when they face death. There are no atheists in the battlefield. But he was aware of divine guidance all of his life; so to pray at life's end was simply a natural outgrowth of a totally committed and useful life.

Reader: (Luke 23:44-46)

Voice: He forgave.

Reader: (Luke 23:34)

Voice: He gave comfort and assurance to someone who asked his help.

Reader: (Luke 23:39-43)

Voice: And he knew, beyond all doubt, that there is more to life than death. Life goes on in a higher plane—the extra-earthly kingdom of God where there is warmth, peace, and security in the very presence of God.

Some look upon Jesus' death as an ending. The cross has been the traditional symbol of Christianity since early times. It is the emblem of death. Perhaps the symbol of our faith should be the empty tomb. The cross was one experience in his life. But he overcame death and lives!

Contrasts

Another Voice:
He was born a human being,
Yet he is God.
He came to bring Good News,
But many thought it was bad.
He did good, fed the hungry, cured the sick,
But they said he was evil.
He taught from the Scriptures,
Yet was called a heretic.
He lived among men,
But his allegiance was to the kingdom of God.
He was friend to many,
And they turned their backs on him.
He lived a life of love,
Yet was hated.
He came to save the world,
But would not spare himself.
He despised evil;
He loved sinners.
He had the universe at his command,
But would rather be with the poor.
He harmed no one,
And in return was harmed.
He was innocent,
Yet was declared guilty.
He came bringing peace,
And was given a cross.
He showed God's love,
But it brought out the worst in many.
He died for us;
What shall we do for him?

Reading

ANOTHER VOICE: Look at the lives which surrounded Jesus as he went to the cross: Peter, Pilate, Barabbas, Mary, Martha, John, Judas, the disciples, the soldiers, two thieves, the other women who were there when he died, and many others. Each had a crucial part in the tragic drama unfolding. Some caused it to happen. Some only allowed it. Some were indifferent. But all were a part.

Perhaps the most courageous were little noticed, like the women who stood by the cross. While Peter and others denied him and refused to associate with him, these women had courage to show themselves in full view. At the hour of his greatest need he was not completely alone, for a small group was brave enough and compassionate enough at least to be there.

ANOTHER VOICE: "While to the reluctant the cross is too heavy to be borne, it grows light to the heart of willing trust.

"The cross of Christ, on which he was extended, points, in the length of it, to heaven and earth, reconciling them together; and in the breadth of it, to former and following ages, as being equally salvation to both.

"The cross of Christ is the sweetest burden I ever bore; it is such a burden as wings are to a bird, or sails to a ship, to carry me forward to my harbor" (Samuel Rutherford).[1]

ANOTHER VOICE: We may grieve at death, particularly the death of Christ, as we reflect on what people have done to cause and allow this tragedy. Yet our grief is cleansing, as a gift from God, for in grief we find healing.

ANOTHER VOICE: "Great grief makes sacred those upon whom its hand is laid.—Joy may elevate, ambition glorify, but only sorrow can consecrate" (Horace Greeley).[2]

[1] Tryon Edwards, comp., *The New Dictionary of Thoughts* (New York: Standard Book Co., 1960), p. 123.
[2] *Ibid.*, p. 251.

Good Grief

Grief

A VOICE: We have been a death-denying society. Most deaths take place in the sterile, clinical, and sometimes impersonal isolation room or intensive care unit of a hospital. Professionals fix up the bodies of the dead and make them look as though they are merely sleeping. When someone is about to die, we are often whisked out of the room so that we can be spared seeing the end of life. Just when a person needs the comfort of another human being—at the hour of death—we usually leave him or her to face the final time alone.

But death is a part of life. It has been defined as the final stage of growth. And only in recent years has our society dared to acknowledge death, to study it, and to try to come to grips with the process of grief.

Jesus' death was untimely and unnatural. He did not die of disease or old age or by accident. He was executed at an age when life should have been full of promise, accomplishment, and hope. Instead, he was cut down, and life was cut short—but for a higher purpose.

We learn a lot about grief from the death of Jesus. On the way to Calvary, he said to the women who were mourning his coming death, "Weep for yourselves . . . . " When we mourn the loss of someone we love, we also are thinking about ourselves, for now we must face life without that person. But deeper still, when we see death, we not only feel for the person who has died, but we also feel for ourselves. We know that we, too, must face the end of our lives.

Jesus took care of some last bit of family business just before he died. He entrusted Mary, his mother, to the care of the disciple John. He was concerned for others even while facing his own death.

READER: (John 19:25-27)

VOICE: He was mindful of God, at first feeling God-forsaken, then trusting his very being to God's care. Most people are mindful of God when they face death. There are no atheists in the battlefield. But he was aware of divine guidance all of his life; so to pray at life's end was simply a natural outgrowth of a totally committed and useful life.

READER: (Luke 23:44-46)

VOICE: He forgave.

READER: (Luke 23:34)

VOICE: He gave comfort and assurance to someone who asked his help.

READER: (Luke 23:39-43)

VOICE: And he knew, beyond all doubt, that there is more to life than death. Life goes on in a higher plane—the extra-earthly kingdom of God where there is warmth, peace, and security in the very presence of God.

Some look upon Jesus' death as an ending. The cross has been the traditional symbol of Christianity since early times. It is the emblem of death. Perhaps the symbol of our faith should be the empty tomb. The cross was one experience in his life. But he overcame death and lives!

Contrasts

ANOTHER VOICE:
He was born a human being,
Yet he is God.
He came to bring Good News,
But many thought it was bad.
He did good, fed the hungry, cured the sick,
But they said he was evil.
He taught from the Scriptures,
Yet was called a heretic.
He lived among men,
But his allegiance was to the kingdom of
    God.
He was friend to many,
And they turned their backs on him.
He lived a life of love,
Yet was hated.
He came to save the world,
But would not spare himself.
He despised evil;
He loved sinners.
He had the universe at his command,
But would rather be with the poor.
He harmed no one,
And in return was harmed.
He was innocent,
Yet was declared guilty.
He came bringing peace,
And was given a cross.
He showed God's love,
But it brought out the worst in many.
He died for us;
What shall we do for him?

Reading

ANOTHER VOICE: Look at the lives which surrounded Jesus as he went to the cross: Peter, Pilate, Barabbas, Mary, Martha, John, Judas, the disciples, the soldiers, two thieves, the other women who were there when he died, and many others. Each had a crucial part in the tragic drama unfolding. Some caused it to happen. Some only allowed it. Some were indifferent. But all were a part.

Perhaps the most courageous were little noticed, like the women who stood by the cross. While Peter and others denied him and refused to associate with him, these women had courage to show themselves in full view. At the hour of his greatest need he was not completely alone, for a small group was brave enough and compassionate enough at least to be there.

ANOTHER VOICE: "While to the reluctant the cross is too heavy to be borne, it grows light to the heart of willing trust.

"The cross of Christ, on which he was extended, points, in the length of it, to heaven and earth, reconciling them together; and in the breadth of it, to former and following ages, as being equally salvation to both.

"The cross of Christ is the sweetest burden I ever bore; it is such a burden as wings are to a bird, or sails to a ship, to carry me forward to my harbor" (Samuel Rutherford).[1]

ANOTHER VOICE: We may grieve at death, particularly the death of Christ, as we reflect on what people have done to cause and allow this tragedy. Yet our grief is cleansing, as a gift from God, for in grief we find healing.

ANOTHER VOICE: "Great grief makes sacred those upon whom its hand is laid.—Joy may elevate, ambition glorify, but only sorrow can consecrate" (Horace Greeley).[2]

[1] Tryon Edwards, comp., *The New Dictionary of Thoughts* (New York: Standard Book Co., 1960), p. 123.
[2] *Ibid.,* p. 251.

Good Grief

Grief

A VOICE: We have been a death-denying society. Most deaths take place in the sterile, clinical, and sometimes impersonal isolation room or intensive care unit of a hospital. Professionals fix up the bodies of the dead and make them look as though they are merely sleeping. When someone is about to die, we are often whisked out of the room so that we can be spared seeing the end of life. Just when a person needs the comfort of another human being—at the hour of death—we usually leave him or her to face the final time alone.

But death is a part of life. It has been defined as the final stage of growth. And only in recent years has our society dared to acknowledge death, to study it, and to try to come to grips with the process of grief.

Jesus' death was untimely and unnatural. He did not die of disease or old age or by accident. He was executed at an age when life should have been full of promise, accomplishment, and hope. Instead, he was cut down, and life was cut short—but for a higher purpose.

We learn a lot about grief from the death of Jesus. On the way to Calvary, he said to the women who were mourning his coming death, "Weep for yourselves . . . . " When we mourn the loss of someone we love, we also are thinking about ourselves, for now we must face life without that person. But deeper still, when we see death, we not only feel for the person who has died, but we also feel for ourselves. We know that we, too, must face the end of our lives.

Jesus took care of some last bit of family business just before he died. He entrusted Mary, his mother, to the care of the disciple John. He was concerned for others even while facing his own death.

READER: (John 19:25-27)

VOICE: He was mindful of God, at first feeling God-forsaken, then trusting his very being to God's care. Most people are mindful of God when they face death. There are no atheists in the battlefield. But he was aware of divine guidance all of his life; so to pray at life's end was simply a natural outgrowth of a totally committed and useful life.

READER: (Luke 23:44-46)

VOICE: He forgave.

READER: (Luke 23:34)

VOICE: He gave comfort and assurance to someone who asked his help.

READER: (Luke 23:39-43)

VOICE: And he knew, beyond all doubt, that there is more to life than death. Life goes on in a higher plane—the extra-earthly kingdom of God where there is warmth, peace, and security in the very presence of God.

Some look upon Jesus' death as an ending. The cross has been the traditional symbol of Christianity since early times. It is the emblem of death. Perhaps the symbol of our faith should be the empty tomb. The cross was one experience in his life. But he overcame death and lives!

Contrasts

ANOTHER VOICE:

He was born a human being,
Yet he is God.
He came to bring Good News,
But many thought it was bad.
He did good, fed the hungry, cured the sick,
But they said he was evil.
He taught from the Scriptures,
Yet was called a heretic.
He lived among men,
But his allegiance was to the kingdom of
    God.
He was friend to many,
And they turned their backs on him.
He lived a life of love,
Yet was hated.
He came to save the world,
But would not spare himself.
He despised evil;
He loved sinners.
He had the universe at his command,
But would rather be with the poor.
He harmed no one,
And in return was harmed.
He was innocent,
Yet was declared guilty.
He came bringing peace,
And was given a cross.
He showed God's love,
But it brought out the worst in many.
He died for us;
What shall we do for him?

Reading

ANOTHER VOICE: Look at the lives which surrounded Jesus as he went to the cross: Peter, Pilate, Barabbas, Mary, Martha, John, Judas, the disciples, the soldiers, two thieves, the other women who were there when he died, and many others. Each had a crucial part in the tragic drama unfolding. Some caused it to happen. Some only allowed it. Some were indifferent. But all were a part.

Perhaps the most courageous were little noticed, like the women who stood by the cross. While Peter and others denied him and refused to associate with him, these women had courage to show themselves in full view. At the hour of his greatest need he was not completely alone, for a small group was brave enough and compassionate enough at least to be there.

ANOTHER VOICE: "While to the reluctant the cross is too heavy to be borne, it grows light to the heart of willing trust.

"The cross of Christ, on which he was extended, points, in the length of it, to heaven and earth, reconciling them together; and in the breadth of it, to former and following ages, as being equally salvation to both.

"The cross of Christ is the sweetest burden I ever bore; it is such a burden as wings are to a bird, or sails to a ship, to carry me forward to my harbor" (Samuel Rutherford).[1]

ANOTHER VOICE: We may grieve at death, particularly the death of Christ, as we reflect on what people have done to cause and allow this tragedy. Yet our grief is cleansing, as a gift from God, for in grief we find healing.

ANOTHER VOICE: "Great grief makes sacred those upon whom its hand is laid.—Joy may elevate, ambition glorify, but only sorrow can consecrate" (Horace Greeley).[2]

[1] Tryon Edwards, comp., *The New Dictionary of Thoughts* (New York: Standard Book Co., 1960), p. 123.
[2] *Ibid.,* p. 251.

Good Grief

Grief

A VOICE: We have been a death-denying society. Most deaths take place in the sterile, clinical, and sometimes impersonal isolation room or intensive care unit of a hospital. Professionals fix up the bodies of the dead and make them look as though they are merely sleeping. When someone is about to die, we are often whisked out of the room so that we can be spared seeing the end of life. Just when a person needs the comfort of another human being—at the hour of death—we usually leave him or her to face the final time alone.

But death is a part of life. It has been defined as the final stage of growth. And only in recent years has our society dared to acknowledge death, to study it, and to try to come to grips with the process of grief.

Jesus' death was untimely and unnatural. He did not die of disease or old age or by accident. He was executed at an age when life should have been full of promise, accomplishment, and hope. Instead, he was cut down, and life was cut short—but for a higher purpose.

We learn a lot about grief from the death of Jesus. On the way to Calvary, he said to the women who were mourning his coming death, "Weep for yourselves . . . ." When we mourn the loss of someone we love, we also are thinking about ourselves, for now we must face life without that person. But deeper still, when we see death, we not only feel for the person who has died, but we also feel for ourselves. We know that we, too, must face the end of our lives.

Jesus took care of some last bit of family business just before he died. He entrusted Mary, his mother, to the care of the disciple John. He was concerned for others even while facing his own death.

READER: (John 19:25-27)

VOICE: He was mindful of God, at first feeling God-forsaken, then trusting his very being to God's care. Most people are mindful of God when they face death. There are no atheists in the battlefield. But he was aware of divine guidance all of his life; so to pray at life's end was simply a natural outgrowth of a totally committed and useful life.

READER: (Luke 23:44-46)

VOICE: He forgave.

READER: (Luke 23:34)

VOICE: He gave comfort and assurance to someone who asked his help.

READER: (Luke 23:39-43)

VOICE: And he knew, beyond all doubt, that there is more to life than death. Life goes on in a higher plane—the extra-earthly kingdom of God where there is warmth, peace, and security in the very presence of God.

Some look upon Jesus' death as an ending. The cross has been the traditional symbol of Christianity since early times. It is the emblem of death. Perhaps the symbol of our faith should be the empty tomb. The cross was one experience in his life. But he overcame death and lives!

Contrasts

ANOTHER VOICE:

He was born a human being,
Yet he is God.
He came to bring Good News,
But many thought it was bad.
He did good, fed the hungry, cured the sick,
But they said he was evil.
He taught from the Scriptures,
Yet was called a heretic.
He lived among men,
But his allegiance was to the kingdom of
    God.
He was friend to many,
And they turned their backs on him.
He lived a life of love,
Yet was hated.
He came to save the world,
But would not spare himself.
He despised evil;
He loved sinners.
He had the universe at his command,
But would rather be with the poor.
He harmed no one,
And in return was harmed.
He was innocent,
Yet was declared guilty.
He came bringing peace,
And was given a cross.
He showed God's love,
But it brought out the worst in many.
He died for us;
What shall we do for him?

Reading

ANOTHER VOICE: Look at the lives which surrounded Jesus as he went to the cross: Peter, Pilate, Barabbas, Mary, Martha, John, Judas, the disciples, the soldiers, two thieves, the other women who were there when he died, and many others. Each had a crucial part in the tragic drama unfolding. Some caused it to happen. Some only allowed it. Some were indifferent. But all were a part.

Perhaps the most courageous were little noticed, like the women who stood by the cross. While Peter and others denied him and refused to associate with him, these women had courage to show themselves in full view. At the hour of his greatest need he was not completely alone, for a small group was brave enough and compassionate enough at least to be there.

ANOTHER VOICE: "While to the reluctant the cross is too heavy to be borne, it grows light to the heart of willing trust.

"The cross of Christ, on which he was extended, points, in the length of it, to heaven and earth, reconciling them together; and in the breadth of it, to former and following ages, as being equally salvation to both.

"The cross of Christ is the sweetest burden I ever bore; it is such a burden as wings are to a bird, or sails to a ship, to carry me forward to my harbor" (Samuel Rutherford).[1]

ANOTHER VOICE: We may grieve at death, particularly the death of Christ, as we reflect on what people have done to cause and allow this tragedy. Yet our grief is cleansing, as a gift from God, for in grief we find healing.

ANOTHER VOICE: "Great grief makes sacred those upon whom its hand is laid.—Joy may elevate, ambition glorify, but only sorrow can consecrate" (Horace Greeley).[2]

[1] Tryon Edwards, comp., *The New Dictionary of Thoughts* (New York: Standard Book Co., 1960), p. 123.
[2] *Ibid.*, p. 251.

Good Grief

Grief

A VOICE: We have been a death-denying society. Most deaths take place in the sterile, clinical, and sometimes impersonal isolation room or intensive care unit of a hospital. Professionals fix up the bodies of the dead and make them look as though they are merely sleeping. When someone is about to die, we are often whisked out of the room so that we can be spared seeing the end of life. Just when a person needs the comfort of another human being—at the hour of death—we usually leave him or her to face the final time alone.

But death is a part of life. It has been defined as the final stage of growth. And only in recent years has our society dared to acknowledge death, to study it, and to try to come to grips with the process of grief.

Jesus' death was untimely and unnatural. He did not die of disease or old age or by accident. He was executed at an age when life should have been full of promise, accomplishment, and hope. Instead, he was cut down, and life was cut short—but for a higher purpose.

We learn a lot about grief from the death of Jesus. On the way to Calvary, he said to the women who were mourning his coming death, "Weep for yourselves . . . . " When we mourn the loss of someone we love, we also are thinking about ourselves, for now we must face life without that person. But deeper still, when we see death, we not only feel for the person who has died, but we also feel for ourselves. We know that we, too, must face the end of our lives.

Jesus took care of some last bit of family business just before he died. He entrusted Mary, his mother, to the care of the disciple John. He was concerned for others even while facing his own death.

READER: (John 19:25-27)

VOICE: He was mindful of God, at first feeling God-forsaken, then trusting his very being to God's care. Most people are mindful of God when they face death. There are no atheists in the battlefield. But he was aware of divine guidance all of his life; so to pray at life's end was simply a natural outgrowth of a totally committed and useful life.

READER: (Luke 23:44-46)

VOICE: He forgave.

READER: (Luke 23:34)

VOICE: He gave comfort and assurance to someone who asked his help.

READER: (Luke 23:39-43)

VOICE: And he knew, beyond all doubt, that there is more to life than death. Life goes on in a higher plane—the extra-earthly kingdom of God where there is warmth, peace, and security in the very presence of God.

Some look upon Jesus' death as an ending. The cross has been the traditional symbol of Christianity since early times. It is the emblem of death. Perhaps the symbol of our faith should be the empty tomb. The cross was one experience in his life. But he overcame death and lives!

Contrasts

ANOTHER VOICE:

He was born a human being,
Yet he is God.
He came to bring Good News,
But many thought it was bad.
He did good, fed the hungry, cured the sick,
But they said he was evil.
He taught from the Scriptures,
Yet was called a heretic.
He lived among men,
But his allegiance was to the kingdom of God.
He was friend to many,
And they turned their backs on him.
He lived a life of love,
Yet was hated.
He came to save the world,
But would not spare himself.
He despised evil;
He loved sinners.
He had the universe at his command,
But would rather be with the poor.
He harmed no one,
And in return was harmed.
He was innocent,
Yet was declared guilty.
He came bringing peace,
And was given a cross.
He showed God's love,
But it brought out the worst in many.
He died for us;
What shall we do for him?

Reading

ANOTHER VOICE: Look at the lives which surrounded Jesus as he went to the cross: Peter, Pilate, Barabbas, Mary, Martha, John, Judas, the disciples, the soldiers, two thieves, the other women who were there when he died, and many others. Each had a crucial part in the tragic drama unfolding. Some caused it to happen. Some only allowed it. Some were indifferent. But all were a part.

Perhaps the most courageous were little noticed, like the women who stood by the cross. While Peter and others denied him and refused to associate with him, these women had courage to show themselves in full view. At the hour of his greatest need he was not completely alone, for a small group was brave enough and compassionate enough at least to be there.

ANOTHER VOICE: "While to the reluctant the cross is too heavy to be borne, it grows light to the heart of willing trust.

"The cross of Christ, on which he was extended, points, in the length of it, to heaven and earth, reconciling them together; and in the breadth of it, to former and following ages, as being equally salvation to both.

"The cross of Christ is the sweetest burden I ever bore; it is such a burden as wings are to a bird, or sails to a ship, to carry me forward to my harbor" (Samuel Rutherford).[1]

ANOTHER VOICE: We may grieve at death, particularly the death of Christ, as we reflect on what people have done to cause and allow this tragedy. Yet our grief is cleansing, as a gift from God, for in grief we find healing.

ANOTHER VOICE: "Great grief makes sacred those upon whom its hand is laid.—Joy may elevate, ambition glorify, but only sorrow can consecrate" (Horace Greeley).[2]

[1] Tryon Edwards, comp., *The New Dictionary of Thoughts* (New York: Standard Book Co., 1960), p. 123.
[2] *Ibid.*, p. 251.

Modern Easter

A Celebration for Easter

This service is one which combines drama with opportunities for reflection and dedication. You may decide to use this material as a part of a special youth program or for an Easter sunrise service.

Preparation

The most effective way to use the playlet in this chapter is to have each participant learn his or her lines. The play is quite short, and memorization should be easy. Encourage the actors to add to the script their own ideas which may have grown out of personal experiences and thoughts. The setting should be kept simple. There are only three characters. Have them sit around a table at the front of your meeting room or sanctuary. Better still, have your meeting area arranged in the round with the table as its center. If lines cannot be memorized, encourage each actor to read over his or her part several times so that proper emphasis can be felt and delivered.

When the time comes for "Reflection," be sure that the questions are read slowly, allowing time for thought.

The Experience

Opening Thought: "Our Lord has written the promise of the resurrection, not in books alone, but in every leaf in spring-time.

"The diamond that shines in the Saviour's crown shall beam in unquenched beauty, at last, on the forehead of every human soul, risen through grace to the immortality of heaven" (Martin Luther).[1]

Hymn: "Christ the Lord Is Risen Today."

Scripture: 1 Corinthians 15:42-53.

The End or the Beginning?: Supplement A.

Scripture: Luke 24:1-12.

Reflections: Supplement A.

Closing: In faith, let us go and do likewise.

[1] Tryon Edwards, comp., *The New Dictionary of Thoughts* (New York: Standard Book Co., 1960), p. 571.

Modern Easter

The End or the Beginning?

This playlet is written for simplicity of presentation and with the minimal use of props. The setting is today. The place is anywhere young people might meet to talk. There are only three characters: Walt, a teenaged boy; Tina, a girl; and Gloria, who is the counselor of the youth group Tina and Walt attend. The subject is death and resurrection; the theme is Easter faith. The three are seated around a table. They are very serious and grief stricken.

WALT: That funeral sort of shook me up. I wish I hadn't gone. Last week Mary was happy and full of life. Today she just lay there, still as anything.

TINA: Why Mary? Why did it have to happen to her?

GLORIA: Why does it happen to anybody? It was an accident. That's all.

TINA: But why did God let it happen?

WALT: He didn't let it happen. If that kid who ran into her had had better training, or if his brakes would have been in better shape. . . .

TINA: If, if, if. What if? We can't change it now no matter what. Bet that kid wishes he had a second chance—bet he'd do differently.

GLORIA: It's all past history now. No one can change what happened. We have to stop thinking about what might have happened and concentrate on how things are today—and tomorrow.

WALT: Tomorrow. What will tomorrow be like for Mary? Or today for that matter? Pastor Williams read those verses about the resurrection and life after death and all, but what does it mean to Mary? Where is she now? Six feet under?

TINA: She's there all right. But I can't stand thinking that she's really gone. There has to be more to life than—death.

WALT: Pastor Williams said there is. I'd like to believe him, but that casket looked pretty final to me. And that's another thing. How come people say "casket" instead of "coffin"?

TINA: Sounds better. Just like they say "passed away" so they don't have to say "died." But Mary didn't just pass away. She's dead! And I feel almost like I died inside—or part of me did.

GLORIA: I've thought a lot about death. Fact is, I used to be terrified to think about my own life coming to an end.

WALT: I know what you mean. Sometimes I'd wake up for no good reason in the middle of the night, thinking that I have to face death myself someday. It's like an impossible thought. I can't even think it through all the way. Me, coming to the end.

GLORIA: But one day I got the idea that if you are no longer conscious after death, if your thinking stops and you disappear, you would be just like you were before you were born—no thoughts, no feelings, just nothingness.

TINA: That gives me the creeps.

GLORIA: Then I had another thought. I have come to believe in Jesus' resurrection, and he said that because he lives, his followers will live, too.

WALT: I'd like to believe that. But what would it be like? And what is Mary experiencing right now?

GLORIA: I think that Mary is the same Mary we knew and loved. She has taken with her all that she was until she died—all her hopes, dreams, expectations—and she will continue to grow as Mary throughout eternity. She'll develop into a higher person than she could have here, but she's building on the foundation of personality she had while she was alive on earth.

TINA: It's like her life here was just a beginning, a starting place. She'll keep on growing and experiencing and loving.

WALT: I get it—only on a much higher level. That's a fantastic thought! You know, one thing that helped me a lot when my granddad died was a thought my kid brother came up with. I thought it was kind of silly at the time, but it sort of helped me get over the hurt a little. He'd had a tooth pulled—a molar—and had quite a time because it was infected. He said that when somebody close to you died, it was something like getting a tooth pulled. It bothered you a lot at first, but then it healed over after a while, and you could even put your tongue in the place that used to hurt. It got all healed up; yet you were always aware that there was a gap there where the tooth used to be. Things felt better, but they were never quite the same.

Reflections

(At this point, someone in your group should ask all present to bow their heads while

the following questions are asked. Pause after each question to allow time for individual thoughts and meditation.)

In the playlet we saw, what came to mind as Tina asked if God allowed the accident to happen? *(Pause)*

When Walt asked where Mary is now? *(Pause)*

When Tina said that there must be more to life than death? *(Pause)*

When Gloria told about her fear of death and her early explanation, comparing death to the time before she was born? *(Pause)*

When Gloria spoke of faith in Jesus' resurrection and her own personal hope? *(Pause)*

When the group talked about life after life as a continuation of our lives on a higher plane? *(Pause)*

When Walt told how he had been helped by a simple illustration from his brother? *(Pause)*

Where do we stand in our faith and hope in the resurrection? *(Pause)*

This is a good moment in time for us to renew our own resurrection faith. *(Pause)* Amen.

Modern Easter

The End or the Beginning?

This playlet is written for simplicity of presentation and with the minimal use of props. The setting is today. The place is anywhere young people might meet to talk. There are only three characters: Walt, a teenaged boy; Tina, a girl; and Gloria, who is the counselor of the youth group Tina and Walt attend. The subject is death and resurrection; the theme is Easter faith. The three are seated around a table. They are very serious and grief stricken.

WALT: That funeral sort of shook me up. I wish I hadn't gone. Last week Mary was happy and full of life. Today she just lay there, still as anything.

TINA: Why Mary? Why did it have to happen to her?

GLORIA: Why does it happen to anybody? It was an accident. That's all.

TINA: But why did God let it happen?

WALT: He didn't let it happen. If that kid who ran into her had had better training, or if his brakes would have been in better shape. . . .

TINA: If, if, if. What if? We can't change it now no matter what. Bet that kid wishes he had a second chance—bet he'd do differently.

GLORIA: It's all past history now. No one can change what happened. We have to stop thinking about what might have happened and concentrate on how things are today—and tomorrow.

WALT: Tomorrow. What will tomorrow be like for Mary? Or today for that matter? Pastor Williams read those verses about the resurrection and life after death and all, but what does it mean to Mary? Where is she now? Six feet under?

TINA: She's there all right. But I can't stand thinking that she's really gone. There has to be more to life than—death.

WALT: Pastor Williams said there is. I'd like to believe him, but that casket looked pretty final to me. And that's another thing. How come people say "casket" instead of "coffin"?

TINA: Sounds better. Just like they say "passed away" so they don't have to say "died." But Mary didn't just pass away. She's dead! And I feel almost like I died inside—or part of me did.

GLORIA: I've thought a lot about death. Fact is, I used to be terrified to think about my own life coming to an end.

WALT: I know what you mean. Sometimes I'd wake up for no good reason in the middle of the night, thinking that I have to face death myself someday. It's like an impossible thought. I can't even think it through all the way. Me, coming to the end.

GLORIA: But one day I got the idea that if you are no longer conscious after death, if your thinking stops and you disappear, you would be just like you were before you were born—no thoughts, no feelings, just nothingness.

TINA: That gives me the creeps.

GLORIA: Then I had another thought. I have come to believe in Jesus' resurrection, and he said that because he lives, his followers will live, too.

WALT: I'd like to believe that. But what would it be like? And what is Mary experiencing right now?

GLORIA: I think that Mary is the same Mary we knew and loved. She has taken with her all that she was until she died—all her hopes, dreams, expectations—and she will continue to grow as Mary throughout eternity. She'll develop into a higher person than she could have here, but she's building on the foundation of personality she had while she was alive on earth.

TINA: It's like her life here was just a beginning, a starting place. She'll keep on growing and experiencing and loving.

WALT: I get it—only on a much higher level. That's a fantastic thought! You know, one thing that helped me a lot when my granddad died was a thought my kid brother came up with. I thought it was kind of silly at the time, but it sort of helped me get over the hurt a little. He'd had a tooth pulled—a molar—and had quite a time because it was infected. He said that when somebody close to you died, it was something like getting a tooth pulled. It bothered you a lot at first, but then it healed over after a while, and you could even put your tongue in the place that used to hurt. It got all healed up; yet you were always aware that there was a gap there where the tooth used to be. Things felt better, but they were never quite the same.

Reflections

(At this point, someone in your group should ask all present to bow their heads while

the following questions are asked. Pause after each question to allow time for individual thoughts and meditation.)

In the playlet we saw, what came to mind as Tina asked if God allowed the accident to happen? *(Pause)*

When Walt asked where Mary is now? *(Pause)*

When Tina said that there must be more to life than death? *(Pause)*

When Gloria told about her fear of death and her early explanation, comparing death to the time before she was born? *(Pause)*

When Gloria spoke of faith in Jesus' resurrection and her own personal hope? *(Pause)*

When the group talked about life after life as a continuation of our lives on a higher plane? *(Pause)*

When Walt told how he had been helped by a simple illustration from his brother? *(Pause)*

Where do we stand in our faith and hope in the resurrection? *(Pause)*

This is a good moment in time for us to renew our own resurrection faith. *(Pause)* Amen.

Modern Easter

The End or the Beginning?

This playlet is written for simplicity of presentation and with the minimal use of props. The setting is today. The place is anywhere young people might meet to talk. There are only three characters: Walt, a teenaged boy; Tina, a girl; and Gloria, who is the counselor of the youth group Tina and Walt attend. The subject is death and resurrection; the theme is Easter faith. The three are seated around a table. They are very serious and grief stricken.

WALT: That funeral sort of shook me up. I wish I hadn't gone. Last week Mary was happy and full of life. Today she just lay there, still as anything.

TINA: Why Mary? Why did it have to happen to her?

GLORIA: Why does it happen to anybody? It was an accident. That's all.

TINA: But why did God let it happen?

WALT: He didn't let it happen. If that kid who ran into her had had better training, or if his brakes would have been in better shape. . . .

TINA: If, if, if. What if? We can't change it now no matter what. Bet that kid wishes he had a second chance—bet he'd do differently.

GLORIA: It's all past history now. No one can change what happened. We have to stop thinking about what might have happened and concentrate on how things are today—and tomorrow.

WALT: Tomorrow. What will tomorrow be like for Mary? Or today for that matter? Pastor Williams read those verses about the resurrection and life after death and all, but what does it mean to Mary? Where is she now? Six feet under?

TINA: She's there all right. But I can't stand thinking that she's really gone. There has to be more to life than—death.

WALT: Pastor Williams said there is. I'd like to believe him, but that casket looked pretty final to me. And that's another thing. How come people say "casket" instead of "coffin"?

TINA: Sounds better. Just like they say "passed away" so they don't have to say "died." But Mary didn't just pass away. She's dead! And I feel almost like I died inside—or part of me did.

GLORIA: I've thought a lot about death. Fact is, I used to be terrified to think about my own life coming to an end.

WALT: I know what you mean. Sometimes I'd wake up for no good reason in the middle of the night, thinking that I have to face death myself someday. It's like an impossible thought. I can't even think it through all the way. Me, coming to the end.

GLORIA: But one day I got the idea that if you are no longer conscious after death, if your thinking stops and you disappear, you would be just like you were before you were born—no thoughts, no feelings, just nothingness.

TINA: That gives me the creeps.

GLORIA: Then I had another thought. I have come to believe in Jesus' resurrection, and he said that because he lives, his followers will live, too.

WALT: I'd like to believe that. But what would it be like? And what is Mary experiencing right now?

GLORIA: I think that Mary is the same Mary we knew and loved. She has taken with her all that she was until she died—all her hopes, dreams, expectations—and she will continue to grow as Mary throughout eternity. She'll develop into a higher person than she could have here, but she's building on the foundation of personality she had while she was alive on earth.

TINA: It's like her life here was just a beginning, a starting place. She'll keep on growing and experiencing and loving.

WALT: I get it—only on a much higher level. That's a fantastic thought! You know, one thing that helped me a lot when my granddad died was a thought my kid brother came up with. I thought it was kind of silly at the time, but it sort of helped me get over the hurt a little. He'd had a tooth pulled—a molar—and had quite a time because it was infected. He said that when somebody close to you died, it was something like getting a tooth pulled. It bothered you a lot at first, but then it healed over after a while, and you could even put your tongue in the place that used to hurt. It got all healed up; yet you were always aware that there was a gap there where the tooth used to be. Things felt better, but they were never quite the same.

Reflections

(At this point, someone in your group should ask all present to bow their heads while

the following questions are asked. Pause after each question to allow time for individual thoughts and meditation.)

In the playlet we saw, what came to mind as Tina asked if God allowed the accident to happen? *(Pause)*

When Walt asked where Mary is now? *(Pause)*

When Tina said that there must be more to life than death? *(Pause)*

When Gloria told about her fear of death and her early explanation, comparing death to the time before she was born? *(Pause)*

When Gloria spoke of faith in Jesus' resurrection and her own personal hope? *(Pause)*

When the group talked about life after life as a continuation of our lives on a higher plane? *(Pause)*

When Walt told how he had been helped by a simple illustration from his brother? *(Pause)*

Where do we stand in our faith and hope in the resurrection? *(Pause)*

This is a good moment in time for us to renew our own resurrection faith. *(Pause)* Amen.

Modern Easter

The End or the Beginning?

This playlet is written for simplicity of presentation and with the minimal use of props. The setting is today. The place is anywhere young people might meet to talk. There are only three characters: Walt, a teenaged boy; Tina, a girl; and Gloria, who is the counselor of the youth group Tina and Walt attend. The subject is death and resurrection; the theme is Easter faith. The three are seated around a table. They are very serious and grief stricken.

WALT: That funeral sort of shook me up. I wish I hadn't gone. Last week Mary was happy and full of life. Today she just lay there, still as anything.

TINA: Why Mary? Why did it have to happen to her?

GLORIA: Why does it happen to anybody? It was an accident. That's all.

TINA: But why did God let it happen?

WALT: He didn't let it happen. If that kid who ran into her had had better training, or if his brakes would have been in better shape. . . .

TINA: If, if, if. What if? We can't change it now no matter what. Bet that kid wishes he had a second chance—bet he'd do differently.

GLORIA: It's all past history now. No one can change what happened. We have to stop thinking about what might have happened and concentrate on how things are today—and tomorrow.

WALT: Tomorrow. What will tomorrow be like for Mary? Or today for that matter? Pastor Williams read those verses about the resurrection and life after death and all, but what does it mean to Mary? Where is she now? Six feet under?

TINA: She's there all right. But I can't stand thinking that she's really gone. There has to be more to life than—death.

WALT: Pastor Williams said there is. I'd like to believe him, but that casket looked pretty final to me. And that's another thing. How come people say "casket" instead of "coffin"?

TINA: Sounds better. Just like they say "passed away" so they don't have to say "died." But Mary didn't just pass away. She's dead! And I feel almost like I died inside—or part of me did.

GLORIA: I've thought a lot about death. Fact is, I used to be terrified to think about my own life coming to an end.

WALT: I know what you mean. Sometimes I'd wake up for no good reason in the middle of the night, thinking that I have to face death myself someday. It's like an impossible thought. I can't even think it through all the way. Me, coming to the end.

GLORIA: But one day I got the idea that if you are no longer conscious after death, if your thinking stops and you disappear, you would be just like you were before you were born—no thoughts, no feelings, just nothingness.

TINA: That gives me the creeps.

GLORIA: Then I had another thought. I have come to believe in Jesus' resurrection, and he said that because he lives, his followers will live, too.

WALT: I'd like to believe that. But what would it be like? And what is Mary experiencing right now?

GLORIA: I think that Mary is the same Mary we knew and loved. She has taken with her all that she was until she died—all her hopes, dreams, expectations—and she will continue to grow as Mary throughout eternity. She'll develop into a higher person than she could have here, but she's building on the foundation of personality she had while she was alive on earth.

TINA: It's like her life here was just a beginning, a starting place. She'll keep on growing and experiencing and loving.

WALT: I get it—only on a much higher level. That's a fantastic thought! You know, one thing that helped me a lot when my granddad died was a thought my kid brother came up with. I thought it was kind of silly at the time, but it sort of helped me get over the hurt a little. He'd had a tooth pulled—a molar—and had quite a time because it was infected. He said that when somebody close to you died, it was something like getting a tooth pulled. It bothered you a lot at first, but then it healed over after a while, and you could even put your tongue in the place that used to hurt. It got all healed up; yet you were always aware that there was a gap there where the tooth used to be. Things felt better, but they were never quite the same.

Reflections

(At this point, someone in your group should ask all present to bow their heads while

the following questions are asked. Pause after each question to allow time for individual thoughts and meditation.)

In the playlet we saw, what came to mind as Tina asked if God allowed the accident to happen? *(Pause)*

When Walt asked where Mary is now? *(Pause)*

When Tina said that there must be more to life than death? *(Pause)*

When Gloria told about her fear of death and her early explanation, comparing death to the time before she was born? *(Pause)*

When Gloria spoke of faith in Jesus' resurrection and her own personal hope? *(Pause)*

When the group talked about life after life as a continuation of our lives on a higher plane? *(Pause)*

When Walt told how he had been helped by a simple illustration from his brother? *(Pause)*

Where do we stand in our faith and hope in the resurrection? *(Pause)*

This is a good moment in time for us to renew our own resurrection faith. *(Pause)* Amen.

Modern Easter

The End or the Beginning?

This playlet is written for simplicity of presentation and with the minimal use of props. The setting is today. The place is anywhere young people might meet to talk. There are only three characters: Walt, a teenaged boy; Tina, a girl; and Gloria, who is the counselor of the youth group Tina and Walt attend. The subject is death and resurrection; the theme is Easter faith. The three are seated around a table. They are very serious and grief stricken.

WALT: That funeral sort of shook me up. I wish I hadn't gone. Last week Mary was happy and full of life. Today she just lay there, still as anything.

TINA: Why Mary? Why did it have to happen to her?

GLORIA: Why does it happen to anybody? It was an accident. That's all.

TINA: But why did God let it happen?

WALT: He didn't let it happen. If that kid who ran into her had had better training, or if his brakes would have been in better shape. . . .

TINA: If, if, if. What if? We can't change it now no matter what. Bet that kid wishes he had a second chance—bet he'd do differently.

GLORIA: It's all past history now. No one can change what happened. We have to stop thinking about what might have happened and concentrate on how things are today—and tomorrow.

WALT: Tomorrow. What will tomorrow be like for Mary? Or today for that matter? Pastor Williams read those verses about the resurrection and life after death and all, but what does it mean to Mary? Where is she now? Six feet under?

TINA: She's there all right. But I can't stand thinking that she's really gone. There has to be more to life than—death.

WALT: Pastor Williams said there is. I'd like to believe him, but that casket looked pretty final to me. And that's another thing. How come people say "casket" instead of "coffin"?

TINA: Sounds better. Just like they say "passed away" so they don't have to say "died." But Mary didn't just pass away. She's dead! And I feel almost like I died inside—or part of me did.

GLORIA: I've thought a lot about death. Fact is, I used to be terrified to think about my own life coming to an end.

WALT: I know what you mean. Sometimes I'd wake up for no good reason in the middle of the night, thinking that I have to face death myself someday. It's like an impossible thought. I can't even think it through all the way. Me, coming to the end.

GLORIA: But one day I got the idea that if you are no longer conscious after death, if your thinking stops and you disappear, you would be just like you were before you were born—no thoughts, no feelings, just nothingness.

TINA: That gives me the creeps.

GLORIA: Then I had another thought. I have come to believe in Jesus' resurrection, and he said that because he lives, his followers will live, too.

WALT: I'd like to believe that. But what would it be like? And what is Mary experiencing right now?

GLORIA: I think that Mary is the same Mary we knew and loved. She has taken with her all that she was until she died—all her hopes, dreams, expectations—and she will continue to grow as Mary throughout eternity. She'll develop into a higher person than she could have here, but she's building on the foundation of personality she had while she was alive on earth.

TINA: It's like her life here was just a beginning, a starting place. She'll keep on growing and experiencing and loving.

WALT: I get it—only on a much higher level. That's a fantastic thought! You know, one thing that helped me a lot when my granddad died was a thought my kid brother came up with. I thought it was kind of silly at the time, but it sort of helped me get over the hurt a little. He'd had a tooth pulled—a molar—and had quite a time because it was infected. He said that when somebody close to you died, it was something like getting a tooth pulled. It bothered you a lot at first, but then it healed over after a while, and you could even put your tongue in the place that used to hurt. It got all healed up; yet you were always aware that there was a gap there where the tooth used to be. Things felt better, but they were never quite the same.

Reflections

(At this point, someone in your group should ask all present to bow their heads while

the following questions are asked. Pause after each question to allow time for individual thoughts and meditation.)

In the playlet we saw, what came to mind as Tina asked if God allowed the accident to happen? *(Pause)*

When Walt asked where Mary is now? *(Pause)*

When Tina said that there must be more to life than death? *(Pause)*

When Gloria told about her fear of death and her early explanation, comparing death to the time before she was born? *(Pause)*

When Gloria spoke of faith in Jesus' resurrection and her own personal hope? *(Pause)*

When the group talked about life after life as a continuation of our lives on a higher plane? *(Pause)*

When Walt told how he had been helped by a simple illustration from his brother? *(Pause)*

Where do we stand in our faith and hope in the resurrection? *(Pause)*

This is a good moment in time for us to renew our own resurrection faith. *(Pause)* Amen.

Easter Reflections

A Celebration for Easter

The material in this chapter provides an alternative to the chapter entitled "Modern Easter." This chapter is designed to follow a more traditional approach to the Easter theme. The service can be adapted to a variety of settings but may be particularly useful as a part of a regular church service or sunrise service.

Preparation

It is vital to the effectiveness of this experience that all who participate in special parts know their material well and that where there are voice parts, they are delivered slowly enough and also with meaning. The voice parts can be used as a choir or choral reading but with slight modification can be used by one or more people as sermon material. If you elect to have a choral reading, those taking part should use the sanctuary platform, standing together as a choir. Otherwise, use the pulpit or lecterns for presentation of this material.

The Experience

Opening Thoughts: Winter's grasp tries desperately to cling on, but opposing forces are too great. Soon the grip will be broken as the endless cycle of seasons rolls on. For even now, life is bursting forth from the ground. Flowers will appear soon, and so will leaves on the trees. The grass will turn velvet with green. Nothing can prevent the resurrection of nature as springtime blossoms forth. This season is a token and reminder of Christ's resurrection and gives us assurance that all who live in him, though they die, shall live.

Hymn: "Christ Arose" ("Up from the Grave He Arose").

Prayer: Lord and Father of mankind, help us to comprehend the meaning of the Easter faith and of the glory of the risen Lord. Amen.

Scripture: Luke 24:13-35.

Choral Reading: Supplement A.

Reading: "If We Can Believe" (Supplement A).

Hymn: "Christ the Lord Is Risen Today" or solo number "I Know That My Redeemer Lives."

Closing: It is a tradition in many churches for all the people to greet each other after the Easter service by shaking hands and saying, "He is risen." Have one member of your group begin this process by turning to someone else and saying, "He is risen," then telling that person to "pass it on."

SUPPLEMENT A

Easter Reflections

Choral Reading

VOICE: It was the very day of the resurrection, and two of Jesus' followers were walking from Jerusalem to Emmaus.

VOICE: Their steps were slow; their hearts were low.

VOICE: They expected a king who would raise an army.

VOICE: But there was no army, only a crown of thorns.

VOICE: They wanted life.

VOICE: They saw only death.

VOICE: They wanted a revolutionary, a militant who would conquer the conquering Romans.

VOICE: But they saw a cross.

VOICE: For Jesus there was no dignity in death.

ALL: It was a public execution.

VOICE: They expected the pride of victory.

ALL: They got shame, fear, and sorrow.

VOICE: Then a stranger approached.

VOICE: He broke into their conversation.

VOICE: Just like he breaks into ours if we let him.

ALL: They walked the road to Emmaus with God.

VOICE: But did not know him.

VOICE: He asked them probing questions, and the two were amazed that he had not heard the sad news.

VOICE: They also had heard other news, for some people had said that Christ came to life again.

ALL: But they were afraid to believe—or even hope.

VOICE: They were not alone in their doubt. We all are doubters.

ALL: But he broke in! Christ broke into their conversation and their lives.

VOICE: And broke down the walls of their fears.

ALL: How foolish we are; how slow to believe!

VOICE: And from the Scriptures, he told them of all that the Messiah must suffer.

ALL: He broke in. Christ broke in.

VOICE: From Moses and the prophets.

ALL: He broke in. Christ broke in.

VOICE: For all mankind.

ALL: (*loud*) He broke in. Christ broke in.

VOICE: For the Jew and the Gentile.

ALL: (*louder*) He broke in. Christ broke in.

VOICE: For you and for me.

ALL: (*very loud*) He broke in. Christ broke in.

VOICE: So they ate together that night, Jesus and the two.

ALL: And still they did not know him.

VOICE: He took bread.

ALL: And still they did not know him.

VOICE: He broke it, just like he did at the Passover.

ALL: And still they did not know him.

VOICE: He gave them bread.

ALL: And somehow they knew!

VOICE: It may have been his voice.

VOICE: They may have seen . . .

ALL: The nail prints in his hands.

VOICE: But their eyes were opened.

ALL: And they knew him.

VOICE: Their hearts were aglow like a fire burning within them.

ALL: And they believed him.

VOICE: He disappeared from their sight.

ALL: Yet, seeing him no more, they loved him.

VOICE: Seeing, believing, and loving compelled them to act. Though the hour was late and the night had fallen . . .

ALL: They got up at once to spread the word—to gossip the Good News.

ALL: He is risen.

(*louder*) He is risen.

(*very loud*) The Lord is risen, indeed!

Reading: "If We Can Believe"

If we can believe—
   That plants can grow,
   That creatures can breathe,
   That an atom can be split,
   That modern medicine can cure disease,
   That we are ingenious enough to probe
      the planets
(And we possess a particle of the power of
   God),

Is it all that hard to believe—
   That God, in whose image people were
      made,
   Could come to earth,
   Be killed by murderous people,
   Yet forgive
   And break the power of death?
Is it all that hard to believe—
   That because Christ lives,
   We, too, shall live?

SUPPLEMENT A

Easter Reflections

Choral Reading

VOICE: It was the very day of the resurrection, and two of Jesus' followers were walking from Jerusalem to Emmaus.

VOICE: Their steps were slow; their hearts were low.

VOICE: They expected a king who would raise an army.

VOICE: But there was no army, only a crown of thorns.

VOICE: They wanted life.

VOICE: They saw only death.

VOICE: They wanted a revolutionary, a militant who would conquer the conquering Romans.

VOICE: But they saw a cross.

VOICE: For Jesus there was no dignity in death.

ALL: It was a public execution.

VOICE: They expected the pride of victory.

ALL: They got shame, fear, and sorrow.

VOICE: Then a stranger approached.

VOICE: He broke into their conversation.

VOICE: Just like he breaks into ours if we let him.

ALL: They walked the road to Emmaus with God.

VOICE: But did not know him.

VOICE: He asked them probing questions, and the two were amazed that he had not heard the sad news.

VOICE: They also had heard other news, for some people had said that Christ came to life again.

ALL: But they were afraid to believe—or even hope.

VOICE: They were not alone in their doubt. We all are doubters.

ALL: But he broke in! Christ broke into their conversation and their lives.

VOICE: And broke down the walls of their fears.

ALL: How foolish we are; how slow to believe!

VOICE: And from the Scriptures, he told them of all that the Messiah must suffer.

ALL: He broke in. Christ broke in.

VOICE: From Moses and the prophets.

ALL: He broke in. Christ broke in.

VOICE: For all mankind.

ALL: (loud) He broke in. Christ broke in.

VOICE: For the Jew and the Gentile.

ALL: (louder) He broke in. Christ broke in.

VOICE: For you and for me.

ALL: (very loud) He broke in. Christ broke in.

VOICE: So they ate together that night, Jesus and the two.

ALL: And still they did not know him.

VOICE: He took bread.

ALL: And still they did not know him.

VOICE: He broke it, just like he did at the Passover.

ALL: And still they did not know him.

VOICE: He gave them bread.

ALL: And somehow they knew!

VOICE: It may have been his voice.

VOICE: They may have seen . . .

ALL: The nail prints in his hands.

VOICE: But their eyes were opened.

ALL: And they knew him.

VOICE: Their hearts were aglow like a fire burning within them.

ALL: And they believed him.

VOICE: He disappeared from their sight.

ALL: Yet, seeing him no more, they loved him.

VOICE: Seeing, believing, and loving compelled them to act. Though the hour was late and the night had fallen . . .

ALL: They got up at once to spread the word—to gossip the Good News.

ALL: He is risen.

(louder) He is risen.

(very loud) The Lord is risen, indeed!

Reading: "If We Can Believe"

If we can believe—
    That plants can grow,
    That creatures can breathe,
    That an atom can be split,
    That modern medicine can cure disease,
    That we are ingenious enough to probe
        the planets
(And we possess a particle of the power of
    God),

Is it all that hard to believe—
    That God, in whose image people were
        made,
    Could come to earth,
    Be killed by murderous people,
    Yet forgive
    And break the power of death?
Is it all that hard to believe—
    That because Christ lives,
    We, too, shall live?

SUPPLEMENT A   ⑧

Easter Reflections

Choral Reading

VOICE: It was the very day of the resurrection, and two of Jesus' followers were walking from Jerusalem to Emmaus.

VOICE: Their steps were slow; their hearts were low.

VOICE: They expected a king who would raise an army.

VOICE: But there was no army, only a crown of thorns.

VOICE: They wanted life.

VOICE: They saw only death.

VOICE: They wanted a revolutionary, a militant who would conquer the conquering Romans.

VOICE: But they saw a cross.

VOICE: For Jesus there was no dignity in death.

ALL: It was a public execution.

VOICE: They expected the pride of victory.

ALL: They got shame, fear, and sorrow.

VOICE: Then a stranger approached.

VOICE: He broke into their conversation.

VOICE: Just like he breaks into ours if we let him.

ALL: They walked the road to Emmaus with God.

VOICE: But did not know him.

VOICE: He asked them probing questions, and the two were amazed that he had not heard the sad news.

VOICE: They also had heard other news, for some people had said that Christ came to life again.

ALL: But they were afraid to believe—or even hope.

VOICE: They were not alone in their doubt. We all are doubters.

ALL: But he broke in! Christ broke into their conversation and their lives.

VOICE: And broke down the walls of their fears.

ALL: How foolish we are; how slow to believe!

VOICE: And from the Scriptures, he told them of all that the Messiah must suffer.

ALL: He broke in. Christ broke in.

VOICE: From Moses and the prophets.

ALL: He broke in. Christ broke in.

VOICE: For all mankind.

ALL: (loud) He broke in. Christ broke in.

VOICE: For the Jew and the Gentile.

ALL: (louder) He broke in. Christ broke in.

VOICE: For you and for me.

ALL: (very loud) He broke in. Christ broke in.

VOICE: So they ate together that night, Jesus and the two.

ALL: And still they did not know him.

VOICE: He took bread.

ALL: And still they did not know him.

VOICE: He broke it, just like he did at the Passover.

ALL: And still they did not know him.

VOICE: He gave them bread.

ALL: And somehow they knew!

VOICE: It may have been his voice.

VOICE: They may have seen . . .

ALL: The nail prints in his hands.

VOICE: But their eyes were opened.

ALL: And they knew him.

VOICE: Their hearts were aglow like a fire burning within them.

ALL: And they believed him.

VOICE: He disappeared from their sight.

ALL: Yet, seeing him no more, they loved him.

VOICE: Seeing, believing, and loving compelled them to act. Though the hour was late and the night had fallen . . .

ALL: They got up at once to spread the word—to gossip the Good News.

ALL: He is risen.

(louder) He is risen.

(very loud) The Lord is risen, indeed!

Reading: "If We Can Believe"

If we can believe—
    That plants can grow,
    That creatures can breathe,
    That an atom can be split,
    That modern medicine can cure disease,
    That we are ingenious enough to probe
      the planets
(And we possess a particle of the power of
    God),

Is it all that hard to believe—
    That God, in whose image people were
      made,
    Could come to earth,
    Be killed by murderous people,
    Yet forgive
    And break the power of death?
Is it all that hard to believe—
    That because Christ lives,
    We, too, shall live?

SUPPLEMENT A

Easter Reflections

Choral Reading

VOICE: It was the very day of the resurrection, and two of Jesus' followers were walking from Jerusalem to Emmaus.

VOICE: Their steps were slow; their hearts were low.

VOICE: They expected a king who would raise an army.

VOICE: But there was no army, only a crown of thorns.

VOICE: They wanted life.

VOICE: They saw only death.

VOICE: They wanted a revolutionary, a militant who would conquer the conquering Romans.

VOICE: But they saw a cross.

VOICE: For Jesus there was no dignity in death.

ALL: It was a public execution.

VOICE: They expected the pride of victory.

ALL: They got shame, fear, and sorrow.

VOICE: Then a stranger approached.

VOICE: He broke into their conversation.

VOICE: Just like he breaks into ours if we let him.

ALL: They walked the road to Emmaus with God.

VOICE: But did not know him.

VOICE: He asked them probing questions, and the two were amazed that he had not heard the sad news.

VOICE: They also had heard other news, for some people had said that Christ came to life again.

ALL: But they were afraid to believe—or even hope.

VOICE: They were not alone in their doubt. We all are doubters.

ALL: But he broke in! Christ broke into their conversation and their lives.

VOICE: And broke down the walls of their fears.

ALL: How foolish we are; how slow to believe!

VOICE: And from the Scriptures, he told them of all that the Messiah must suffer.

ALL: He broke in. Christ broke in.

VOICE: From Moses and the prophets.

ALL: He broke in. Christ broke in.

VOICE: For all mankind.

ALL: (loud) He broke in. Christ broke in.

VOICE: For the Jew and the Gentile.

ALL: (louder) He broke in. Christ broke in.

VOICE: For you and for me.

ALL: (very loud) He broke in. Christ broke in.

VOICE: So they ate together that night, Jesus and the two.

ALL: And still they did not know him.

VOICE: He took bread.

ALL: And still they did not know him.

VOICE: He broke it, just like he did at the Passover.

ALL: And still they did not know him.

VOICE: He gave them bread.

ALL: And somehow they knew!

VOICE: It may have been his voice.

VOICE: They may have seen . . .

ALL: The nail prints in his hands.

VOICE: But their eyes were opened.

ALL: And they knew him.

VOICE: Their hearts were aglow like a fire burning within them.

ALL: And they believed him.

VOICE: He disappeared from their sight.

ALL: Yet, seeing him no more, they loved him.

VOICE: Seeing, believing, and loving compelled them to act. Though the hour was late and the night had fallen . . .

ALL: They got up at once to spread the word—to gossip the Good News.

ALL: He is risen.

(louder) He is risen.

(very loud) The Lord is risen, indeed!

Reading: "If We Can Believe"

If we can believe—
    That plants can grow,
    That creatures can breathe,
    That an atom can be split,
    That modern medicine can cure disease,
    That we are ingenious enough to probe
      the planets
(And we possess a particle of the power of
    God),

Is it all that hard to believe—
    That God, in whose image people were
      made,
    Could come to earth,
    Be killed by murderous people,
    Yet forgive
    And break the power of death?
Is it all that hard to believe—
    That because Christ lives,
    We, too, shall live?

Parents' Day

A Celebration for Mother's Day and Father's Day

We live in a day when much is written and said about sex discrimination. The material in this chapter is designed to supersede both Mother's Day and Father's Day because it concentrates on parents. It can be used on either of these special days but includes both parents. Some people have two parents, some one, some none. Every person usually has a "parent figure" who may be a grandparent, a sister or brother, or an older friend. If either or both of your parents cannot come to this special worship celebration, then invite a parent figure or some older person who is particularly close to you.

Consider having a special "parents" celebration. Put on a dinner or banquet for parents, and be sure youth group members do all the setting up, cooking, planning, and cleanup. Provide entertainment, but instead of an after-dinner speaker, use this worship idea, tailored to fit the particular personality of your group.

The suggestion has been made throughout this book that worship be thought of as a celebration. In keeping with this concept, have decorations, balloons, and even a special "parent" cake. Also consider inviting parents to participate in the leadership and speaking parts of this service.

This material may also be used quite apart from a banquet or dinner idea.

Preparation

A key to this service is the selection entitled "Thoughts Out Loud." In it, two people will interpret a parent's thoughts and feelings and a youth's thoughts and feelings in a kind of antiphonal or back-and-forth way. A parent might do the "parent" readings and a young person, the "youth" readings.

The idea here is to create the impression that these two people are thinking aloud. The young person speaks about some facet of youth life, and the parent responds with his or her feelings and the experiences through which he or she is living. This approach may well produce better understanding between members of your group and their parents.

The Experience
Opening Thought

"The father and mother of an unnoticed family, who in their seclusion awakened the mind of one child to the idea and love of goodness, who awaken in him a strength of will to repel temptation, and who send him [the child] out prepared to profit by the conflicts of life, surpass in influence a Napoleon breaking the world to his sway" (William Channing).[1]

Hymn: Choose a hymn or song which is a familiar favorite of your group.

Scripture: Psalm 36:5-10; Luke 2:41-52.

Thoughts Out Loud: Supplement A.

Guided Prayer: Supplement A.

Closing: Form a fellowship circle and include parents. Sing a verse of a favorite hymn or say a familiar benediction together.

[1]Tryon Edwards, comp., *The New Dictionary of Thoughts* (New York: Standard Book Co., 1960), p. 463.

Parents' Day

Thoughts Out Loud

YOUTH: "Why have you done this to us? Your father and I have been terribly worried...." Sure sounds familiar. My parents are really rough on me. They are strict sometimes. They won't let me do anything on my own. They don't trust me. They treat me like a baby.

PARENT: I remember my younger years. I felt my parents really cramped my style. They hovered over me to protect me. Now I know the source of our tension. I was growing, developing, looking ahead to adult years, and trying out my independence. But they lovingly guided me, reluctant to let go, yet knowing they couldn't hang on. They said it was for my own sake, my own good. Maybe it really was for their own sake. I have the same feelings of hanging on while gradually letting go. I trust my children; yet I feel the need to shield them from harm. But do they understand? Do they understand that I have a need to hang on, if not for their sake, for mine?

YOUTH: Really though, there is security in knowing that they care—that if I really need them, they'll be there. I am a strange mixture of wanting the responsibilities and freedoms of being grown-up, yet knowing my insecurities and immaturities. It's a mixed-up feeling.

PARENT: Sometimes I feel mixed-up. But I'd never let on. Got to keep that perfect parent image. There are times when I almost resent the kids. I want my freedom, too, and I've been tied to them a long, long time. Guess I'll be sad but glad when they are on their own. Got to get them ready for it now. Got to get me ready for it. I need to have time for myself, to develop my own talents, to pursue my own interests, to do my own thing. But I can't now—not yet. I'm a parent, with all the responsibilities that implies. I'm a parent, but that's not all I am. There is another me inside, too, which needs nurture and growth quite apart from the kids. Sort of makes me feel guilty to think the thought. Sounds so selfish. What will I do; who will I be when they go?

YOUTH: Sometimes I feel guilty. I want to please my parents, to do the things they say. But sometimes, somehow, I end up doing just the opposite. Wonder how they feel?

PARENT: When I've been particularly tough on the kids, I end up feeling guilty—terribly guilty. My dad used to say, "This hurts me more than it hurts you." Now I know exactly what he meant.

YOUTH: I get into trouble when I hang around whoever my parents think is the wrong crowd, the wrong people. But I like some of those people. Some of them are really neat.

PARENT: I want my children to have the freedom to choose their own friends. But I have reservations—yes, fears—that others will be a negative influence. Maybe it's a lack of confidence in my own influence and a lack of trust in their own inner strength. But how can I take the chance? Soon they will be beyond my control. Got to guide them in the right paths now—while there is still time. Maybe they don't always care for my friends either.

YOUTH: I want to have my own car—to drive—to go places and do things. And I want it now.

PARENT: I want my kids to go places, to drive, to have cars. But I don't want their lives to be broken or destroyed because of inexperience or underdeveloped judgment. They have to learn. The only way to learn is through experience. It's one of life's risks I must take. But it must be a calculated risk. I'll have to do all I can to train and guide them, but then it's up to them. They are part of me, an extension of myself. That part of me, somehow has to be let go. But only after I have done my best.

YOUTH: I am muddled by morality. I'm finding out that the old saying is true—anything any fun is either immoral, illegal, or fattening. My parents can't possibly know my feelings.

PARENT: I know the feelings because I've been there. Had them as a youth and still have them in one way or another. My kids have to find a moral and ethical attitude of their own. All I can do is share with them my own sense of right and wrong. Sometimes it's so hard to talk to them when I know my own actions speak louder than my words. Lord, help me in this. Help me to know how solid a foundation my own life is based on. I cannot teach what I am not or expect others to do as I do not.

YOUTH: And then there is the church and God. I see things in some church people that

really turn me off. I want a faith of my own, to make what little I know of Christ a part of me—a center for my soul, a focal point for my being.

PARENT: Faith for me has not come cheap. I had my own doubts and fears. Still do sometimes, for that matter. As a youth, I was a strange combination of believing and doubting, being faithful and being self-willed, feeling like a saint and a sinner all in one. I had faith then; I have a stronger faith now. It's been an up-and-down experience; yet with each new day, my faith grows stronger, more mature. I am not yet what I hope to become. I am far from perfect; yet I strive for perfection. I'd like my kids to see me as perfect, but to say I am is being phony. Lord, all I ask is that in some little way, others will see some of your goodness in me.

YOUTH: We didn't cover everything, not the innermost things that really concern us most. But it's a start, a beginning. If we could see and feel as parents feel! They have the advantage. They know how we feel. They've been there. If only they could share some of those feelings and experiences, but it's hard, very hard.

Lord, increase our faith; help us to understand and appreciate each other, to feel and think each other's thoughts—in spite of ourselves.

Guided Prayer: (This is a guided prayer in which a leader suggests ideas for thought, then pauses briefly to allow worshipers to add their concerns and offer their prayers silently.)

As we think of kids and parents, help us, Lord, to be open, as open as we can be, and to trust each other. (*Pause*)

Help us, together, to trust you. (*Pause*)

Give us grace to understand each other. (*Pause*)

Grant us the will to forgive each other. (*Pause*)

Let there be good times along with the sad. (*Pause*)

Let there be harmony in spite of tensions. (*Pause*)

If we disagree, let us disagree agreeably. (*Pause*)

Grant us the goodness to allow each other to be the persons we want to be. (*Pause*)

Help us to help each other in achieving life's possibilities, to do all that is humanly possible for each other, to bring happiness, meaning, and beauty to each other. (*Pause*)

Help us to let go gracefully, to understand our wanting to hang on to each other, to walk together as people concerned for each other. (*Pause*)

In all our clinging to and letting go, we need to hold on to you, our God and Father. Amen.

SUPPLEMENT A

Parents' Day

Thoughts Out Loud

YOUTH: "Why have you done this to us? Your father and I have been terribly worried...." Sure sounds familiar. My parents are really rough on me. They are strict sometimes. They won't let me do anything on my own. They don't trust me. They treat me like a baby.

PARENT: I remember my younger years. I felt my parents really cramped my style. They hovered over me to protect me. Now I know the source of our tension. I was growing, developing, looking ahead to adult years, and trying out my independence. But they lovingly guided me, reluctant to let go, yet knowing they couldn't hang on. They said it was for my own sake, my own good. Maybe it really was for their own sake. I have the same feelings of hanging on while gradually letting go. I trust my children; yet I feel the need to shield them from harm. But do they understand? Do they understand that I have a need to hang on, if not for their sake, for mine?

YOUTH: Really though, there is security in knowing that they care—that if I really need them, they'll be there. I am a strange mixture of wanting the responsibilities and freedoms of being grown-up, yet knowing my insecurities and immaturities. It's a mixed-up feeling.

PARENT: Sometimes I feel mixed-up. But I'd never let on. Got to keep that perfect parent image. There are times when I almost resent the kids. I want my freedom, too, and I've been tied to them a long, long time. Guess I'll be sad but glad when they are on their own. Got to get them ready for it now. Got to get me ready for it. I need to have time for myself, to develop my own talents, to pursue my own interests, to do my own thing. But I can't now—not yet. I'm a parent, with all the responsibilities that implies. I'm a parent, but that's not all I am. There is another me inside, too, which needs nurture and growth quite apart from the kids. Sort of makes me feel guilty to think the thought. Sounds so selfish. What will I do; who will I be when they go?

YOUTH: Sometimes I feel guilty. I want to please my parents, to do the things they say. But sometimes, somehow, I end up doing just the opposite. Wonder how they feel?

PARENT: When I've been particularly tough on the kids, I end up feeling guilty—terribly guilty. My dad used to say, "This hurts me more than it hurts you." Now I know exactly what he meant.

YOUTH: I get into trouble when I hang around whoever my parents think is the wrong crowd, the wrong people. But I like some of those people. Some of them are really neat.

PARENT: I want my children to have the freedom to choose their own friends. But I have reservations—yes, fears—that others will be a negative influence. Maybe it's a lack of confidence in my own influence and a lack of trust in their own inner strength. But how can I take the chance? Soon they will be beyond my control. Got to guide them in the right paths now—while there is still time. Maybe they don't always care for my friends either.

YOUTH: I want to have my own car—to drive—to go places and do things. And I want it now.

PARENT: I want my kids to go places, to drive, to have cars. But I don't want their lives to be broken or destroyed because of inexperience or underdeveloped judgment. They have to learn. The only way to learn is through experience. It's one of life's risks I must take. But it must be a calculated risk. I'll have to do all I can to train and guide them, but then it's up to them. They are part of me, an extension of myself. That part of me, somehow has to be let go. But only after I have done my best.

YOUTH: I am muddled by morality. I'm finding out that the old saying is true—anything any fun is either immoral, illegal, or fattening. My parents can't possibly know my feelings.

PARENT: I know the feelings because I've been there. Had them as a youth and still have them in one way or another. My kids have to find a moral and ethical attitude of their own. All I can do is share with them my own sense of right and wrong. Sometimes it's so hard to talk to them when I know my own actions speak louder than my words. Lord, help me in this. Help me to know how solid a foundation my own life is based on. I cannot teach what I am not or expect others to do as I do not.

YOUTH: And then there is the church and God. I see things in some church people that

really turn me off. I want a faith of my own, to make what little I know of Christ a part of me—a center for my soul, a focal point for my being.

PARENT: Faith for me has not come cheap. I had my own doubts and fears. Still do sometimes, for that matter. As a youth, I was a strange combination of believing and doubting, being faithful and being self-willed, feeling like a saint and a sinner all in one. I had faith then; I have a stronger faith now. It's been an up-and-down experience; yet with each new day, my faith grows stronger, more mature. I am not yet what I hope to become. I am far from perfect; yet I strive for perfection. I'd like my kids to see me as perfect, but to say I am is being phony. Lord, all I ask is that in some little way, others will see some of your goodness in me.

YOUTH: We didn't cover everything, not the innermost things that really concern us most. But it's a start, a beginning. If we could see and feel as parents feel! They have the advantage. They know how we feel. They've been there. If only they could share some of those feelings and experiences, but it's hard, very hard.

Lord, increase our faith; help us to understand and appreciate each other, to feel and think each other's thoughts—in spite of ourselves.

Guided Prayer: (This is a guided prayer in which a leader suggests ideas for thought, then pauses briefly to allow worshipers to add their concerns and offer their prayers silently.)

As we think of kids and parents, help us, Lord, to be open, as open as we can be, and to trust each other. (*Pause*)

Help us, together, to trust you. (*Pause*)

Give us grace to understand each other. (*Pause*)

Grant us the will to forgive each other. (*Pause*)

Let there be good times along with the sad. (*Pause*)

Let there be harmony in spite of tensions. (*Pause*)

If we disagree, let us disagree agreeably. (*Pause*)

Grant us the goodness to allow each other to be the persons we want to be. (*Pause*)

Help us to help each other in achieving life's possibilities, to do all that is humanly possible for each other, to bring happiness, meaning, and beauty to each other. (*Pause*)

Help us to let go gracefully, to understand our wanting to hang on to each other, to walk together as people concerned for each other. (*Pause*)

In all our clinging to and letting go, we need to hold on to you, our God and Father. Amen.

Parents' Day

Thoughts Out Loud

YOUTH: "Why have you done this to us? Your father and I have been terribly worried. . . ." Sure sounds familiar. My parents are really rough on me. They are strict sometimes. They won't let me do anything on my own. They don't trust me. They treat me like a baby.

PARENT: I remember my younger years. I felt my parents really cramped my style. They hovered over me to protect me. Now I know the source of our tension. I was growing, developing, looking ahead to adult years, and trying out my independence. But they lovingly guided me, reluctant to let go, yet knowing they couldn't hang on. They said it was for my own sake, my own good. Maybe it really was for their own sake. I have the same feelings of hanging on while gradually letting go. I trust my children; yet I feel the need to shield them from harm. But do they understand? Do they understand that I have a need to hang on, if not for their sake, for mine?

YOUTH: Really though, there is security in knowing that they care—that if I really need them, they'll be there. I am a strange mixture of wanting the responsibilities and freedoms of being grown-up, yet knowing my insecurities and immaturities. It's a mixed-up feeling.

PARENT: Sometimes I feel mixed-up. But I'd never let on. Got to keep that perfect parent image. There are times when I almost resent the kids. I want my freedom, too, and I've been tied to them a long, long time. Guess I'll be sad but glad when they are on their own. Got to get them ready for it now. Got to get me ready for it. I need to have time for myself, to develop my own talents, to pursue my own interests, to do my own thing. But I can't now—not yet. I'm a parent, with all the responsibilities that implies. I'm a parent, but that's not all I am. There is another me inside, too, which needs nurture and growth quite apart from the kids. Sort of makes me feel guilty to think the thought. Sounds so selfish. What will I do; who will I be when they go?

YOUTH: Sometimes I feel guilty. I want to please my parents, to do the things they say. But sometimes, somehow, I end up doing just the opposite. Wonder how they feel?

PARENT: When I've been particularly tough on the kids, I end up feeling guilty—terribly guilty. My dad used to say, "This hurts me more than it hurts you." Now I know exactly what he meant.

YOUTH: I get into trouble when I hang around whoever my parents think is the wrong crowd, the wrong people. But I like some of those people. Some of them are really neat.

PARENT: I want my children to have the freedom to choose their own friends. But I have reservations—yes, fears—that others will be a negative influence. Maybe it's a lack of confidence in my own influence and a lack of trust in their own inner strength. But how can I take the chance? Soon they will be beyond my control. Got to guide them in the right paths now—while there is still time. Maybe they don't always care for my friends either.

YOUTH: I want to have my own car—to drive—to go places and do things. And I want it now.

PARENT: I want my kids to go places, to drive, to have cars. But I don't want their lives to be broken or destroyed because of inexperience or underdeveloped judgment. They have to learn. The only way to learn is through experience. It's one of life's risks I must take. But it must be a calculated risk. I'll have to do all I can to train and guide them, but then it's up to them. They are part of me, an extension of myself. That part of me, somehow has to be let go. But only after I have done my best.

YOUTH: I am muddled by morality. I'm finding out that the old saying is true—anything any fun is either immoral, illegal, or fattening. My parents can't possibly know my feelings.

PARENT: I know the feelings because I've been there. Had them as a youth and still have them in one way or another. My kids have to find a moral and ethical attitude of their own. All I can do is share with them my own sense of right and wrong. Sometimes it's so hard to talk to them when I know my own actions speak louder than my words. Lord, help me in this. Help me to know how solid a foundation my own life is based on. I cannot teach what I am not or expect others to do as I do not.

YOUTH: And then there is the church and God. I see things in some church people that

really turn me off. I want a faith of my own, to make what little I know of Christ a part of me—a center for my soul, a focal point for my being.

PARENT: Faith for me has not come cheap. I had my own doubts and fears. Still do sometimes, for that matter. As a youth, I was a strange combination of believing and doubting, being faithful and being self-willed, feeling like a saint and a sinner all in one. I had faith then; I have a stronger faith now. It's been an up-and-down experience; yet with each new day, my faith grows stronger, more mature. I am not yet what I hope to become. I am far from perfect; yet I strive for perfection. I'd like my kids to see me as perfect, but to say I am is being phony. Lord, all I ask is that in some little way, others will see some of your goodness in me.

YOUTH: We didn't cover everything, not the innermost things that really concern us most. But it's a start, a beginning. If we could see and feel as parents feel! They have the advantage. They know how we feel. They've been there. If only they could share some of those feelings and experiences, but it's hard, very hard.

Lord, increase our faith; help us to understand and appreciate each other, to feel and think each other's thoughts—in spite of ourselves.

Guided Prayer: (This is a guided prayer in which a leader suggests ideas for thought, then pauses briefly to allow worshipers to add their concerns and offer their prayers silently.)

As we think of kids and parents, help us, Lord, to be open, as open as we can be, and to trust each other. (*Pause*)

Help us, together, to trust you. (*Pause*)

Give us grace to understand each other. (*Pause*)

Grant us the will to forgive each other. (*Pause*)

Let there be good times along with the sad. (*Pause*)

Let there be harmony in spite of tensions. (*Pause*)

If we disagree, let us disagree agreeably. (*Pause*)

Grant us the goodness to allow each other to be the persons we want to be. (*Pause*)

Help us to help each other in achieving life's possibilities, to do all that is humanly possible for each other, to bring happiness, meaning, and beauty to each other. (*Pause*)

Help us to let go gracefully, to understand our wanting to hang on to each other, to walk together as people concerned for each other. (*Pause*)

In all our clinging to and letting go, we need to hold on to you, our God and Father. Amen.

The World Looks On

A Celebration for an Outdoor Vesper Service

Your group may be planning an outing— a bike hike, a campout, a canoe trip—or you may be looking for meaningful devotional material for a general or special occasion. Perhaps you plan to host another youth group or some special gathering of your particular congregation. The following material is designed to provide a group worship experience which can have deep meaning in light of the vast gap which exists between the rich and the poor, the "haves" and the "have-nots," the full and the hungry of our world. Not only are there rich and poor nations of the world, but, as inconsistent as it may seem, there are also hungry people in our land, in our very midst. What is the message of Jesus in this regard? You will attempt to make vivid the facts of our world and the implications of that message through readings and an actual experience of plenty and poverty.

Preparation

The place of your meeting is not important. It may be out-of-doors in the sun or under the stars. It may be a church meeting room or sanctuary. If it is possible, have the group sit in a circle with no visible leader. Each person who has a preassigned part should take his or her place anywhere in the group. As the group arrives or enters the meeting place, give every other person either a candy bar, a cookie, or a piece of fruit. Give those without a "goodie" a slice of bread, preferably semidry or crusty. Tell everyone to start eating. If you have been on a hike or bike hike, an alternative to this might be to offer half the group a bottle of soda pop, lemonade, or iced tea and the other half some not-so-cold water.

There will probably be some joking and laughter in the group as they realize that some have been more fortunate than others. This is perfectly alright. The point of this "feast" will become clear as you progress.

The Experience

Voice Readings: Supplement A.
Litany: Group Litany using the response "O Lord, Deliver Us."
Hymn: The suggested hymn is "O Jesus, I Have Promised," though a hymn of your choice or one which is familiar to the group may be used. If the setting of your meeting is out-of-doors, you probably will not have hymnals or songbooks available. You might also want to use a folk song here, especially if there is an appropriate one which is popular at the time of your group gathering.
Thoughts: A meditation or prayer based on "Thoughts" (Supplement A).
Scripture: Luke 10:30-37; Matthew 10:37-42.
Poem: "Today" (Supplement A).
Closing: As the worshipers begin to leave the meeting area, if possible, pour each person a glass of cold water.

The World Looks On

Voice Readings

A VOICE: This candy bar (cookie, etc.) is really good. Can I have more?

ANOTHER VOICE: More? You want more when all I got was a crust of bread? I'll give you my bread for whatever is left of your candy.

VOICE: No way! That's just your tough luck. Some people rate the goodies, and some people don't.

ANOTHER VOICE: What do you mean, "rate"? I had no choice. I was just handed whatever they wanted to hand me.

VOICE: We must have done something right.

ANOTHER VOICE: This isn't fair. We all should have been treated the same.

VOICE: Let's form a club just for us people with goodies.

ANOTHER VOICE: Then we'll form a club for people with only bread. (*Pause*)

ANOTHER VOICE: I am from an isolated village in South America. The average wage here is less than one thousand dollars a year.

VOICE: My dad makes more than that in a month.

ANOTHER VOICE: The person from South America is fortunate. I am from central India where the annual wage is six hundred dollars a year!

VOICE: Why, my family spends more than that just for eating out, or vacationing, or entertainment.

ANOTHER VOICE: Not everyone in India or South America is poor. There are wealthy people as well.

VOICE: And not everyone in America is rich. There are poor people here, too.

ANOTHER VOICE: Even most of the poor in America are well off by world standards.

ANOTHER VOICE: In my village, a baby died for lack of even a crust of bread.

ANOTHER VOICE: In my nation, thousands will die this year. Some are dying right this minute.

ANOTHER VOICE: In my part of the world there is enough food and clothing, but civil war has prevented it from being shipped to our village.

VOICE: Can't the world raise its own food like we do here?

ANOTHER VOICE: Can't we raise enough right here in our country to feed the world?

ANOTHER VOICE: In my land, the people don't have enough money to build up the soil, to plant the seed. They have crude tools and little background in efficient farming methods. Perhaps the rich of the world can raise enough for all the world, but then there are shipping and distribution problems. You have had two hundred years' growth since the best, most knowledgeable tradesmen, technicians, and farmers came from every part of the world. You have grown and prospered while we have remained the same.

ANOTHER VOICE: It is not particularly the fault of the rich nor of the poor of the world. But some of the best resources in both people and materials have accumulated in America.

VOICE: The poor want what the rich have, and the rich fear and despise those who might try to take away their wealth.

ANOTHER VOICE: Is it wrong to want some of the better things in life?

VOICE: Is it wrong to be rich?

ANOTHER VOICE: It is not wrong to have things, but listen to these words of a man who preferred the company of the poor, the miserable, and the oppressed:

"I was hungry and you fed me, thirsty and you gave me a drink; I was a stranger and you received me in your homes, naked and you clothed me; I was sick and you took care of me, in prison and you visited me. The righteous will then answer him, 'When, Lord, did we ever see you hungry and feed you, or thirsty and give you a drink? When did we ever see you a stranger and welcome you in our homes, or naked and clothe you? When did we ever see you sick or in prison, and visit you? The King will reply, 'I tell you, whenever you did this for one of the least important of these brothers of mine, you did it for me!'" (Matthew 25:35-40).

VOICE: These are hard words. They stab our consciences and grip our hearts. But they were intended to do just that.

Litany

(Instruct the group to respond by saying, "O Lord, Deliver Us" each time the VOICE pauses for response.)

VOICE: From the pride of the rich who feel they, of their own goodness or initiative, have brought themselves plenty;

VOICE: From hatred, fear, or scorn of those less fortunate;

VOICE: From envy of those who have more than we do;

VOICE: From apathy or insensitivity;

VOICE: From false sympathy or concern;

VOICE: From an unwillingness to look for ways of helping these brothers of Christ;

VOICE: From a refusal to identify ourselves with the poor, the hungry, the miserable, and the oppressed:

Thoughts: (To be used as a brief meditation or as a prayer.)

We want more independence, while millions simply want to be free. We want sweets and steaks, while others would be happy with rice. We want higher education, while thousands cannot even read. We want spending money, while others don't even know what currency looks like. We want the best in medical care and medical insurance, while others have never seen a doctor. We want the latest fads and styles in clothes, while many have only rags. We want friends, while others are alone. We want to be popular, while thousands are nameless and forgotten. We want cars and bikes, while others would settle for a shelter from the storm. We want fun and good times, while others drown in boredom, meaninglessness, and despair. We want love, while others are despised. We want jobs, while others only want to survive.

Poem

To be read slowly so that no meaning is lost.

"Today"

So here hath been dawning
  Another blue Day;
Think, wilt thou let it
  Slip useless away?

Out of Eternity
  This new Day is born;
Into Eternity
  At night, will return.

Behold it aforetime
  No eye ever did:
So soon it for ever
  From all eyes is hid.

Here hath been dawning
  Another blue Day;
Think, wilt thou let it
  Slip useless away?

Thomas Carlyle

SUPPLEMENT A

The World Looks On

Voice Readings

A VOICE: This candy bar (cookie, etc.) is really good. Can I have more?

ANOTHER VOICE: More? You want more when all I got was a crust of bread? I'll give you my bread for whatever is left of your candy.

VOICE: No way! That's just your tough luck. Some people rate the goodies, and some people don't.

ANOTHER VOICE: What do you mean, "rate"? I had no choice. I was just handed whatever they wanted to hand me.

VOICE: We must have done something right.

ANOTHER VOICE: This isn't fair. We all should have been treated the same.

VOICE: Let's form a club just for us people with goodies.

ANOTHER VOICE: Then we'll form a club for people with only bread. (*Pause*)

ANOTHER VOICE: I am from an isolated village in South America. The average wage here is less than one thousand dollars a year.

VOICE: My dad makes more than that in a month.

ANOTHER VOICE: The person from South America is fortunate. I am from central India where the annual wage is six hundred dollars a year!

VOICE: Why, my family spends more than that just for eating out, or vacationing, or entertainment.

ANOTHER VOICE: Not everyone in India or South America is poor. There are wealthy people as well.

VOICE: And not everyone in America is rich. There are poor people here, too.

ANOTHER VOICE: Even most of the poor in America are well off by world standards.

ANOTHER VOICE: In my village, a baby died for lack of even a crust of bread.

ANOTHER VOICE: In my nation, thousands will die this year. Some are dying right this minute.

ANOTHER VOICE: In my part of the world there is enough food and clothing, but civil war has prevented it from being shipped to our village.

VOICE: Can't the world raise its own food like we do here?

ANOTHER VOICE: Can't we raise enough right here in our country to feed the world?

ANOTHER VOICE: In my land, the people don't have enough money to build up the soil, to plant the seed. They have crude tools and little background in efficient farming methods. Perhaps the rich of the world can raise enough for all the world, but then there are shipping and distribution problems. You have had two hundred years' growth since the best, most knowledgeable tradesmen, technicians, and farmers came from every part of the world. You have grown and prospered while we have remained the same.

ANOTHER VOICE: It is not particularly the fault of the rich nor of the poor of the world. But some of the best resources in both people and materials have accumulated in America.

VOICE: The poor want what the rich have, and the rich fear and despise those who might try to take away their wealth.

ANOTHER VOICE: Is it wrong to want some of the better things in life?

VOICE: Is it wrong to be rich?

ANOTHER VOICE: It is not wrong to have things, but listen to these words of a man who preferred the company of the poor, the miserable, and the oppressed:

"I was hungry and you fed me, thirsty and you gave me a drink; I was a stranger and you received me in your homes, naked and you clothed me; I was sick and you took care of me, in prison and you visited me. The righteous will then answer him, 'When, Lord, did we ever see you hungry and feed you, or thirsty and give you a drink? When did we ever see you a stranger and welcome you in our homes, or naked and clothe you? When did we ever see you sick or in prison, and visit you? The King will reply, 'I tell you, whenever you did this for one of the least important of these brothers of mine, you did it for me!'" (Matthew 25:35-40).

VOICE: These are hard words. They stab our consciences and grip our hearts. But they were intended to do just that.

Litany

(Instruct the group to respond by saying, "O Lord, Deliver Us" each time the VOICE pauses for response.)

VOICE: From the pride of the rich who feel they, of their own goodness or initiative, have brought themselves plenty;

VOICE: From hatred, fear, or scorn of those less fortunate;

VOICE: From envy of those who have more than we do;

VOICE: From apathy or insensitivity;

VOICE: From false sympathy or concern;

VOICE: From an unwillingness to look for ways of helping these brothers of Christ;

VOICE: From a refusal to identify ourselves with the poor, the hungry, the miserable, and the oppressed:

Thoughts: (To be used as a brief meditation or as a prayer.)

We want more independence, while millions simply want to be free. We want sweets and steaks, while others would be happy with rice. We want higher education, while thousands cannot even read. We want spending money, while others don't even know what currency looks like. We want the best in medical care and medical insurance, while others have never seen a doctor. We want the latest fads and styles in clothes, while many have only rags. We want friends, while others are alone. We want to be popular, while thousands are nameless and forgotten. We want cars and bikes, while others would settle for a shelter from the storm. We want fun and good times, while others drown in boredom, meaninglessness, and despair. We want love, while others are despised. We want jobs, while others only want to survive.

Poem

To be read slowly so that no meaning is lost.

"Today"

So here hath been dawning
   Another blue Day;
Think, wilt thou let it
   Slip useless away?

Out of Eternity
   This new Day is born;
Into Eternity
   At night, will return.

Behold it aforetime
   No eye ever did:
So soon it for ever
   From all eyes is hid.

Here hath been dawning
   Another blue Day;
Think, wilt thou let it
   Slip useless away?

               Thomas Carlyle

The World Looks On

Voice Readings

A VOICE: This candy bar (cookie, etc.) is really good. Can I have more?

ANOTHER VOICE: More? You want more when all I got was a crust of bread? I'll give you my bread for whatever is left of your candy.

VOICE: No way! That's just your tough luck. Some people rate the goodies, and some people don't.

ANOTHER VOICE: What do you mean, "rate"? I had no choice. I was just handed whatever they wanted to hand me.

VOICE: We must have done something right.

ANOTHER VOICE: This isn't fair. We all should have been treated the same.

VOICE: Let's form a club just for us people with goodies.

ANOTHER VOICE: Then we'll form a club for people with only bread. (*Pause*)

ANOTHER VOICE: I am from an isolated village in South America. The average wage here is less than one thousand dollars a year.

VOICE: My dad makes more than that in a month.

ANOTHER VOICE: The person from South America is fortunate. I am from central India where the annual wage is six hundred dollars a year!

VOICE: Why, my family spends more than that just for eating out, or vacationing, or entertainment.

ANOTHER VOICE: Not everyone in India or South America is poor. There are wealthy people as well.

VOICE: And not everyone in America is rich. There are poor people here, too.

ANOTHER VOICE: Even most of the poor in America are well off by world standards.

ANOTHER VOICE: In my village, a baby died for lack of even a crust of bread.

ANOTHER VOICE: In my nation, thousands will die this year. Some are dying right this minute.

ANOTHER VOICE: In my part of the world there is enough food and clothing, but civil war has prevented it from being shipped to our village.

VOICE: Can't the world raise its own food like we do here?

ANOTHER VOICE: Can't we raise enough right here in our country to feed the world?

ANOTHER VOICE: In my land, the people don't have enough money to build up the soil, to plant the seed. They have crude tools and little background in efficient farming methods. Perhaps the rich of the world can raise enough for all the world, but then there are shipping and distribution problems. You have had two hundred years' growth since the best, most knowledgeable tradesmen, technicians, and farmers came from every part of the world. You have grown and prospered while we have remained the same.

ANOTHER VOICE: It is not particularly the fault of the rich nor of the poor of the world. But some of the best resources in both people and materials have accumulated in America.

VOICE: The poor want what the rich have, and the rich fear and despise those who might try to take away their wealth.

ANOTHER VOICE: Is it wrong to want some of the better things in life?

VOICE: Is it wrong to be rich?

ANOTHER VOICE: It is not wrong to have things, but listen to these words of a man who preferred the company of the poor, the miserable, and the oppressed:

"I was hungry and you fed me, thirsty and you gave me a drink; I was a stranger and you received me in your homes, naked and you clothed me; I was sick and you took care of me, in prison and you visited me. The righteous will then answer him, 'When, Lord, did we ever see you hungry and feed you, or thirsty and give you a drink? When did we ever see you a stranger and welcome you in our homes, or naked and clothe you? When did we ever see you sick or in prison, and visit you? The King will reply, 'I tell you, whenever you did this for one of the least important of these brothers of mine, you did it for me!'" (Matthew 25:35-40).

VOICE: These are hard words. They stab our consciences and grip our hearts. But they were intended to do just that.

Litany

(Instruct the group to respond by saying, "O Lord, Deliver Us" each time the VOICE pauses for response.)

VOICE: From the pride of the rich who feel they, of their own goodness or initiative, have brought themselves plenty;

VOICE: From hatred, fear, or scorn of those less fortunate;

VOICE: From envy of those who have more than we do;

VOICE: From apathy or insensitivity;

VOICE: From false sympathy or concern;

VOICE: From an unwillingness to look for ways of helping these brothers of Christ;

VOICE: From a refusal to identify ourselves with the poor, the hungry, the miserable, and the oppressed:

Thoughts: (To be used as a brief meditation or as a prayer.)

We want more independence, while millions simply want to be free. We want sweets and steaks, while others would be happy with rice. We want higher education, while thousands cannot even read. We want spending money, while others don't even know what currency looks like. We want the best in medical care and medical insurance, while others have never seen a doctor. We want the latest fads and styles in clothes, while many have only rags. We want friends, while others are alone. We want to be popular, while thousands are nameless and forgotten. We want cars and bikes, while others would settle for a shelter from the storm. We want fun and good times, while others drown in boredom, meaninglessness, and despair. We want love, while others are despised. We want jobs, while others only want to survive.

Poem

To be read slowly so that no meaning is lost.

"Today"

So here hath been dawning
   Another blue Day;
Think, wilt thou let it
   Slip useless away?

Out of Eternity
   This new Day is born;
Into Eternity
   At night, will return.

Behold it aforetime
   No eye ever did:
So soon it for ever
   From all eyes is hid.

Here hath been dawning
   Another blue Day;
Think, wilt thou let it
   Slip useless away?

          Thomas Carlyle

The World Looks On

Voice Readings

A VOICE: This candy bar (cookie, etc.) is really good. Can I have more?

ANOTHER VOICE: More? You want more when all I got was a crust of bread? I'll give you my bread for whatever is left of your candy.

VOICE: No way! That's just your tough luck. Some people rate the goodies, and some people don't.

ANOTHER VOICE: What do you mean, "rate"? I had no choice. I was just handed whatever they wanted to hand me.

VOICE: We must have done something right.

ANOTHER VOICE: This isn't fair. We all should have been treated the same.

VOICE: Let's form a club just for us people with goodies.

ANOTHER VOICE: Then we'll form a club for people with only bread. (*Pause*)

ANOTHER VOICE: I am from an isolated village in South America. The average wage here is less than one thousand dollars a year.

VOICE: My dad makes more than that in a month.

ANOTHER VOICE: The person from South America is fortunate. I am from central India where the annual wage is six hundred dollars a year!

VOICE: Why, my family spends more than that just for eating out, or vacationing, or entertainment.

ANOTHER VOICE: Not everyone in India or South America is poor. There are wealthy people as well.

VOICE: And not everyone in America is rich. There are poor people here, too.

ANOTHER VOICE: Even most of the poor in America are well off by world standards.

ANOTHER VOICE: In my village, a baby died for lack of even a crust of bread.

ANOTHER VOICE: In my nation, thousands will die this year. Some are dying right this minute.

ANOTHER VOICE: In my part of the world there is enough food and clothing, but civil war has prevented it from being shipped to our village.

VOICE: Can't the world raise its own food like we do here?

ANOTHER VOICE: Can't we raise enough right here in our country to feed the world?

ANOTHER VOICE: In my land, the people don't have enough money to build up the soil, to plant the seed. They have crude tools and little background in efficient farming methods. Perhaps the rich of the world can raise enough for all the world, but then there are shipping and distribution problems. You have had two hundred years' growth since the best, most knowledgeable tradesmen, technicians, and farmers came from every part of the world. You have grown and prospered while we have remained the same.

ANOTHER VOICE: It is not particularly the fault of the rich nor of the poor of the world. But some of the best resources in both people and materials have accumulated in America.

VOICE: The poor want what the rich have, and the rich fear and despise those who might try to take away their wealth.

ANOTHER VOICE: Is it wrong to want some of the better things in life?

VOICE: Is it wrong to be rich?

ANOTHER VOICE: It is not wrong to have things, but listen to these words of a man who preferred the company of the poor, the miserable, and the oppressed:

"I was hungry and you fed me, thirsty and you gave me a drink; I was a stranger and you received me in your homes, naked and you clothed me; I was sick and you took care of me, in prison and you visited me. The righteous will then answer him, 'When, Lord, did we ever see you hungry and feed you, or thirsty and give you a drink? When did we ever see you a stranger and welcome you in our homes, or naked and clothe you? When did we ever see you sick or in prison, and visit you? The King will reply, 'I tell you, whenever you did this for one of the least important of these brothers of mine, you did it for me!'" (Matthew 25:35-40).

VOICE: These are hard words. They stab our consciences and grip our hearts. But they were intended to do just that.

Litany

(Instruct the group to respond by saying, "O Lord, Deliver Us" each time the VOICE pauses for response.)

VOICE: From the pride of the rich who feel they, of their own goodness or initiative, have brought themselves plenty;

VOICE: From hatred, fear, or scorn of those less fortunate;

VOICE: From envy of those who have more than we do;

VOICE: From apathy or insensitivity;

VOICE: From false sympathy or concern;

VOICE: From an unwillingness to look for ways of helping these brothers of Christ;

VOICE: From a refusal to identify ourselves with the poor, the hungry, the miserable, and the oppressed:

Thoughts: (To be used as a brief meditation or as a prayer.)

We want more independence, while millions simply want to be free. We want sweets and steaks, while others would be happy with rice. We want higher education, while thousands cannot even read. We want spending money, while others don't even know what currency looks like. We want the best in medical care and medical insurance, while others have never seen a doctor. We want the latest fads and styles in clothes, while many have only rags. We want friends, while others are alone. We want to be popular, while thousands are nameless and forgotten. We want cars and bikes, while others would settle for a shelter from the storm. We want fun and good times, while others drown in boredom, meaninglessness, and despair. We want love, while others are despised. We want jobs, while others only want to survive.

Poem

To be read slowly so that no meaning is lost.

"Today"

So here hath been dawning
   Another blue Day;
Think, wilt thou let it
   Slip useless away?

Out of Eternity
   This new Day is born;
Into Eternity
   At night, will return.

Behold it aforetime
   No eye ever did:
So soon it for ever
   From all eyes is hid.

Here hath been dawning
   Another blue Day;
Think, wilt thou let it
   Slip useless away?

             Thomas Carlyle

This Land Is Your Land

A Celebration for a National Holiday

We live in an era when patriotism seems passé. For one reason or another, we are reluctant or ashamed to show loyalty and love for our country, to wave our flag, and to declare to all that we are proud to be citizens of this land. Our nation, like all other nations, has in its past history those things for which it might be ashamed. No nation, family, or individual is without its darker side.

But we can and should celebrate the good things about our country. This service is designed to interpret our national history in light of both positive and negative aspects and to focus our attention on the God who is Lord of all humankind.

Preparation

The material in this chapter can be used in a variety of group settings, including a special Fourth of July or national holiday outing, or for a general theme on national patriotism. A time of confession and renewal, both of loyalty to country and dedication to Christ, is suggested. Add elements of your own creativity and imagination to this material.

The Experience

Beginning Thoughts: "After what I owe to God, nothing should be more dear or more sacred than the love and respect I owe to my country" (François de Thou).[1]

"Let our object be our country, our whole country, and nothing but our country. And, by the blessing of God, may that country itself become a vast and splendid monument, not of oppression and terror, but of wisdom, of peace, and of liberty, upon which the world may gaze with admiration . . ." (Daniel Webster).[2]

Song or Hymn: "America the Beautiful" (Or use "This Land Is Your Land" by Woody Guthrie or "The Power and the Glory" by Phil Ochs—Electra Records, EKL 269).

Scripture: Psalm 21:1-7.

Reflections: "Gott Mit Uns" (Supplement A).

Reading: "Frustrated Flag Waver" (Supplement A).

Guided Prayer: Supplement A.

[1] Tryon Edwards, comp., *The New Dictionary of Thoughts* (New York: Standard Book, Co., 1960), p. 471.

[2] *Ibid.*

This Land Is Your Land

Reflections: "Gott Mit Uns"

During World War II, some of the Nazi troops under Hitler had inscribed on their belt buckles these words: "Gott mit uns." Translated it means, "God with us." Even the German armies felt that theirs was a holy cause, that they had God on their side.

Nearly every nation in history has felt that God, gods, or deities were on its side, guiding it, protecting it, and looking upon it with favor. But the only assurance the Bible gives as to God's favor is in passages like this: ". . . the LORD has told us what is good. What he requires of us is this: to do what is just, to show constant love, and to live in humble fellowship with our God" (Micah 6:8).

We would be the most arrogant people on earth to say that God is with us more than with any other nation or to the exclusion of other nations. To the extent that the people and leaders of a nation give their allegiance first to God and his kingdom, that is a key to God's favor. But even history itself does not set this up as a firm rule because there have been nations which have prospered regardless of religious or national philosophies—prospered at least for a time.

Our history as a nation is one of ups and downs, success and failure, faithfulness to the God of Abraham, Isaac, and Jacob, and deeds of terror and injustice. The founding idea of liberty and justice for all is noble and worthy of our loyalty. Yet we must confess that it has not always been our practice. For example, consider what this nation did to a noble, free, and deeply spiritual race of people we call the American Indian. We labeled him a savage worthy of extinction, and in our zeal to destroy him, called upon the name of God. What we did as a people was a grave mark upon our history. Consider these words of Chief Standing Bear of the Oglala band of the Sioux nation.

"We did not think of the great open plains, the beautiful rolling hills, and the winding streams with tangled growth as wild. Only to the white man was nature a wilderness and only to him was the land infested with wild animals and savage people. To us it was tame. Earth was beautiful and we were surrounded with the blessings of the Great Mystery. Not until the hairy man from the east came and with brutal frenzy heaped injustices upon us and the families we loved was it wild for us. When the very animals of the forest began fleeing from his approach, then it was for us that the 'Wild West' began."[1]

But there is another side of our nation which is positive and good. For in this land of ours live some of the most compassionate people in the world, people who always come to the aid of others in other nations who have suffered disasters and injustices. And at least in ideal, we do have opportunity for all citizens to achieve the highest level of living each is capable of attaining.

Reading: "Frustrated Flag Waver"

Over suburbs and slums, rich folks and
  bums.
The star-spangled banner waves.
Over peace and prosperity, strife and
  disparity,
War crops of cold, early graves.

Our flag is still there, through soil and tear,
With pride and shame combined.
Our history is mixed, though we wish it were
  fixed
In the righteous, the true, and the kind.

An ambivalent state, still the greatest of
  great,
We see in the picture all told,
The good and the bad, the happy, the sad,
The weak, the strong, and the bold.

Oh say, can you see, we're supposed to be
  free.
We're equal, we all should agree.
But why is it so, I see as I go,
Injustice and tyranny?

It's hard to conceive, let alone to believe,
The contrasts in haves and have-nots.
Oh say, can you see frustration in me?
Vast riches and poor, ragged tots!

But I sure don't know, where else you could
  go
To get what we've got here at home.
The poorest of poor have a whole lot more

[1] Taken from a display at the Cleveland Museum of Natural History.

Than anywhere else you might roam.

I'll stay here, I guess, regardless the mess
We get ourselves into, you know.
At least we have choice; we do have a voice
In electing who's running this show.

We all have a shot to get to the spot
In life we'd all like to be.
The decisions are ours; we all have great
    powers,
To live life creatively.

By the dawn's early light, I'll struggle and
    fight
To correct the wrongs that I see.
At least there's a start, a beginning part,
In this place called the land of the free.

In the rocket's red glare, I confess I do care,
Though I criticize, rant, and rave.
So love this young land; even strike up the
    band,
And rejoice in the home of the brave!

Guided Prayer: (This is·a guided prayer in which a leader suggests ideas for thought, then pauses briefly to allow worshipers to add their concerns and offer their prayers silently.)

We confess that we as a nation have not always done right in your sight, O Lord. *(Pause)*

We acknowledge our sins before you. *(Pause)*

Not only the errors of the past history, but our own personal sins. *(Pause)*

We confess that we also have neglected opportunities to do good. *(Pause)*

Lord, forgive us. And we know we are forgiven, for you have said that if we confess our sins, you are just and faithful to forgive. *(Pause)*

Bless our nation. There is much which is good and pleasing throughout our land. *(Pause)*

Continue to help us become the people you want us to be, through Christ our Lord. *(Pause)* Amen.

This Land Is Your Land

Reflections: "Gott Mit Uns"

During World War II, some of the Nazi troops under Hitler had inscribed on their belt buckles these words: "Gott mit uns." Translated it means, "God with us." Even the German armies felt that theirs was a holy cause, that they had God on their side.

Nearly every nation in history has felt that God, gods, or deities were on its side, guiding it, protecting it, and looking upon it with favor. But the only assurance the Bible gives as to God's favor is in passages like this: ". . . the LORD has told us what is good. What he requires of us is this: to do what is just, to show constant love, and to live in humble fellowship with our God" (Micah 6:8).

We would be the most arrogant people on earth to say that God is with us more than with any other nation or to the exclusion of other nations. To the extent that the people and leaders of a nation give their allegiance first to God and his kingdom, that is a key to God's favor. But even history itself does not set this up as a firm rule because there have been nations which have prospered regardless of religious or national philosophies—prospered at least for a time.

Our history as a nation is one of ups and downs, success and failure, faithfulness to the God of Abraham, Isaac, and Jacob, and deeds of terror and injustice. The founding idea of liberty and justice for all is noble and worthy of our loyalty. Yet we must confess that it has not always been our practice. For example, consider what this nation did to a noble, free, and deeply spiritual race of people we call the American Indian. We labeled him a savage worthy of extinction, and in our zeal to destroy him, called upon the name of God. What we did as a people was a grave mark upon our history. Consider these words of Chief Standing Bear of the Oglala band of the Sioux nation.

"We did not think of the great open plains, the beautiful rolling hills, and the winding streams with tangled growth as wild. Only to the white man was nature a wilderness and only to him was the land infested with wild animals and savage people. To us it was tame. Earth was beautiful and we were surrounded with the blessings of the Great Mystery. Not until the hairy man from the east came and with brutal frenzy heaped injustices upon us and the families we loved was it wild for us. When the very animals of the forest began fleeing from his approach, then it was for us that the 'Wild West' began." [1]

But there is another side of our nation which is positive and good. For in this land of ours live some of the most compassionate people in the world, people who always come to the aid of others in other nations who have suffered disasters and injustices. And at least in ideal, we do have opportunity for all citizens to achieve the highest level of living each is capable of attaining.

Reading: "Frustrated Flag Waver"

> Over suburbs and slums, rich folks and bums.
> The star-spangled banner waves.
> Over peace and prosperity, strife and disparity,
> War crops of cold, early graves.
>
> Our flag is still there, through soil and tear,
> With pride and shame combined.
> Our history is mixed, though we wish it were fixed
> In the righteous, the true, and the kind.
>
> An ambivalent state, still the greatest of great,
> We see in the picture all told,
> The good and the bad, the happy, the sad,
> The weak, the strong, and the bold.
>
> Oh say, can you see, we're supposed to be free.
> We're equal, we all should agree.
> But why is it so, I see as I go,
> Injustice and tyranny?
>
> It's hard to conceive, let alone to believe,
> The contrasts in haves and have-nots.
> Oh say, can you see frustration in me?
> Vast riches and poor, ragged tots!
>
> But I sure don't know, where else you could go
> To get what we've got here at home.
> The poorest of poor have a whole lot more

[1] Taken from a display at the Cleveland Museum of Natural History.

Than anywhere else you might roam.

I'll stay here, I guess, regardless the mess
We get ourselves into, you know.
At least we have choice; we do have a voice
In electing who's running this show.

We all have a shot to get to the spot
In life we'd all like to be.
The decisions are ours; we all have great
       powers,
To live life creatively.

By the dawn's early light, I'll struggle and
       fight
To correct the wrongs that I see.
At least there's a start, a beginning part,
In this place called the land of the free.

In the rocket's red glare, I confess I do care,
Though I criticize, rant, and rave.
So love this young land; even strike up the
       band,
And rejoice in the home of the brave!

Guided Prayer: (This is a guided prayer in which a leader suggests ideas for thought, then pauses briefly to allow worshipers to add their concerns and offer their prayers silently.)

We confess that we as a nation have not always done right in your sight, O Lord. *(Pause)*

We acknowledge our sins before you. *(Pause)*

Not only the errors of the past history, but our own personal sins. *(Pause)*

We confess that we also have neglected opportunities to do good. *(Pause)*

Lord, forgive us. And we know we are forgiven, for you have said that if we confess our sins, you are just and faithful to forgive. *(Pause)*

Bless our nation. There is much which is good and pleasing throughout our land. *(Pause)*

Continue to help us become the people you want us to be, through Christ our Lord. *(Pause)* Amen.

This Land Is Your Land

Reflections: "Gott Mit Uns"

During World War II, some of the Nazi troops under Hitler had inscribed on their belt buckles these words: "Gott mit uns." Translated it means, "God with us." Even the German armies felt that theirs was a holy cause, that they had God on their side.

Nearly every nation in history has felt that God, gods, or deities were on its side, guiding it, protecting it, and looking upon it with favor. But the only assurance the Bible gives as to God's favor is in passages like this: ". . . the LORD has told us what is good. What he requires of us is this: to do what is just, to show constant love, and to live in humble fellowship with our God" (Micah 6:8).

We would be the most arrogant people on earth to say that God is with us more than with any other nation or to the exclusion of other nations. To the extent that the people and leaders of a nation give their allegiance first to God and his kingdom, that is a key to God's favor. But even history itself does not set this up as a firm rule because there have been nations which have prospered regardless of religious or national philosophies—prospered at least for a time.

Our history as a nation is one of ups and downs, success and failure, faithfulness to the God of Abraham, Isaac, and Jacob, and deeds of terror and injustice. The founding idea of liberty and justice for all is noble and worthy of our loyalty. Yet we must confess that it has not always been our practice. For example, consider what this nation did to a noble, free, and deeply spiritual race of people we call the American Indian. We labeled him a savage worthy of extinction, and in our zeal to destroy him, called upon the name of God. What we did as a people was a grave mark upon our history. Consider these words of Chief Standing Bear of the Oglala band of the Sioux nation.

"We did not think of the great open plains, the beautiful rolling hills, and the winding streams with tangled growth as wild. Only to the white man was nature a wilderness and only to him was the land infested with wild animals and savage people. To us it was tame. Earth was beautiful and we were surrounded with the blessings of the Great Mystery. Not until the hairy man from the east came and with brutal frenzy heaped injustices upon us and the families we loved was it wild for us. When the very animals of the forest began fleeing from his approach, then it was for us that the 'Wild West' began." [1]

But there is another side of our nation which is positive and good. For in this land of ours live some of the most compassionate people in the world, people who always come to the aid of others in other nations who have suffered disasters and injustices. And at least in ideal, we do have opportunity for all citizens to achieve the highest level of living each is capable of attaining.

Reading: "Frustrated Flag Waver"

Over suburbs and slums, rich folks and bums.
The star-spangled banner waves.
Over peace and prosperity, strife and disparity,
War crops of cold, early graves.

Our flag is still there, through soil and tear,
With pride and shame combined.
Our history is mixed, though we wish it were fixed
In the righteous, the true, and the kind.

An ambivalent state, still the greatest of great,
We see in the picture all told,
The good and the bad, the happy, the sad,
The weak, the strong, and the bold.

Oh say, can you see, we're supposed to be free.
We're equal, we all should agree.
But why is it so, I see as I go,
Injustice and tyranny?

It's hard to conceive, let alone to believe,
The contrasts in haves and have-nots.
Oh say, can you see frustration in me?
Vast riches and poor, ragged tots!

But I sure don't know, where else you could go
To get what we've got here at home.
The poorest of poor have a whole lot more

[1] Taken from a display at the Cleveland Museum of Natural History.

Than anywhere else you might roam.

I'll stay here, I guess, regardless the mess
We get ourselves into, you know.
At least we have choice; we do have a voice
In electing who's running this show.

We all have a shot to get to the spot
In life we'd all like to be.
The decisions are ours; we all have great
    powers,
To live life creatively.

By the dawn's early light, I'll struggle and
    fight
To correct the wrongs that I see.
At least there's a start, a beginning part,
In this place called the land of the free.

In the rocket's red glare, I confess I do care,
Though I criticize, rant, and rave.
So love this young land; even strike up the
    band,
And rejoice in the home of the brave!

Guided Prayer: (This is a guided prayer in which a leader suggests ideas for thought, then pauses briefly to allow worshipers to add their concerns and offer their prayers silently.)

We confess that we as a nation have not always done right in your sight, O Lord. *(Pause)*

We acknowledge our sins before you. *(Pause)*

Not only the errors of the past history, but our own personal sins. *(Pause)*

We confess that we also have neglected opportunities to do good. *(Pause)*

Lord, forgive us. And we know we are forgiven, for you have said that if we confess our sins, you are just and faithful to forgive. *(Pause)*

Bless our nation. There is much which is good and pleasing throughout our land. *(Pause)*

Continue to help us become the people you want us to be, through Christ our Lord. *(Pause)* Amen.

This Land Is Your Land

Reflections: "Gott Mit Uns"

During World War II, some of the Nazi troops under Hitler had inscribed on their belt buckles these words: "Gott mit uns." Translated it means, "God with us." Even the German armies felt that theirs was a holy cause, that they had God on their side.

Nearly every nation in history has felt that God, gods, or deities were on its side, guiding it, protecting it, and looking upon it with favor. But the only assurance the Bible gives as to God's favor is in passages like this: ". . . the LORD has told us what is good. What he requires of us is this: to do what is just, to show constant love, and to live in humble fellowship with our God" (Micah 6:8).

We would be the most arrogant people on earth to say that God is with us more than with any other nation or to the exclusion of other nations. To the extent that the people and leaders of a nation give their allegiance first to God and his kingdom, that is a key to God's favor. But even history itself does not set this up as a firm rule because there have been nations which have prospered regardless of religious or national philosophies—prospered at least for a time.

Our history as a nation is one of ups and downs, success and failure, faithfulness to the God of Abraham, Isaac, and Jacob, and deeds of terror and injustice. The founding idea of liberty and justice for all is noble and worthy of our loyalty. Yet we must confess that it has not always been our practice. For example, consider what this nation did to a noble, free, and deeply spiritual race of people we call the American Indian. We labeled him a savage worthy of extinction, and in our zeal to destroy him, called upon the name of God. What we did as a people was a grave mark upon our history. Consider these words of Chief Standing Bear of the Oglala band of the Sioux nation.

"We did not think of the great open plains, the beautiful rolling hills, and the winding streams with tangled growth as wild. Only to the white man was nature a wilderness and only to him was the land infested with wild animals and savage people. To us it was tame. Earth was beautiful and we were surrounded with the blessings of the Great Mystery. Not until the hairy man from the east came and with brutal frenzy heaped injustices upon us and the families we loved was it wild for us. When the very animals of the forest began fleeing from his approach, then it was for us that the 'Wild West' began."[1]

But there is another side of our nation which is positive and good. For in this land of ours live some of the most compassionate people in the world, people who always come to the aid of others in other nations who have suffered disasters and injustices. And at least in ideal, we do have opportunity for all citizens to achieve the highest level of living each is capable of attaining.

Reading: "Frustrated Flag Waver"

Over suburbs and slums, rich folks and
    bums.
The star-spangled banner waves.
Over peace and prosperity, strife and
    disparity,
War crops of cold, early graves.

Our flag is still there, through soil and tear,
With pride and shame combined.
Our history is mixed, though we wish it were
    fixed
In the righteous, the true, and the kind.

An ambivalent state, still the greatest of
    great,
We see in the picture all told,
The good and the bad, the happy, the sad,
The weak, the strong, and the bold.

Oh say, can you see, we're supposed to be
    free.
We're equal, we all should agree.
But why is it so, I see as I go,
Injustice and tyranny?

It's hard to conceive, let alone to believe,
The contrasts in haves and have-nots.
Oh say, can you see frustration in me?
Vast riches and poor, ragged tots!

But I sure don't know, where else you could
    go
To get what we've got here at home.
The poorest of poor have a whole lot more

[1] Taken from a display at the Cleveland Museum of Natural History.

Than anywhere else you might roam.

I'll stay here, I guess, regardless the mess
We get ourselves into, you know.
At least we have choice; we do have a voice
In electing who's running this show.

We all have a shot to get to the spot
In life we'd all like to be.
The decisions are ours; we all have great
    powers,
To live life creatively.

By the dawn's early light, I'll struggle and
    fight
To correct the wrongs that I see.
At least there's a start, a beginning part,
In this place called the land of the free.

In the rocket's red glare, I confess I do care,
Though I criticize, rant, and rave.
So love this young land; even strike up the
    band,
And rejoice in the home of the brave!

Guided Prayer: (This is a guided prayer in which a leader suggests ideas for thought, then pauses briefly to allow worshipers to add their concerns and offer their prayers silently.)

We confess that we as a nation have not always done right in your sight, O Lord. *(Pause)*

We acknowledge our sins before you. *(Pause)*

Not only the errors of the past history, but our own personal sins. *(Pause)*

We confess that we also have neglected opportunities to do good. *(Pause)*

Lord, forgive us. And we know we are forgiven, for you have said that if we confess our sins, you are just and faithful to forgive. *(Pause)*

Bless our nation. There is much which is good and pleasing throughout our land. *(Pause)*

Continue to help us become the people you want us to be, through Christ our Lord. *(Pause)* Amen.

My Father Is Always Working

A Celebration for Labor Day, Life Service Sunday, or a Vesper Service

The following material can be adapted easily for a variety of occasions, from an outdoor worship service to a Labor Day theme. You will find "The Making of a Jet—An Unholy Parable" unusual. Because it is so ridiculous and unbelievable, it probably will bring laughter. This is acceptable because the message behind it is forceful and should show creation and the labors of God in a new light.

Preparation

This material can be used for a special Labor Day emphasis for your group or may be used as a culmination to a group outing or camping experience. You may want to fashion a simple display to be used as a focal point or worship center. Select a variety of carpentry or wood-working tools, garden tools, or other items which will speak to your group of labor. The theme is God as a worker and his labors in the creation process. The voice parts can be delivered from various parts of your room or meeting place (which may be around a campfire or in an open field) or may be spoken from a sanctuary lectern or pulpit.

The Experience

Opening Thought: "You and I toiling for earth, may at the same time be toiling for heaven, and every day's work may be a Jacob's ladder reaching up nearer to God" (Theodore Parker).[1]

Hymn or Song: "For the Beauty of the Earth" (Also consider a folk song here such as "Rocky Mountain High" by John Denver or some other song which may have an appropriate theme which is popular at the time of your group's gathering).

Scripture: John 5:17.

Contemplation on Creation: Supplement A.

Scripture: Genesis 1:1-5; Psalm 19:1-6, 14.

Closing Hymn: "The Spacious Firmament on High."

[1] Tryon Edwards, comp., *The New Dictionary of Thoughts* (New York: Standard Book Co., 1960), p. 338.

My Father Is Always Working

Contemplation on Creation

A VOICE: "The Making of a Jet—An Unholy Parable"

Have you ever watched jet trails overhead or seen these huge metal monsters at an airport or flown inside one of them? It seems unbelievable that such a contraption, weighing tons and tons, could ever lift itself off the ground and slice its way through the sky at a speed of hundreds of miles per hour.

Have you ever wondered how such a machine ever came to be? That is the most fascinating part of all. Most people believe that these planes are made in manufacturing plants as are boats or cars. But I want to let you in on the secret. They are not manufactured at all. As strange and unbelievable as it may seem, these giants of the air seem to build themselves.

That's right! For on a secluded island, a strange phenomenon takes place. The island is rich in mineral ores, and at its very center there is a volcano. The ores are transformed into the various metals necessary for a jet, and the rest of the island yields the necessary rubber and fabric for its completion.

These metals come together as if by magic when there are changes in the weather or when the volcano becomes active. First the inner structure—the beams and braces of the jet—appears. Then the covering metal sheets come up out of the volcano and fuse to the outside of the plane. Rivets appear from virtually nowhere. And when it rains, the various chemicals and gases from the volcano oxidize and form paint.

It all happens without planning, preparation, or human ingenuity. It is just as simple as that.

They are looking for a good crop of jets this year because the conditions on the island have been ideal.

ANOTHER VOICE: And there are those who would have us believe that creation took place in a similar fashion—no planning, no purpose, no design—just the evolutionary process, bringing something out of nothing.

ANOTHER VOICE: How could life, motion, light, beauty, and intelligence have appeared from no place without a Creator?

ANOTHER VOICE: Do you ever wonder how this vast universe came to be? How did God create it? Was it just by the wave of an Almighty arm and—behold? The disciplines of science tell us that the universe evolved, unfolded, over an incomprehensible span of time. The science book is a "how" book. It describes to us, as accurately as it is capable of doing, how the galaxies and all the bodies of the heavens came about. And remember that science is still in its infancy. The Bible, on the other hand, is a "who" and a "why" book. It tells, in picturesque terms, about a Person—God the Creator—who purposefully brought the worlds into being.

Creation is still going on. If you doubt it, consider how suns burn out and are replaced by new ones, how worlds begin. Consider the birth of a baby. This is all a continuation of the creation process. If nature were not creating and renewing and replenishing itself all the time, all existence would cease.

And were the suns, moons, planets, comets, and galaxies merely flung from the fingers of God on some whim? No! There was careful planning, as a master craftsman creates from a blueprint.

Was it easy?

Jesus tells us that it took work—vast amounts of work—to bring the universe into being. The Father is a worker! It took careful long-range planning, skillful engineering, and continual maintenance.

It didn't all happen at once. It didn't happen by chance. It didn't happen on a whim. It isn't completed yet. Creation is still going on, and it took real labor to do it. God is at work still in creation and in our lives.

ANOTHER VOICE: When I look at the sky on a clear, star-studded night, I can't help but think of the vastness of it. We live on a very minor planet with only one moon, in a solar system which, because of its size, can be described as second-rate. There are stars in our galaxy which dwarf our sun. We are a speck, a particle in the Milky Way. And the Milky Way, with its tens of thousands of stars and other bodies, is but one galaxy in a whole network of galaxies in the universe. There seems to be no end to them. The universe stretches on and on, perhaps without end. And after all, what is humankind in

comparison to all the vastness around us?

Stars burn out and grow dim, and new ones appear. The universe is alive with action, with creation, most of it stretching over millions and billions of years. And there are such distances between stars, planets, and galaxies that the mind cannot grasp—cannot comprehend—the vastness of it all.

ANOTHER VOICE: Consider how diligently people in all walks of life, in every profession, must labor. Think about the most basic workman, the agriculturalist. The farmer thinks nothing of putting in a ten- or twelve-hour day during planting or harvest seasons. He plows and fits the soil, plants and fertilizes, cultivates, harvests, refines, and stores or sells the crop. It is hard work. It takes physical labor as well as careful long-range planning. And the hard work comes almost as a second nature.

ANOTHER VOICE: Can we be so naive as to think that God the Creator just threw it all together in a flash? No. There was careful consideration of all the long-range aspects and consequences of creation. And remember how long "long-range" can mean when we are talking about the universe. Ancient people did not have the benefit of modern science when they recorded the book of Genesis. If we had been there and told them even one facet of what we know today—for instance, that the earth is egg-shaped and revolves around the sun—they wouldn't have had the experience, knowledge, or scientific background either to understand or to believe us.

So they described the creation in a beautiful way, in parable or story form. It took God just seven days. And to them, a day was a day. But now we must ask, "Whose day?" A Martian day or a Saturnian day or one of God's days? And remember how long his days can be—the Bible tells us that a thousand years is like a day (or less) in the sight of God. Yes, those were long days in the creation process, indeed, days which are still going on. God has yet to put the finishing touches on it all—to "call it a day." Creation is still going on, evolving, developing, growing, unfolding.

It didn't happen overnight or at the snap of a finger. God is a worker. It took hard work to plan it all and to carry it out, not to mention maintenance, expansion, and improvement.

ANOTHER VOICE: There is no particular conflict between the biblical account of creation and what we know to be true scientifically about the development of the universe. These are two different, yet related and complementary disciplines. Science tells how it all happened; the Bible speaks of a Creator who is working, and it interprets meaning in all things created.

ANOTHER VOICE: The universe seems to be an interdependent system full of unfathomable mysteries and complexities. There is breathtaking beauty as well as celestial accidents, explosions, and collisions. There are heat and light, melting and cooling, heaving and disturbances. Creation, like birth, seems not without its pain and struggle.

There is also humor in creation. Who would have thought to build an elephant?

People seem to be industrious, ingenious, ambitious, innovative by nature. We are inventors, explorers, creators, workers. Could this also be the meaning of the image of God, the *imago Dei?*

My Father Is Always Working

Contemplation on Creation

A VOICE: "The Making of a Jet—An Unholy Parable"

Have you ever watched jet trails overhead or seen these huge metal monsters at an airport or flown inside one of them? It seems unbelievable that such a contraption, weighing tons and tons, could ever lift itself off the ground and slice its way through the sky at a speed of hundreds of miles per hour.

Have you ever wondered how such a machine ever came to be? That is the most fascinating part of all. Most people believe that these planes are made in manufacturing plants as are boats or cars. But I want to let you in on the secret. They are not manufactured at all. As strange and unbelievable as it may seem, these giants of the air seem to build themselves.

That's right! For on a secluded island, a strange phenomenon takes place. The island is rich in mineral ores, and at its very center there is a volcano. The ores are transformed into the various metals necessary for a jet, and the rest of the island yields the necessary rubber and fabric for its completion.

These metals come together as if by magic when there are changes in the weather or when the volcano becomes active. First the inner structure—the beams and braces of the jet—appears. Then the covering metal sheets come up out of the volcano and fuse to the outside of the plane. Rivets appear from virtually nowhere. And when it rains, the various chemicals and gases from the volcano oxidize and form paint.

It all happens without planning, preparation, or human ingenuity. It is just as simple as that.

They are looking for a good crop of jets this year because the conditions on the island have been ideal.

ANOTHER VOICE: And there are those who would have us believe that creation took place in a similar fashion—no planning, no purpose, no design—just the evolutionary process, bringing something out of nothing.

ANOTHER VOICE: How could life, motion, light, beauty, and intelligence have appeared from no place without a Creator?

ANOTHER VOICE: Do you ever wonder how this vast universe came to be? How did God create it? Was it just by the wave of an Almighty arm and—behold? The disciplines of science tell us that the universe evolved, unfolded, over an incomprehensible span of time. The science book is a "how" book. It describes to us, as accurately as it is capable of doing, how the galaxies and all the bodies of the heavens came about. And remember that science is still in its infancy. The Bible, on the other hand, is a "who" and a "why" book. It tells, in picturesque terms, about a Person—God the Creator—who purposefully brought the worlds into being.

Creation is still going on. If you doubt it, consider how suns burn out and are replaced by new ones, how worlds begin. Consider the birth of a baby. This is all a continuation of the creation process. If nature were not creating and renewing and replenishing itself all the time, all existence would cease.

And were the suns, moons, planets, comets, and galaxies merely flung from the fingers of God on some whim? No! There was careful planning, as a master craftsman creates from a blueprint.

Was it easy?

Jesus tells us that it took work—vast amounts of work—to bring the universe into being. The Father is a worker! It took careful long-range planning, skillful engineering, and continual maintenance.

It didn't all happen at once. It didn't happen by chance. It didn't happen on a whim. It isn't completed yet. Creation is still going on, and it took real labor to do it. God is at work still in creation and in our lives.

ANOTHER VOICE: When I look at the sky on a clear, star-studded night, I can't help but think of the vastness of it. We live on a very minor planet with only one moon, in a solar system which, because of its size, can be described as second-rate. There are stars in our galaxy which dwarf our sun. We are a speck, a particle in the Milky Way. And the Milky Way, with its tens of thousands of stars and other bodies, is but one galaxy in a whole network of galaxies in the universe. There seems to be no end to them. The universe stretches on and on, perhaps without end. And after all, what is humankind in

comparison to all the vastness around us?

Stars burn out and grow dim, and new ones appear. The universe is alive with action, with creation, most of it stretching over millions and billions of years. And there are such distances between stars, planets, and galaxies that the mind cannot grasp—cannot comprehend—the vastness of it all.

ANOTHER VOICE: Consider how diligently people in all walks of life, in every profession, must labor. Think about the most basic workman, the agriculturalist. The farmer thinks nothing of putting in a ten- or twelve-hour day during planting or harvest seasons. He plows and fits the soil, plants and fertilizes, cultivates, harvests, refines, and stores or sells the crop. It is hard work. It takes physical labor as well as careful long-range planning. And the hard work comes almost as a second nature.

ANOTHER VOICE: Can we be so naive as to think that God the Creator just threw it all together in a flash? No. There was careful consideration of all the long-range aspects and consequences of creation. And remember how long "long-range" can mean when we are talking about the universe. Ancient people did not have the benefit of modern science when they recorded the book of Genesis. If we had been there and told them even one facet of what we know today—for instance, that the earth is egg-shaped and revolves around the sun—they wouldn't have had the experience, knowledge, or scientific background either to understand or to believe us.

So they described the creation in a beautiful way, in parable or story form. It took God just seven days. And to them, a day was a day. But now we must ask, "Whose day?" A Martian day or a Saturnian day or one of God's days? And remember how long his days can be—the Bible tells us that a thousand years is like a day (or less) in the sight of God. Yes, those were long days in the creation process, indeed, days which are still going on. God has yet to put the finishing touches on it all—to "call it a day." Creation is still going on, evolving, developing, growing, unfolding.

It didn't happen overnight or at the snap of a finger. God is a worker. It took hard work to plan it all and to carry it out, not to mention maintenance, expansion, and improvement.

ANOTHER VOICE: There is no particular conflict between the biblical account of creation and what we know to be true scientifically about the development of the universe. These are two different, yet related and complementary disciplines. Science tells how it all happened; the Bible speaks of a Creator who is working, and it interprets meaning in all things created.

ANOTHER VOICE: The universe seems to be an interdependent system full of unfathomable mysteries and complexities. There is breathtaking beauty as well as celestial accidents, explosions, and collisions. There are heat and light, melting and cooling, heaving and disturbances. Creation, like birth, seems not without its pain and struggle.

There is also humor in creation. Who would have thought to build an elephant?

People seem to be industrious, ingenious, ambitious, innovative by nature. We are inventors, explorers, creators, workers. Could this also be the meaning of the image of God, the *imago Dei?*

My Father Is Always Working

Contemplation on Creation

A VOICE: "The Making of a Jet—An Unholy Parable"

Have you ever watched jet trails overhead or seen these huge metal monsters at an airport or flown inside one of them? It seems unbelievable that such a contraption, weighing tons and tons, could ever lift itself off the ground and slice its way through the sky at a speed of hundreds of miles per hour.

Have you ever wondered how such a machine ever came to be? That is the most fascinating part of all. Most people believe that these planes are made in manufacturing plants as are boats or cars. But I want to let you in on the secret. They are not manufactured at all. As strange and unbelievable as it may seem, these giants of the air seem to build themselves.

That's right! For on a secluded island, a strange phenomenon takes place. The island is rich in mineral ores, and at its very center there is a volcano. The ores are transformed into the various metals necessary for a jet, and the rest of the island yields the necessary rubber and fabric for its completion.

These metals come together as if by magic when there are changes in the weather or when the volcano becomes active. First the inner structure—the beams and braces of the jet—appears. Then the covering metal sheets come up out of the volcano and fuse to the outside of the plane. Rivets appear from virtually nowhere. And when it rains, the various chemicals and gases from the volcano oxidize and form paint.

It all happens without planning, preparation, or human ingenuity. It is just as simple as that.

They are looking for a good crop of jets this year because the conditions on the island have been ideal.

ANOTHER VOICE: And there are those who would have us believe that creation took place in a similar fashion—no planning, no purpose, no design—just the evolutionary process, bringing something out of nothing.

ANOTHER VOICE: How could life, motion, light, beauty, and intelligence have appeared from no place without a Creator?

ANOTHER VOICE: Do you ever wonder how this vast universe came to be? How did God create it? Was it just by the wave of an Almighty arm and—behold? The disciplines of science tell us that the universe evolved, unfolded, over an incomprehensible span of time. The science book is a "how" book. It describes to us, as accurately as it is capable of doing, how the galaxies and all the bodies of the heavens came about. And remember that science is still in its infancy. The Bible, on the other hand, is a "who" and a "why" book. It tells, in picturesque terms, about a Person—God the Creator—who purposefully brought the worlds into being.

Creation is still going on. If you doubt it, consider how suns burn out and are replaced by new ones, how worlds begin. Consider the birth of a baby. This is all a continuation of the creation process. If nature were not creating and renewing and replenishing itself all the time, all existence would cease.

And were the suns, moons, planets, comets, and galaxies merely flung from the fingers of God on some whim? No! There was careful planning, as a master craftsman creates from a blueprint.

Was it easy?

Jesus tells us that it took work—vast amounts of work—to bring the universe into being. The Father is a worker! It took careful long-range planning, skillful engineering, and continual maintenance.

It didn't all happen at once. It didn't happen by chance. It didn't happen on a whim. It isn't completed yet. Creation is still going on, and it took real labor to do it. God is at work still in creation and in our lives.

ANOTHER VOICE: When I look at the sky on a clear, star-studded night, I can't help but think of the vastness of it. We live on a very minor planet with only one moon, in a solar system which, because of its size, can be described as second-rate. There are stars in our galaxy which dwarf our sun. We are a speck, a particle in the Milky Way. And the Milky Way, with its tens of thousands of stars and other bodies, is but one galaxy in a whole network of galaxies in the universe. There seems to be no end to them. The universe stretches on and on, perhaps without end. And after all, what is humankind in

comparison to all the vastness around us?

Stars burn out and grow dim, and new ones appear. The universe is alive with action, with creation, most of it stretching over millions and billions of years. And there are such distances between stars, planets, and galaxies that the mind cannot grasp—cannot comprehend—the vastness of it all.

ANOTHER VOICE: Consider how diligently people in all walks of life, in every profession, must labor. Think about the most basic workman, the agriculturalist. The farmer thinks nothing of putting in a ten- or twelve-hour day during planting or harvest seasons. He plows and fits the soil, plants and fertilizes, cultivates, harvests, refines, and stores or sells the crop. It is hard work. It takes physical labor as well as careful long-range planning. And the hard work comes almost as a second nature.

ANOTHER VOICE: Can we be so naive as to think that God the Creator just threw it all together in a flash? No. There was careful consideration of all the long-range aspects and consequences of creation. And remember how long "long-range" can mean when we are talking about the universe. Ancient people did not have the benefit of modern science when they recorded the book of Genesis. If we had been there and told them even one facet of what we know today—for instance, that the earth is egg-shaped and revolves around the sun—they wouldn't have had the experience, knowledge, or scientific background either to understand or to believe us.

So they described the creation in a beautiful way, in parable or story form. It took God just seven days. And to them, a day was a day. But now we must ask, "Whose day?" A Martian day or a Saturnian day or one of God's days? And remember how long his days can be—the Bible tells us that a thousand years is like a day (or less) in the sight of God. Yes, those were long days in the creation process, indeed, days which are still going on. God has yet to put the finishing touches on it all—to "call it a day." Creation is still going on, evolving, developing, growing, unfolding.

It didn't happen overnight or at the snap of a finger. God is a worker. It took hard work to plan it all and to carry it out, not to mention maintenance, expansion, and improvement.

ANOTHER VOICE: There is no particular conflict between the biblical account of creation and what we know to be true scientifically about the development of the universe. These are two different, yet related and complementary disciplines. Science tells how it all happened; the Bible speaks of a Creator who is working, and it interprets meaning in all things created.

ANOTHER VOICE: The universe seems to be an interdependent system full of unfathomable mysteries and complexities. There is breathtaking beauty as well as celestial accidents, explosions, and collisions. There are heat and light, melting and cooling, heaving and disturbances. Creation, like birth, seems not without its pain and struggle.

There is also humor in creation. Who would have thought to build an elephant?

People seem to be industrious, ingenious, ambitious, innovative by nature. We are inventors, explorers, creators, workers. Could this also be the meaning of the image of God, the *imago Dei?*

My Father Is Always Working

Contemplation on Creation

A VOICE: "The Making of a Jet—An Unholy Parable"

Have you ever watched jet trails overhead or seen these huge metal monsters at an airport or flown inside one of them? It seems unbelievable that such a contraption, weighing tons and tons, could ever lift itself off the ground and slice its way through the sky at a speed of hundreds of miles per hour.

Have you ever wondered how such a machine ever came to be? That is the most fascinating part of all. Most people believe that these planes are made in manufacturing plants as are boats or cars. But I want to let you in on the secret. They are not manufactured at all. As strange and unbelievable as it may seem, these giants of the air seem to build themselves.

That's right! For on a secluded island, a strange phenomenon takes place. The island is rich in mineral ores, and at its very center there is a volcano. The ores are transformed into the various metals necessary for a jet, and the rest of the island yields the necessary rubber and fabric for its completion.

These metals come together as if by magic when there are changes in the weather or when the volcano becomes active. First the inner structure—the beams and braces of the jet—appears. Then the covering metal sheets come up out of the volcano and fuse to the outside of the plane. Rivets appear from virtually nowhere. And when it rains, the various chemicals and gases from the volcano oxidize and form paint.

It all happens without planning, preparation, or human ingenuity. It is just as simple as that.

They are looking for a good crop of jets this year because the conditions on the island have been ideal.

ANOTHER VOICE: And there are those who would have us believe that creation took place in a similar fashion—no planning, no purpose, no design—just the evolutionary process, bringing something out of nothing.

ANOTHER VOICE: How could life, motion, light, beauty, and intelligence have appeared from no place without a Creator?

ANOTHER VOICE: Do you ever wonder how this vast universe came to be? How did God create it? Was it just by the wave of an Almighty arm and—behold? The disciplines of science tell us that the universe evolved, unfolded, over an incomprehensible span of time. The science book is a "how" book. It describes to us, as accurately as it is capable of doing, how the galaxies and all the bodies of the heavens came about. And remember that science is still in its infancy. The Bible, on the other hand, is a "who" and a "why" book. It tells, in picturesque terms, about a Person—God the Creator—who purposefully brought the worlds into being.

Creation is still going on. If you doubt it, consider how suns burn out and are replaced by new ones, how worlds begin. Consider the birth of a baby. This is all a continuation of the creation process. If nature were not creating and renewing and replenishing itself all the time, all existence would cease.

And were the suns, moons, planets, comets, and galaxies merely flung from the fingers of God on some whim? No! There was careful planning, as a master craftsman creates from a blueprint.

Was it easy?

Jesus tells us that it took work—vast amounts of work—to bring the universe into being. The Father is a worker! It took careful long-range planning, skillful engineering, and continual maintenance.

It didn't all happen at once. It didn't happen by chance. It didn't happen on a whim. It isn't completed yet. Creation is still going on, and it took real labor to do it. God is at work still in creation and in our lives.

ANOTHER VOICE: When I look at the sky on a clear, star-studded night, I can't help but think of the vastness of it. We live on a very minor planet with only one moon, in a solar system which, because of its size, can be described as second-rate. There are stars in our galaxy which dwarf our sun. We are a speck, a particle in the Milky Way. And the Milky Way, with its tens of thousands of stars and other bodies, is but one galaxy in a whole network of galaxies in the universe. There seems to be no end to them. The universe stretches on and on, perhaps without end. And after all, what is humankind in

comparison to all the vastness around us?

Stars burn out and grow dim, and new ones appear. The universe is alive with action, with creation, most of it stretching over millions and billions of years. And there are such distances between stars, planets, and galaxies that the mind cannot grasp—cannot comprehend—the vastness of it all.

ANOTHER VOICE: Consider how diligently people in all walks of life, in every profession, must labor. Think about the most basic workman, the agriculturalist. The farmer thinks nothing of putting in a ten- or twelve-hour day during planting or harvest seasons. He plows and fits the soil, plants and fertilizes, cultivates, harvests, refines, and stores or sells the crop. It is hard work. It takes physical labor as well as careful long-range planning. And the hard work comes almost as a second nature.

ANOTHER VOICE: Can we be so naive as to think that God the Creator just threw it all together in a flash? No. There was careful consideration of all the long-range aspects and consequences of creation. And remember how long "long-range" can mean when we are talking about the universe. Ancient people did not have the benefit of modern science when they recorded the book of Genesis. If we had been there and told them even one facet of what we know today—for instance, that the earth is egg-shaped and revolves around the sun—they wouldn't have had the experience, knowledge, or scientific background either to understand or to believe us.

So they described the creation in a beautiful way, in parable or story form. It took God just seven days. And to them, a day was a day. But now we must ask, "Whose day?" A Martian day or a Saturnian day or one of God's days? And remember how long his days can be—the Bible tells us that a thousand years is like a day (or less) in the sight of God. Yes, those were long days in the creation process, indeed, days which are still going on. God has yet to put the finishing touches on it all—to "call it a day." Creation is still going on, evolving, developing, growing, unfolding.

It didn't happen overnight or at the snap of a finger. God is a worker. It took hard work to plan it all and to carry it out, not to mention maintenance, expansion, and improvement.

ANOTHER VOICE: There is no particular conflict between the biblical account of creation and what we know to be true scientifically about the development of the universe. These are two different, yet related and complementary disciplines. Science tells how it all happened; the Bible speaks of a Creator who is working, and it interprets meaning in all things created.

ANOTHER VOICE: The universe seems to be an interdependent system full of unfathomable mysteries and complexities. There is breathtaking beauty as well as celestial accidents, explosions, and collisions. There are heat and light, melting and cooling, heaving and disturbances. Creation, like birth, seems not without its pain and struggle.

There is also humor in creation. Who would have thought to build an elephant?

People seem to be industrious, ingenious, ambitious, innovative by nature. We are inventors, explorers, creators, workers. Could this also be the meaning of the image of God, the *imago Dei?*

My Father Is Always Working

Contemplation on Creation

A VOICE: "The Making of a Jet—An Unholy Parable"

Have you ever watched jet trails overhead or seen these huge metal monsters at an airport or flown inside one of them? It seems unbelievable that such a contraption, weighing tons and tons, could ever lift itself off the ground and slice its way through the sky at a speed of hundreds of miles per hour.

Have you ever wondered how such a machine ever came to be? That is the most fascinating part of all. Most people believe that these planes are made in manufacturing plants as are boats or cars. But I want to let you in on the secret. They are not manufactured at all. As strange and unbelievable as it may seem, these giants of the air seem to build themselves.

That's right! For on a secluded island, a strange phenomenon takes place. The island is rich in mineral ores, and at its very center there is a volcano. The ores are transformed into the various metals necessary for a jet, and the rest of the island yields the necessary rubber and fabric for its completion.

These metals come together as if by magic when there are changes in the weather or when the volcano becomes active. First the inner structure—the beams and braces of the jet—appears. Then the covering metal sheets come up out of the volcano and fuse to the outside of the plane. Rivets appear from virtually nowhere. And when it rains, the various chemicals and gases from the volcano oxidize and form paint.

It all happens without planning, preparation, or human ingenuity. It is just as simple as that.

They are looking for a good crop of jets this year because the conditions on the island have been ideal.

ANOTHER VOICE: And there are those who would have us believe that creation took place in a similar fashion—no planning, no purpose, no design—just the evolutionary process, bringing something out of nothing.

ANOTHER VOICE: How could life, motion, light, beauty, and intelligence have appeared from no place without a Creator?

ANOTHER VOICE: Do you ever wonder how this vast universe came to be? How did God create it? Was it just by the wave of an Almighty arm and—behold? The disciplines of science tell us that the universe evolved, unfolded, over an incomprehensible span of time. The science book is a "how" book. It describes to us, as accurately as it is capable of doing, how the galaxies and all the bodies of the heavens came about. And remember that science is still in its infancy. The Bible, on the other hand, is a "who" and a "why" book. It tells, in picturesque terms, about a Person—God the Creator—who purposefully brought the worlds into being.

Creation is still going on. If you doubt it, consider how suns burn out and are replaced by new ones, how worlds begin. Consider the birth of a baby. This is all a continuation of the creation process. If nature were not creating and renewing and replenishing itself all the time, all existence would cease.

And were the suns, moons, planets, comets, and galaxies merely flung from the fingers of God on some whim? No! There was careful planning, as a master craftsman creates from a blueprint.

Was it easy?

Jesus tells us that it took work—vast amounts of work—to bring the universe into being. The Father is a worker! It took careful long-range planning, skillful engineering, and continual maintenance.

It didn't all happen at once. It didn't happen by chance. It didn't happen on a whim. It isn't completed yet. Creation is still going on, and it took real labor to do it. God is at work still in creation and in our lives.

ANOTHER VOICE: When I look at the sky on a clear, star-studded night, I can't help but think of the vastness of it. We live on a very minor planet with only one moon, in a solar system which, because of its size, can be described as second-rate. There are stars in our galaxy which dwarf our sun. We are a speck, a particle in the Milky Way. And the Milky Way, with its tens of thousands of stars and other bodies, is but one galaxy in a whole network of galaxies in the universe. There seems to be no end to them. The universe stretches on and on, perhaps without end. And after all, what is humankind in

comparison to all the vastness around us?

Stars burn out and grow dim, and new ones appear. The universe is alive with action, with creation, most of it stretching over millions and billions of years. And there are such distances between stars, planets, and galaxies that the mind cannot grasp—cannot comprehend—the vastness of it all.

ANOTHER VOICE: Consider how diligently people in all walks of life, in every profession, must labor. Think about the most basic workman, the agriculturalist. The farmer thinks nothing of putting in a ten- or twelve-hour day during planting or harvest seasons. He plows and fits the soil, plants and fertilizes, cultivates, harvests, refines, and stores or sells the crop. It is hard work. It takes physical labor as well as careful long-range planning. And the hard work comes almost as a second nature.

ANOTHER VOICE: Can we be so naive as to think that God the Creator just threw it all together in a flash? No. There was careful consideration of all the long-range aspects and consequences of creation. And remember how long "long-range" can mean when we are talking about the universe. Ancient people did not have the benefit of modern science when they recorded the book of Genesis. If we had been there and told them even one facet of what we know today—for instance, that the earth is egg-shaped and revolves around the sun—they wouldn't have had the experience, knowledge, or scientific background either to understand or to believe us.

So they described the creation in a beautiful way, in parable or story form. It took God just seven days. And to them, a day was a day. But now we must ask, "Whose day?" A Martian day or a Saturnian day or one of God's days? And remember how long his days can be—the Bible tells us that a thousand years is like a day (or less) in the sight of God. Yes, those were long days in the creation process, indeed, days which are still going on. God has yet to put the finishing touches on it all—to "call it a day." Creation is still going on, evolving, developing, growing, unfolding.

It didn't happen overnight or at the snap of a finger. God is a worker. It took hard work to plan it all and to carry it out, not to mention maintenance, expansion, and improvement.

ANOTHER VOICE: There is no particular conflict between the biblical account of creation and what we know to be true scientifically about the development of the universe. These are two different, yet related and complementary disciplines. Science tells how it all happened; the Bible speaks of a Creator who is working, and it interprets meaning in all things created.

ANOTHER VOICE: The universe seems to be an interdependent system full of unfathomable mysteries and complexities. There is breathtaking beauty as well as celestial accidents, explosions, and collisions. There are heat and light, melting and cooling, heaving and disturbances. Creation, like birth, seems not without its pain and struggle.

There is also humor in creation. Who would have thought to build an elephant?

People seem to be industrious, ingenious, ambitious, innovative by nature. We are inventors, explorers, creators, workers. Could this also be the meaning of the image of God, the *imago Dei?*

Let's Celebrate School

Celebrating Who We Are as Students

The material in this chapter might be used best around the beginning of the school year. Most youth groups have a special meeting or party as a kind of "kick off" to begin the fall season. Summer vacations and activities often curtail church youth group activities, but the beginning of school seems to be a time when we get back into the routines and challenges of group activities. When we are young, our chief occupation is that of being a student. The world is full of work to do, and most of our adult lives will be occupied with earning a living. Youth is a time when people devote nearly full time to earning an education. It is this phase of life that we celebrate.

Preparation

Consider creating a worship center composed of things which remind you of the many facets of school life. These might include books, footballs or basketballs, paper and pencils, audiovisual equipment, band hats or uniforms. Every young person has many mixed feelings about school. Some may dread it; others enjoy school life to its fullest. Some like the studies; others live only for school activities. Regardless of your particular feelings, this is a time in life which will pass all too quickly, never to be repeated. As you prepare for this worship experience, reflect on the meaning of your own education and the opportunities it provides.

Prepare your meeting place with chairs arranged in circular seating around a table on which are displayed the worship center items. Special leadership and parts should be spoken from within the group, and anyone having a special part should sit within the group.

The Experience

Beginning Thought: "The school should always have as its aim that the young person leave it as a harmonious personality, not as a specialist. . . . It is essential that the student acquire an understanding of and a lively feeling for values. He must acquire a vivid sense of the beautiful and of the morally good. Otherwise he—with his specialized knowledge—more closely resembles a well-trained dog than a harmoniously developed person" (Albert Einstein).[1]

A Song: At this point, play a record of a song which is popular currently. This will help remind individuals of their life apart from the group and the fact that all experiences, listening to popular music included, are not separate from devotional life. Life should be one, not divided into "secular" and "sacred."

Hymn: "Now in the Days of Youth."

Scripture: 2 Timothy 2:8-19.

Reading: "Fall and All" (Supplement A).

Litany of Celebration: Supplement A.

Reading: "Youth" (Supplement A).

Hymn: "I Would Be True."

Sharing, Caring: In this concluding part of the service, ask group members to gather in groups of threes. Then invite them to share briefly with each other the following:

My hopes for school this year.

My hopes for the life of our youth group.

My personal goals, hopes, and ambitions for this school year.

Allow about ten minutes for this time of sharing. Then have the group join together in a friendship circle, holding hands. Allow a brief time for individuals to share with the total group the ideas and feelings expressed in the smaller groups. Close with a group benediction or a favorite and familiar song or hymn.

[1] Tryon Edwards, comp., *The New Dictionary of Thoughts* (New York: Standard Book Co., 1960), p. 164.

Let's Celebrate School

Reading: "Fall and All"

There is something about fall. Winter still sleeps; the joys of summer are fresh in mind and it's time for hayrides and hot dogs, bands and bleachers, touchdowns and tears, the passing pride of victory, the momentary melancholy of defeat.

Fall—and Halloween, and Thanksgiving, and Christmas . . .

And all.

Each with a special feeling all its own.

Is there another season with as many familiar sounds, sights and smells, activities and challenges, expectations and emotions?

Litany of Celebration

(Each time the leader pauses, instruct the group to respond with the words "We celebrate your love and blessing, O Lord.")

For the fall season and the beginning of school. *(Pause)*

For all our teachers, counselors, and instructors, those we especially love and those who make us study hard. *(Pause)*

For all our friends, old and new. *(Pause)*

For the chance to study and learn. *(Pause)*

For our chief occupation as students. *(Pause)*

For all of the opportunities, challenges, and even the frustrations of student life. *(Pause)*

For every opportunity which helps us grow. *(Pause)*

Lord, this is a time in our lives which is brief, elusive, fleeting. Help us to live it to its fullest, knowing that we shall never pass this way again. Save us from wishing so much for tomorrow that we miss today. Amen.

Reading: "Youth"

Action, activity, vitality, briskness,
liveliness, animation, snap, spirit,
go, energy, vim, vigor, eagerness, and
enthusiasm
are what young people are made of.
But not always.
Sometimes they are quiet and thoughtful,

alone, dreamy, frustrated, insecure,
disappointed, depressed, down.
People are sometimes
shocked, shook, terrified, mystified,
horrified, frightened, appalled, speechless,
hopeless, or helpless in their presence.
At other times people are
delighted, pleased, encouraged, enchanted,
gratified, surprised, inspired, uplifted.
These years are a time of
being and becoming,
questioning and discovering,
doubting and believing,
maturing and being immature,
loving and hating (sometimes the same
person at the same time),
being silly and serious,
being both child and adult,
rebelling and conforming,
wanting independence and wanting
the security of authority,
desiring to be grown-up and
feeling guilty for acting childish.
It's a time when people say,
"Grow up and accept responsibility,"
then turn right around and say,
"You can't do that; you're too young."
Sound familiar?
Or confusing?
It is! Sometimes.
But mostly it's great,
just great!

Hear now an indictment: "Our youth now love luxury; they have bad manners and contempt for authority. They show disrespect for their elders and love idle chatter in place of exercise. Children are now tyrants—not servants of their households. They no longer rise when elders enter the room. They disrespect their parents, chatter before company, gobble their food, and tyrannize their teachers." This statement was written by the Greek philosopher Socrates in the fifth century B.C.!

Let's Celebrate School

Reading: "Fall and All"

There is something about fall. Winter still sleeps; the joys of summer are fresh in mind and it's time for hayrides and hot dogs, bands and bleachers, touchdowns and tears, the passing pride of victory, the momentary melancholy of defeat.

Fall—and Halloween, and Thanksgiving, and Christmas . . .

And all.

Each with a special feeling all its own.

Is there another season with as many familiar sounds, sights and smells, activities and challenges, expectations and emotions?

Litany of Celebration

(Each time the leader pauses, instruct the group to respond with the words "We celebrate your love and blessing, O Lord.")

For the fall season and the beginning of school. *(Pause)*

For all our teachers, counselors, and instructors, those we especially love and those who make us study hard. *(Pause)*

For all our friends, old and new. *(Pause)*

For the chance to study and learn. *(Pause)*

For our chief occupation as students. *(Pause)*

For all of the opportunities, challenges, and even the frustrations of student life. *(Pause)*

For every opportunity which helps us grow. *(Pause)*

Lord, this is a time in our lives which is brief, elusive, fleeting. Help us to live it to its fullest, knowing that we shall never pass this way again. Save us from wishing so much for tomorrow that we miss today. Amen.

Reading: "Youth"

Action, activity, vitality, briskness,
liveliness, animation, snap, spirit,
go, energy, vim, vigor, eagerness, and
   enthusiasm
are what young people are made of.
But not always.
Sometimes they are quiet and thoughtful,
alone, dreamy, frustrated, insecure,
disappointed, depressed, down.
People are sometimes
shocked, shook, terrified, mystified,
horrified, frightened, appalled, speechless,
hopeless, or helpless in their presence.
At other times people are
delighted, pleased, encouraged, enchanted,
gratified, surprised, inspired, uplifted.
These years are a time of
being and becoming,
questioning and discovering,
doubting and believing,
maturing and being immature,
loving and hating (sometimes the same
   person at the same time),
being silly and serious,
being both child and adult,
rebelling and conforming,
wanting independence and wanting
the security of authority,
desiring to be grown-up and
feeling guilty for acting childish.
It's a time when people say,
"Grow up and accept responsibility,"
then turn right around and say,
"You can't do that; you're too young."
Sound familiar?
Or confusing?
It is! Sometimes.
But mostly it's great,
just great!

Hear now an indictment: "Our youth now love luxury; they have bad manners and contempt for authority. They show disrespect for their elders and love idle chatter in place of exercise. Children are now tyrants—not servants of their households. They no longer rise when elders enter the room. They disrespect their parents, chatter before company, gobble their food, and tyrannize their teachers." This statement was written by the Greek philosopher Socrates in the fifth century B.C.!

Let's Celebrate School

Reading: "Fall and All"

There is something about fall. Winter still sleeps; the joys of summer are fresh in mind and it's time for hayrides and hot dogs, bands and bleachers, touchdowns and tears, the passing pride of victory, the momentary melancholy of defeat.

Fall—and Halloween, and Thanksgiving, and Christmas . . .

And all.

Each with a special feeling all its own.

Is there another season with as many familiar sounds, sights and smells, activities and challenges, expectations and emotions?

Litany of Celebration

(Each time the leader pauses, instruct the group to respond with the words "We celebrate your love and blessing, O Lord.")

For the fall season and the beginning of school. *(Pause)*

For all our teachers, counselors, and instructors, those we especially love and those who make us study hard. *(Pause)*

For all our friends, old and new. *(Pause)*

For the chance to study and learn. *(Pause)*

For our chief occupation as students. *(Pause)*

For all of the opportunities, challenges, and even the frustrations of student life. *(Pause)*

For every opportunity which helps us grow. *(Pause)*

Lord, this is a time in our lives which is brief, elusive, fleeting. Help us to live it to its fullest, knowing that we shall never pass this way again. Save us from wishing so much for tomorrow that we miss today. Amen.

Reading: "Youth"

Action, activity, vitality, briskness,
liveliness, animation, snap, spirit,
go, energy, vim, vigor, eagerness, and
    enthusiasm
are what young people are made of.
But not always.
Sometimes they are quiet and thoughtful,
alone, dreamy, frustrated, insecure,
disappointed, depressed, down.
People are sometimes
shocked, shook, terrified, mystified,
horrified, frightened, appalled, speechless,
hopeless, or helpless in their presence.
At other times people are
delighted, pleased, encouraged, enchanted,
gratified, surprised, inspired, uplifted.
These years are a time of
being and becoming,
questioning and discovering,
doubting and believing,
maturing and being immature,
loving and hating (sometimes the same
    person at the same time),
being silly and serious,
being both child and adult,
rebelling and conforming,
wanting independence and wanting
the security of authority,
desiring to be grown-up and
feeling guilty for acting childish.
It's a time when people say,
"Grow up and accept responsibility,"
then turn right around and say,
"You can't do that; you're too young."
Sound familiar?
Or confusing?
It is! Sometimes.
But mostly it's great,
just great!

Hear now an indictment: "Our youth now love luxury; they have bad manners and contempt for authority. They show disrespect for their elders and love idle chatter in place of exercise. Children are now tyrants—not servants of their households. They no longer rise when elders enter the room. They disrespect their parents, chatter before company, gobble their food, and tyrannize their teachers." This statement was written by the Greek philosopher Socrates in the fifth century B.C.!

Let's Celebrate School

Reading: "Fall and All"

There is something about fall. Winter still sleeps; the joys of summer are fresh in mind and it's time for hayrides and hot dogs, bands and bleachers, touchdowns and tears, the passing pride of victory, the momentary melancholy of defeat.

Fall—and Halloween, and Thanksgiving, and Christmas . . .

And all.

Each with a special feeling all its own.

Is there another season with as many familiar sounds, sights and smells, activities and challenges, expectations and emotions?

Litany of Celebration

(Each time the leader pauses, instruct the group to respond with the words "We celebrate your love and blessing, O Lord.")

For the fall season and the beginning of school. *(Pause)*

For all our teachers, counselors, and instructors, those we especially love and those who make us study hard. *(Pause)*

For all our friends, old and new. *(Pause)*

For the chance to study and learn. *(Pause)*

For our chief occupation as students. *(Pause)*

For all of the opportunities, challenges, and even the frustrations of student life. *(Pause)*

For every opportunity which helps us grow. *(Pause)*

Lord, this is a time in our lives which is brief, elusive, fleeting. Help us to live it to its fullest, knowing that we shall never pass this way again. Save us from wishing so much for tomorrow that we miss today. Amen.

Reading: "Youth"

Action, activity, vitality, briskness,
liveliness, animation, snap, spirit,
go, energy, vim, vigor, eagerness, and
    enthusiasm
are what young people are made of.
But not always.
Sometimes they are quiet and thoughtful,
alone, dreamy, frustrated, insecure,
disappointed, depressed, down.
People are sometimes
shocked, shook, terrified, mystified,
horrified, frightened, appalled, speechless,
hopeless, or helpless in their presence.
At other times people are
delighted, pleased, encouraged, enchanted,
gratified, surprised, inspired, uplifted.
These years are a time of
being and becoming,
questioning and discovering,
doubting and believing,
maturing and being immature,
loving and hating (sometimes the same
    person at the same time),
being silly and serious,
being both child and adult,
rebelling and conforming,
wanting independence and wanting
the security of authority,
desiring to be grown-up and
feeling guilty for acting childish.
It's a time when people say,
"Grow up and accept responsibility,"
then turn right around and say,
"You can't do that; you're too young."
Sound familiar?
Or confusing?
It is! Sometimes.
But mostly it's great,
just great!

Hear now an indictment: "Our youth now love luxury; they have bad manners and contempt for authority. They show disrespect for their elders and love idle chatter in place of exercise. Children are now tyrants—not servants of their households. They no longer rise when elders enter the room. They disrespect their parents, chatter before company, gobble their food, and tyrannize their teachers." This statement was written by the Greek philosopher Socrates in the fifth century B.C.!

Celebrating Life

A Celebration for a General Occasion or Service Project

The material in this chapter may inspire your group to undertake a special service project. It covers several phases of life and concludes with a stirring poem about the elderly. You may decide to visit a geriatric center, nursing home, or county home. Most of these places have a rather full schedule of religious services sponsored by various faiths and church groups. Try something different. Put on your own live entertainment for the elderly. Individuals in your group probably have talent you never knew they had! Include such things as baton twirling, interpretive dance, group singing, solos, comedy routines, sing-alongs, and anything that would entertain. You will brighten the day for these elderly people because some of them receive few visitors and have little contact with the outside world. Contact the director or social services person in a nursing home near you and set up a date when your group can visit. It will be an experience you'll not forget, and you will be doing an act of Christian service. The project will be enlightening to every member of your group.

Before you go to the nursing home, have your group participate in this worship service. It will help you understand not only the elderly but also life itself, regardless of age.

Use this service for any other occasion. It need not be tied in with a service project.

Preparation

This experience is a celebration of all of life. It concentrates on the youth years, adult life, and later life. Worship is a celebration. To emphasize this, some groups have gone so far as to serve refreshments and have party favors to make the experience more like celebrations to which we are accustomed. A worship center idea might be to have a table in the center of a circle of chairs. On the table could be a cake with streamers. Those having special parts in the service can speak from wherever they happen to be seated within the group.

The Experience

Song: Use a fun song or camp song familiar to your group, such as "Viva la Company," "Father Abraham," a song with motions, or a "round." The use of such a song should give the group a sense of relaxation, fun, and joy to begin the worship celebration.

Opening Thought: We are here today to celebrate life and to give thanks to God, the author and giver of all life.

Hymn: Use a favorite, familiar hymn. An unusual but timely suggestion is "Joy to the World," even though it isn't Christmas!

Scripture: Ecclesiastes 9; 12:1-5, 14.

Reading: "Youth Years" (Or use the reading entitled "Youth" from the chapter "Let's Celebrate School") Supplement A.

Reading: "Adult Years" (Supplement A).

Reading: "Crabby Old Woman" (Supplement A).

Closing Moments: Have your group form a fellowship circle and say a favorite benediction together.

Celebrating Life

Reading: "Youth Years"

We didn't become who we are as young people overnight. Our personalities, emotions, feelings, beliefs, mannerisms, likes, and dislikes took years to develop. So did our fears, frustrations, apprehensions, and antagonisms. We were born mere babes. We lived and were loved, learned to crawl, said our first word, and managed messily to feed ourselves. Do you have a baby picture of *you?* Does it bring you embarrassment each time you see it or when Mom affectionately shows it to someone?

Remember an early Christmas? *(Pause)*

Remember your first day at school? *(Pause)*

Did you cry? *(Pause)*

Remember your childhood toys—trucks, tops, dolls, or stuffed animals? *(Pause)*

Remember your first day at junior high or high school? *(Pause)*

Were you afraid? *(Pause)*

Remember the first fellow or girl you had a crush on? *(Pause)*

Your first date? *(Pause)*

A kiss? *(Pause)*

What stands out in your mind and your feelings as the happiest time of your young years? *(Pause)*

How do you feel about the sad times? *(Pause)*

But you were not alone. You were surrounded by people who influenced you: parents, brothers and sisters, friends, teachers. They all made their mark in molding you into who you are and who you will become. You are a different you now. Yet you are still the same you you were at birth, changed by experiences, learnings, and growth. And you will be the same you as you grow older, yet changed by time and the unknown events, persons, feelings, adventures, and experiences which are ahead.

We celebrate who we are and who we will become. We praise God, giver of all life, who will guide our growth if we give him the chance.

Reading: "Adult Years"

Have you ever wondered who people really are? Parents, teachers, merchants, preachers? There is no mystery. They once sat where we sit. They were babes, too, and learned to walk. They had their first day at school (and probably cried), their first crush, their first kiss. They, too, had their time of not knowing what to do with their lives. They had to find out, sometimes painfully, who they were and where they were heading.

For them, life was both kind and cruel, up and down, rewarding and frustrating. They are who they were as children and as teenagers. Yet they are different, mellowed and molded by life and the passing of time.

Think for a moment about the adult you admire most. *(Pause)*

Think how that adult may have spent his or her young years. *(Pause)*

Think about him or her as a teenager. What was he or she like? *(Pause)*

Now let us thank God for that adult's life and how he or she inspires us.

We celebrate life and give thanks to God, the giver of all life.

Reading

This poem was found among the possessions of an elderly lady who died in a geriatric hospital.

"Crabby Old Woman"

What do you see, nurses, what do you see?
What are you thinking when you look at me?
A crabby old woman, not very wise,
Uncertain of habit, with faraway eyes,
Who dribbles her food and makes no reply
When you say in a loud voice, "I do wish you'd try."
Who seems not to notice the things that you do
And forever is losing a stocking or shoe.
Who, resisting or not, lets you do as you will
With bathing and feeding, the long day to fill.
Is that what you're thinking; is that what you see?
Then open your eyes; you're not looking at me.
I'll tell you who I am as I sit here so still,
As I move at your bidding, as I eat at your will.
I'm a small child of ten with father and mother,
Brothers and sisters who love one another.

A young girl at sixteen with wings on her
feet,
Dreaming that soon now a lover she'll meet.
A bride soon at twenty; my heart gives a
leap,
Remembering the vows that I promised to
keep.
At twenty-five, now I have young of my own
Who need me to build a secure, happy
home.
A woman of thirty, my young now grow
fast,
Bound to each other with ties that should
last.
At forty, my young now will soon be gone,
But my man stays beside me to see I don't
mourn.
At fifty, once more babes play round my
knee,
Again we know children, my loved one and
me.
Dark days are upon me; my husband is
dead.
I look to the future; I shudder in dread.
For my young are all busy rearing young of
their own,

And I think of the years and the love that
I've known.
I'm an old woman now, and nature seems
cruel.
'Tis her jest to make old age look like a fool.
The body it crumbles; grace and vigor
depart.
Now it seems like a stone where I once had a
heart.
But inside this old carcass a young girl still
dwells,
And now and again my battered heart
swells.
I remember the joys; I remember the pain,
And I'm loving and living life over again.
I think of the years, all too few—gone so
fast—
And accept the stark fact that nothing can
last.
So open your eyes, nurses, open and see
Not a crabby old woman; look closer—see
me.

We celebrate life, and thank God who has
created us. O Lord, help me to be the best me I
can be—the "me" in me I like the best. Amen.

Celebrating Life

Reading: "Youth Years"

We didn't become who we are as young people overnight. Our personalities, emotions, feelings, beliefs, mannerisms, likes, and dislikes took years to develop. So did our fears, frustrations, apprehensions, and antagonisms. We were born mere babes. We lived and were loved, learned to crawl, said our first word, and managed messily to feed ourselves. Do you have a baby picture of *you?* Does it bring you embarrassment each time you see it or when Mom affectionately shows it to someone?

Remember an early Christmas? *(Pause)*

Remember your first day at school? *(Pause)*

Did you cry? *(Pause)*

Remember your childhood toys—trucks, tops, dolls, or stuffed animals? *(Pause)*

Remember your first day at junior high or high school? *(Pause)*

Were you afraid? *(Pause)*

Remember the first fellow or girl you had a crush on? *(Pause)*

Your first date? *(Pause)*

A kiss? *(Pause)*

What stands out in your mind and your feelings as the happiest time of your young years? *(Pause)*

How do you feel about the sad times? *(Pause)*

But you were not alone. You were surrounded by people who influenced you: parents, brothers and sisters, friends, teachers. They all made their mark in molding you into who you are and who you will become. You are a different you now. Yet you are still the same you you were at birth, changed by experiences, learnings, and growth. And you will be the same you as you grow older, yet changed by time and the unknown events, persons, feelings, adventures, and experiences which are ahead.

We celebrate who we are and who we will become. We praise God, giver of all life, who will guide our growth if we give him the chance.

Reading: "Adult Years"

Have you ever wondered who people really are? Parents, teachers, merchants, preachers? There is no mystery. They once sat where we sit. They were babes, too, and learned to walk. They had their first day at school (and probably cried), their first crush, their first kiss. They, too, had their time of not knowing what to do with their lives. They had to find out, sometimes painfully, who they were and where they were heading.

For them, life was both kind and cruel, up and down, rewarding and frustrating. They are who they were as children and as teenagers. Yet they are different, mellowed and molded by life and the passing of time.

Think for a moment about the adult you admire most. *(Pause)*

Think how that adult may have spent his or her young years. *(Pause)*

Think about him or her as a teenager. What was he or she like? *(Pause)*

Now let us thank God for that adult's life and how he or she inspires us.

We celebrate life and give thanks to God, the giver of all life.

Reading

This poem was found among the possessions of an elderly lady who died in a geriatric hospital.

"Crabby Old Woman"

What do you see, nurses, what do you see?
What are you thinking when you look at me?
A crabby old woman, not very wise,
Uncertain of habit, with faraway eyes,
Who dribbles her food and makes no reply
When you say in a loud voice, "I do wish you'd try."
Who seems not to notice the things that you do
And forever is losing a stocking or shoe.
Who, resisting or not, lets you do as you will
With bathing and feeding, the long day to fill.
Is that what you're thinking; is that what you see?
Then open your eyes; you're not looking at me.
I'll tell you who I am as I sit here so still,
As I move at your bidding, as I eat at your will.
I'm a small child of ten with father and mother,
Brothers and sisters who love one another.

A young girl at sixteen with wings on her
feet,
Dreaming that soon now a lover she'll meet.
A bride soon at twenty; my heart gives a
leap,
Remembering the vows that I promised to
keep.
At twenty-five, now I have young of my own
Who need me to build a secure, happy
home.
A woman of thirty, my young now grow
fast,
Bound to each other with ties that should
last.
At forty, my young now will soon be gone,
But my man stays beside me to see I don't
mourn.
At fifty, once more babes play round my
knee,
Again we know children, my loved one and
me.
Dark days are upon me; my husband is
dead.
I look to the future; I shudder in dread.
For my young are all busy rearing young of
their own,

And I think of the years and the love that
I've known.
I'm an old woman now, and nature seems
cruel.
'Tis her jest to make old age look like a fool.
The body it crumbles; grace and vigor
depart.
Now it seems like a stone where I once had a
heart.
But inside this old carcass a young girl still
dwells,
And now and again my battered heart
swells.
I remember the joys; I remember the pain,
And I'm loving and living life over again.
I think of the years, all too few—gone so
fast—
And accept the stark fact that nothing can
last.
So open your eyes, nurses, open and see
Not a crabby old woman; look closer—see
me.

We celebrate life, and thank God who has
created us. O Lord, help me to be the best me I
can be—the "me" in me I like the best. Amen.

Celebrating Life

Reading: "Youth Years"

We didn't become who we are as young people overnight. Our personalities, emotions, feelings, beliefs, mannerisms, likes, and dislikes took years to develop. So did our fears, frustrations, apprehensions, and antagonisms. We were born mere babes. We lived and were loved, learned to crawl, said our first word, and managed messily to feed ourselves. Do you have a baby picture of *you?* Does it bring you embarrassment each time you see it or when Mom affectionately shows it to someone?

Remember an early Christmas? *(Pause)*

Remember your first day at school? *(Pause)*

Did you cry? *(Pause)*

Remember your childhood toys—trucks, tops, dolls, or stuffed animals? *(Pause)*

Remember your first day at junior high or high school? *(Pause)*

Were you afraid? *(Pause)*

Remember the first fellow or girl you had a crush on? *(Pause)*

Your first date? *(Pause)*

A kiss? *(Pause)*

What stands out in your mind and your feelings as the happiest time of your young years? *(Pause)*

How do you feel about the sad times? *(Pause)*

But you were not alone. You were surrounded by people who influenced you: parents, brothers and sisters, friends, teachers. They all made their mark in molding you into who you are and who you will become. You are a different you now. Yet you are still the same you you were at birth, changed by experiences, learnings, and growth. And you will be the same you as you grow older, yet changed by time and the unknown events, persons, feelings, adventures, and experiences which are ahead.

We celebrate who we are and who we will become. We praise God, giver of all life, who will guide our growth if we give him the chance.

Reading: "Adult Years"

Have you ever wondered who people really are? Parents, teachers, merchants, preachers? There is no mystery. They once sat where we sit. They were babes, too, and learned to walk. They had their first day at school (and probably cried), their first crush, their first kiss. They, too, had their time of not knowing what to do with their lives. They had to find out, sometimes painfully, who they were and where they were heading.

For them, life was both kind and cruel, up and down, rewarding and frustrating. They are who they were as children and as teenagers. Yet they are different, mellowed and molded by life and the passing of time.

Think for a moment about the adult you admire most. *(Pause)*

Think how that adult may have spent his or her young years. *(Pause)*

Think about him or her as a teenager. What was he or she like? *(Pause)*

Now let us thank God for that adult's life and how he or she inspires us.

We celebrate life and give thanks to God, the giver of all life.

Reading

This poem was found among the possessions of an elderly lady who died in a geriatric hospital.

"Crabby Old Woman"

What do you see, nurses, what do you see?
What are you thinking when you look at me?
A crabby old woman, not very wise,
Uncertain of habit, with faraway eyes,
Who dribbles her food and makes no reply
When you say in a loud voice, "I do wish you'd try."
Who seems not to notice the things that you do
And forever is losing a stocking or shoe.
Who, resisting or not, lets you do as you will
With bathing and feeding, the long day to fill.
Is that what you're thinking; is that what you see?
Then open your eyes; you're not looking at me.
I'll tell you who I am as I sit here so still,
As I move at your bidding, as I eat at your will.
I'm a small child of ten with father and mother,
Brothers and sisters who love one another.

A young girl at sixteen with wings on her feet,
Dreaming that soon now a lover she'll meet.
A bride soon at twenty; my heart gives a leap,
Remembering the vows that I promised to keep.
At twenty-five, now I have young of my own
Who need me to build a secure, happy home.
A woman of thirty, my young now grow fast,
Bound to each other with ties that should last.
At forty, my young now will soon be gone,
But my man stays beside me to see I don't mourn.
At fifty, once more babes play round my knee,
Again we know children, my loved one and me.
Dark days are upon me; my husband is dead.
I look to the future; I shudder in dread.
For my young are all busy rearing young of their own,
And I think of the years and the love that I've known.
I'm an old woman now, and nature seems cruel.
'Tis her jest to make old age look like a fool.
The body it crumbles; grace and vigor depart.
Now it seems like a stone where I once had a heart.
But inside this old carcass a young girl still dwells,
And now and again my battered heart swells.
I remember the joys; I remember the pain,
And I'm loving and living life over again.
I think of the years, all too few—gone so fast—
And accept the stark fact that nothing can last.
So open your eyes, nurses, open and see
Not a crabby old woman; look closer—see me.

We celebrate life, and thank God who has created us. O Lord, help me to be the best me I can be—the "me" in me I like the best. Amen.

Celebrating Life

Reading: "Youth Years"

We didn't become who we are as young people overnight. Our personalities, emotions, feelings, beliefs, mannerisms, likes, and dislikes took years to develop. So did our fears, frustrations, apprehensions, and antagonisms. We were born mere babes. We lived and were loved, learned to crawl, said our first word, and managed messily to feed ourselves. Do you have a baby picture of *you?* Does it bring you embarrassment each time you see it or when Mom affectionately shows it to someone?

Remember an early Christmas? *(Pause)*

Remember your first day at school? *(Pause)*

Did you cry? *(Pause)*

Remember your childhood toys—trucks, tops, dolls, or stuffed animals? *(Pause)*

Remember your first day at junior high or high school? *(Pause)*

Were you afraid? *(Pause)*

Remember the first fellow or girl you had a crush on? *(Pause)*

Your first date? *(Pause)*

A kiss? *(Pause)*

What stands out in your mind and your feelings as the happiest time of your young years? *(Pause)*

How do you feel about the sad times? *(Pause)*

But you were not alone. You were surrounded by people who influenced you: parents, brothers and sisters, friends, teachers. They all made their mark in molding you into who you are and who you will become. You are a different you now. Yet you are still the same you you were at birth, changed by experiences, learnings, and growth. And you will be the same you as you grow older, yet changed by time and the unknown events, persons, feelings, adventures, and experiences which are ahead.

We celebrate who we are and who we will become. We praise God, giver of all life, who will guide our growth if we give him the chance.

Reading: "Adult Years"

Have you ever wondered who people really are? Parents, teachers, merchants, preachers? There is no mystery. They once sat where we sit. They were babes, too, and learned to walk. They had their first day at school (and probably cried), their first crush, their first kiss. They, too, had their time of not knowing what to do with their lives. They had to find out, sometimes painfully, who they were and where they were heading.

For them, life was both kind and cruel, up and down, rewarding and frustrating. They are who they were as children and as teenagers. Yet they are different, mellowed and molded by life and the passing of time.

Think for a moment about the adult you admire most. *(Pause)*

Think how that adult may have spent his or her young years. *(Pause)*

Think about him or her as a teenager. What was he or she like? *(Pause)*

Now let us thank God for that adult's life and how he or she inspires us.

We celebrate life and give thanks to God, the giver of all life.

Reading

This poem was found among the possessions of an elderly lady who died in a geriatric hospital.

"Crabby Old Woman"

What do you see, nurses, what do you see?
What are you thinking when you look at
    me?
A crabby old woman, not very wise,
Uncertain of habit, with faraway eyes,
Who dribbles her food and makes no reply
When you say in a loud voice, "I do wish
    you'd try."
Who seems not to notice the things that you
    do
And forever is losing a stocking or shoe.
Who, resisting or not, lets you do as you will
With bathing and feeding, the long day to
    fill.
Is that what you're thinking; is that what
    you see?
Then open your eyes; you're not looking at
    me.
I'll tell you who I am as I sit here so still,
As I move at your bidding, as I eat at your
    will.
I'm a small child of ten with father and
    mother,
Brothers and sisters who love one another.

A young girl at sixteen with wings on her feet,
Dreaming that soon now a lover she'll meet.
A bride soon at twenty; my heart gives a leap,
Remembering the vows that I promised to keep.
At twenty-five, now I have young of my own
Who need me to build a secure, happy home.
A woman of thirty, my young now grow fast,
Bound to each other with ties that should last.
At forty, my young now will soon be gone,
But my man stays beside me to see I don't mourn.
At fifty, once more babes play round my knee,
Again we know children, my loved one and me.
Dark days are upon me; my husband is dead.
I look to the future; I shudder in dread.
For my young are all busy rearing young of their own,
And I think of the years and the love that I've known.
I'm an old woman now, and nature seems cruel.
'Tis her jest to make old age look like a fool.
The body it crumbles; grace and vigor depart.
Now it seems like a stone where I once had a heart.
But inside this old carcass a young girl still dwells,
And now and again my battered heart swells.
I remember the joys; I remember the pain,
And I'm loving and living life over again.
I think of the years, all too few—gone so fast—
And accept the stark fact that nothing can last.
So open your eyes, nurses, open and see
Not a crabby old woman; look closer—see me.

We celebrate life, and thank God who has created us. O Lord, help me to be the best me I can be—the "me" in me I like the best. Amen.

Rights Are Right

A Celebration with a Brotherhood Theme

The material in this chapter centers on the rights of human beings throughout the world. For many people at home and abroad, these rights have not become realities. We pray that humankind will dedicate itself to achieving equality for all. With God's help, it can be a reality.

A major part of this devotional experience will be contemplating the meaning of the Universal Declaration of Human Rights as set forth by the United Nations General Assembly. This declaration is one of the most powerful and stirring documents ever conceived by humans.

Preparation

Consider inviting young people from another religious, racial, or ethnic group to participate in this service. You might even consider making this an occasion to enjoy food, fellowship, and entertainment together. There may be a group in your locality which could demonstrate ethnic customs through song, dance, art, or music. Invite members of the visiting group to share in the reading of the Universal Declaration of Human Rights. Note how the declaration parallels the Bill of Rights of the United States.

You might want to have someone summarize the following comments as an introduction. One of the first things the United Nations did when it was formed was to draw up what history will record as one of the greatest human documents ever written. Since its writing in 1948, the world has changed. New nations have been born; new powers have emerged; new alliances have been made. Not included in the Universal Declaration of Human Rights are such concepts as equality for women, the rights of the handicapped, and additional human rights (though sex discrimination is mentioned).

This document, like our Bill of Rights, is an ideal, a goal, a model. We have not fully achieved these goals; indeed, we are far from them, but we work toward them in the strength which God gives us.

Because the Declaration is long, have at least two or more different people share in its reading. Divide it as you see fit. You may decide to use only selected portions. Be sure those who read it have gone over it in advance, thus eliminating embarrassing pauses and mistakes. Above all, remember the theme of this Declaration: dignity and reverence for human life.

The Experience

Opening Thought: We have come here on this occasion to celebrate our God-given rights and dignity as members of the human race. We pray that even in our day, these rights may become realities for all of us.

Hymn: "Once to Every Man and Nation."

Scripture: Proverbs 29:2-14.

The Universal Declaration of Human Rights: Supplement A.

Ending Prayer: God of people and of nations, help us to help make human rights real and workable for the people we know and for the millions we do not know. Amen.

Rights Are Right

The Universal Declaration of Human Rights:

Article 1. All human beings are born free and equal in dignity and rights. They are endowed with reason and conscience and should act towards one another in a spirit of brotherhood.

Article 2. Everyone is entitled to all the rights and freedoms set forth in this Declaration, without distinction of any kind, such as race, colour, sex, language, religion, political or other opinion, national or social origin, property, birth or other status.

Furthermore, no distinction shall be made on the basis of the political, jurisdictional or international status of the country or territory to which a person belongs, whether it be independent, trust, non-self-governing or under any other limitation of sovereignty.

Article 3. Everyone has the right to life, liberty and security of person.

Article 4. No one shall be held in slavery or servitude; slavery and the slave trade shall be prohibited in all their forms.

Article 5. No one shall be subjected to torture or cruel, inhuman or degrading treatment or punishment.

Article 6. Everyone has the right to recognition everywhere as a person before the law.

Article 7. All are equal before the law and are entitled without any discrimination to equal protection of the law. All are entitled to equal protection against any discrimination in violation of this Declaration and against any incitement to such discrimination.

Article 8. Everyone has the right to an effective remedy by the competent national tribunals for acts violating the fundamental rights granted him by the constitution or by law.

Article 9. No one shall be subject to arbitrary arrest, detention or exile.

Article 10. Everyone is entitled in full equality to a fair and public hearing by an independent and impartial tribunal, in the determination of his rights and obligations and of any criminal charges against him.

Article 11. (1) Everyone charged with a penal offense has the right to be presumed innocent until proved guilty according to law in a public trial at which he has had all the guarantees necessary for his defense.

(2) No one shall be held guilty of any penal offence on account of any act or omission which did not constitute a penal offence, under national or international law, at the time when it was committed. Nor shall a heavier penalty be imposed than the one that was applicable at the time the penal offence was committed.

Article 12. No one shall be subjected to arbitrary interference with his privacy, family, home or correspondence, nor to attacks upon his honour and reputation. Everyone has the right to the protection of the law against such interference or attacks.

Article 13. (1) Everyone has the right to freedom of movement and residence within the borders of each state.

(2) Everyone has the right to leave any country, including his own, and to return to his country.

Article 14. (1) Everyone has the right to seek and to enjoy in other countries asylum from persecution.

(2) This right may not be invoked in the case of prosecutions genuinely arising from non-political crimes or from acts contrary to the purposes and principles of the United Nations.

Article 15. (1) Everyone has the right to a nationality.

(2) No one shall be arbitrarily deprived of his nationality nor denied the right to change his nationality.

Article 16. (1) Men and women of full age, without any limitation due to race, nationality or religion, have the right to marry and to found a family. They are entitled to equal rights as to marriage, during marriage and its dissolution.

(2) Marriage shall be entered into only with the free and full consent of the intending spouses.

(3) The family is the natural and fundamental group unit of society and is entitled to protection by society and the State.

Article 17. (1) Everyone has the right to own property alone as well as in association with others.

(2) No one shall be arbitrarily deprived of his property.

Article 18. Everyone has the right to freedom of thought, conscience and religion; this right includes freedom to change his religion or belief, and freedom, either alone or in community with

others and in public or private, to manifest his religion or belief in teaching, practice, worship and observance.

Article 19. Everyone has the right to freedom of opinion and expression; this right includes freedom to hold opinions without interference and to seek, receive and impart information and ideas through any media and regardless of frontiers.

Article 20. (1) Everyone has the right to freedom of peaceful assembly and association.

(2) No one may be compelled to belong to an association.

Article 21. (1) Everyone has the right to take part in the government of his country, directly or through freely chosen representatives.

(2) Everyone has the right of equal access to public service in his country.

(3) The will of the people shall be the basis of the authority of government; this will shall be expressed in periodic and genuine elections which shall be by universal and equal suffrage and shall be held by secret vote or by equivalent free voting procedures.

Article 22. Everyone, as a member of society, has the right to social security and is entitled to realization, through national effort and international co-operation and in accordance with the organization and resources of each State, of the economic, social and cultural rights indispensable for his dignity and the free development of his personality.

Article 23. (1) Everyone has the right to work, to free choice of employment, to just and favorable conditions of work and to protection against unemployment.

(2) Everyone, without any discrimination, has the right to equal pay for equal work.

(3) Everyone who works has the right to just and favourable remuneration ensuring for himself and his family an existence worthy of human dignity, and supplemented, if necessary, by other means of social protection.

(4) Everyone has the right to form and to join trade unions for the protection of his interests.

Article 24. Everyone has the right to rest and leisure, including reasonable limitation of working hours and periodic holidays with pay.

Article 25. (1) Everyone has the right to a standard of living adequate for the health and well-being of himself and of his family, including food, clothing, housing and medical care and necessary social services, and the right to security

in the event of unemployment, sickness, disability, widowhood, old age or other lack of livelihood in circumstances beyond his control.

(2) Motherhood and childhood are entitled to special care and assistance. All children, whether born in or out of wedlock, shall enjoy the same social protection.

Article 26. (1) Everyone has the right to education. Education shall be free, at least in the elementary and fundamental stages. Elementary education shall be compulsory. Technical and professional education shall be made generally available and higher education shall be equally accessible to all on the basis of merit.

(2) Education shall be directed to the full development of the human personality and to the strengthening of respect for human rights and fundamental freedoms. It shall promote understanding, tolerance and friendship among all nations, racial or religious groups, and shall further the activities of the United Nations for the maintenance of peace.

(3) Parents have a prior right to choose the kind of education that shall be given to their children.

Article 27. (1) Everyone has the right freely to participate in the cultural life of the community, to enjoy the arts and to share in scientific advancement and its benefits.

(2) Everyone has the right to the protection of the moral and material interests resulting from any scientific, literary or artistic production of which he is author.

Article 28. Everyone is entitled to a social and international order in which the rights and freedoms set forth in this Declaration can be fully realized.

Article 29. (1) Everyone has duties to the community in which alone the free and full development of his personality is possible.

(2) In the exercise of his rights and freedoms, everyone shall be subject only to such limitations as are determined by law solely for the purpose of securing due recognition and respect for the rights and freedoms of others and of meeting the just requirements of morality, public order and the general welfare in a democratic society.

(3) These rights and freedoms may in no case be exercised contrary to the purposes and principles of the United Nations.

Article 30. Nothing in this Declaration may be interpreted as implying for any State, group or person any right to engage in any activity or to perform any act aimed at the destruction of any of the rights and freedoms set forth herein.

Rights Are Right

The Universal Declaration of Human Rights:

Article 1. All human beings are born free and equal in dignity and rights. They are endowed with reason and conscience and should act towards one another in a spirit of brotherhood.

Article 2. Everyone is entitled to all the rights and freedoms set forth in this Declaration, without distinction of any kind, such as race, colour, sex, language, religion, political or other opinion, national or social origin, property, birth or other status.

Furthermore, no distinction shall be made on the basis of the political, jurisdictional or international status of the country or territory to which a person belongs, whether it be independent, trust, non-self-governing or under any other limitation of sovereignty.

Article 3. Everyone has the right to life, liberty and security of person.

Article 4. No one shall be held in slavery or servitude; slavery and the slave trade shall be prohibited in all their forms.

Article 5. No one shall be subjected to torture or cruel, inhuman or degrading treatment or punishment.

Article 6. Everyone has the right to recognition everywhere as a person before the law.

Article 7. All are equal before the law and are entitled without any discrimination to equal protection of the law. All are entitled to equal protection against any discrimination in violation of this Declaration and against any incitement to such discrimination.

Article 8. Everyone has the right to an effective remedy by the competent national tribunals for acts violating the fundamental rights granted him by the constitution or by law.

Article 9. No one shall be subject to arbitrary arrest, detention or exile.

Article 10. Everyone is entitled in full equality to a fair and public hearing by an independent and impartial tribunal, in the determination of his rights and obligations and of any criminal charges against him.

Article 11. (1) Everyone charged with a penal offense has the right to be presumed innocent until proved guilty according to law in a public trial at which he has had all the guarantees necessary for his defense.

(2) No one shall be held guilty of any penal offence on account of any act or omission which did not constitute a penal offence, under national or international law, at the time when it was committed. Nor shall a heavier penalty be imposed than the one that was applicable at the time the penal offence was committed.

Article 12. No one shall be subjected to arbitrary interference with his privacy, family, home or correspondence, nor to attacks upon his honour and reputation. Everyone has the right to the protection of the law against such interference or attacks.

Article 13. (1) Everyone has the right to freedom of movement and residence within the borders of each state.

(2) Everyone has the right to leave any country, including his own, and to return to his country.

Article 14. (1) Everyone has the right to seek and to enjoy in other countries asylum from persecution.

(2) This right may not be invoked in the case of prosecutions genuinely arising from non-political crimes or from acts contrary to the purposes and principles of the United Nations.

Article 15. (1) Everyone has the right to a nationality.

(2) No one shall be arbitrarily deprived of his nationality nor denied the right to change his nationality.

Article 16. (1) Men and women of full age, without any limitation due to race, nationality or religion, have the right to marry and to found a family. They are entitled to equal rights as to marriage, during marriage and its dissolution.

(2) Marriage shall be entered into only with the free and full consent of the intending spouses.

(3) The family is the natural and fundamental group unit of society and is entitled to protection by society and the State.

Article 17. (1) Everyone has the right to own property alone as well as in association with others.

(2) No one shall be arbitrarily deprived of his property.

Article 18. Everyone has the right to freedom of thought, conscience and religion; this right includes freedom to change his religion or belief, and freedom, either alone or in community with

others and in public or private, to manifest his religion or belief in teaching, practice, worship and observance.

Article 19. Everyone has the right to freedom of opinion and expression; this right includes freedom to hold opinions without interference and to seek, receive and impart information and ideas through any media and regardless of frontiers.

Article 20. (1) Everyone has the right to freedom of peaceful assembly and association.

(2) No one may be compelled to belong to an association.

Article 21. (1) Everyone has the right to take part in the government of his country, directly or through freely chosen representatives.

(2) Everyone has the right of equal access to public service in his country.

(3) The will of the people shall be the basis of the authority of government; this will shall be expressed in periodic and genuine elections which shall be by universal and equal suffrage and shall be held by secret vote or by equivalent free voting procedures.

Article 22. Everyone, as a member of society, has the right to social security and is entitled to realization, through national effort and international co-operation and in accordance with the organization and resources of each State, of the economic, social and cultural rights indispensable for his dignity and the free development of his personality.

Article 23. (1) Everyone has the right to work, to free choice of employment, to just and favorable conditions of work and to protection against unemployment.

(2) Everyone, without any discrimination, has the right to equal pay for equal work.

(3) Everyone who works has the right to just and favourable remuneration ensuring for himself and his family an existence worthy of human dignity, and supplemented, if necessary, by other means of social protection.

(4) Everyone has the right to form and to join trade unions for the protection of his interests.

Article 24. Everyone has the right to rest and leisure, including reasonable limitation of working hours and periodic holidays with pay.

Article 25. (1) Everyone has the right to a standard of living adequate for the health and well-being of himself and of his family, including food, clothing, housing and medical care and necessary social services, and the right to security

in the event of unemployment, sickness, disability, widowhood, old age or other lack of livelihood in circumstances beyond his control.

(2) Motherhood and childhood are entitled to special care and assistance. All children, whether born in or out of wedlock, shall enjoy the same social protection.

Article 26. (1) Everyone has the right to education. Education shall be free, at least in the elementary and fundamental stages. Elementary education shall be compulsory. Technical and professional education shall be made generally available and higher education shall be equally accessible to all on the basis of merit.

(2) Education shall be directed to the full development of the human personality and to the strengthening of respect for human rights and fundamental freedoms. It shall promote understanding, tolerance and friendship among all nations, racial or religious groups, and shall further the activities of the United Nations for the maintenance of peace.

(3) Parents have a prior right to choose the kind of education that shall be given to their children.

Article 27. (1) Everyone has the right freely to participate in the cultural life of the community, to enjoy the arts and to share in scientific advancement and its benefits.

(2) Everyone has the right to the protection of the moral and material interests resulting from any scientific, literary or artistic production of which he is author.

Article 28. Everyone is entitled to a social and international order in which the rights and freedoms set forth in this Declaration can be fully realized.

Article 29. (1) Everyone has duties to the community in which alone the free and full development of his personality is possible.

(2) In the exercise of his rights and freedoms, everyone shall be subject only to such limitations as are determined by law solely for the purpose of securing due recognition and respect for the rights and freedoms of others and of meeting the just requirements of morality, public order and the general welfare in a democratic society.

(3) These rights and freedoms may in no case be exercised contrary to the purposes and principles of the United Nations.

Article 30. Nothing in this Declaration may be interpreted as implying for any State, group or person any right to engage in any activity or to perform any act aimed at the destruction of any of the rights and freedoms set forth herein.

Rights Are Right

The Universal Declaration of Human Rights:

Article 1. All human beings are born free and equal in dignity and rights. They are endowed with reason and conscience and should act towards one another in a spirit of brotherhood.

Article 2. Everyone is entitled to all the rights and freedoms set forth in this Declaration, without distinction of any kind, such as race, colour, sex, language, religion, political or other opinion, national or social origin, property, birth or other status.

Furthermore, no distinction shall be made on the basis of the political, jurisdictional or international status of the country or territory to which a person belongs, whether it be independent, trust, non-self-governing or under any other limitation of sovereignty.

Article 3. Everyone has the right to life, liberty and security of person.

Article 4. No one shall be held in slavery or servitude; slavery and the slave trade shall be prohibited in all their forms.

Article 5. No one shall be subjected to torture or cruel, inhuman or degrading treatment or punishment.

Article 6. Everyone has the right to recognition everywhere as a person before the law.

Article 7. All are equal before the law and are entitled without any discrimination to equal protection of the law. All are entitled to equal protection against any discrimination in violation of this Declaration and against any incitement to such discrimination.

Article 8. Everyone has the right to an effective remedy by the competent national tribunals for acts violating the fundamental rights granted him by the constitution or by law.

Article 9. No one shall be subject to arbitrary arrest, detention or exile.

Article 10. Everyone is entitled in full equality to a fair and public hearing by an independent and impartial tribunal, in the determination of his rights and obligations and of any criminal charges against him.

Article 11. (1) Everyone charged with a penal offense has the right to be presumed innocent until proved guilty according to law in a public trial at which he has had all the guarantees necessary for his defense.

(2) No one shall be held guilty of any penal offence on account of any act or omission which did not constitute a penal offence, under national or international law, at the time when it was committed. Nor shall a heavier penalty be imposed than the one that was applicable at the time the penal offence was committed.

Article 12. No one shall be subjected to arbitrary interference with his privacy, family, home or correspondence, nor to attacks upon his honour and reputation. Everyone has the right to the protection of the law against such interference or attacks.

Article 13. (1) Everyone has the right to freedom of movement and residence within the borders of each state.

(2) Everyone has the right to leave any country, including his own, and to return to his country.

Article 14. (1) Everyone has the right to seek and to enjoy in other countries asylum from persecution.

(2) This right may not be invoked in the case of prosecutions genuinely arising from non-political crimes or from acts contrary to the purposes and principles of the United Nations.

Article 15. (1) Everyone has the right to a nationality.

(2) No one shall be arbitrarily deprived of his nationality nor denied the right to change his nationality.

Article 16. (1) Men and women of full age, without any limitation due to race, nationality or religion, have the right to marry and to found a family. They are entitled to equal rights as to marriage, during marriage and its dissolution.

(2) Marriage shall be entered into only with the free and full consent of the intending spouses.

(3) The family is the natural and fundamental group unit of society and is entitled to protection by society and the State.

Article 17. (1) Everyone has the right to own property alone as well as in association with others.

(2) No one shall be arbitrarily deprived of his property.

Article 18. Everyone has the right to freedom of thought, conscience and religion; this right includes freedom to change his religion or belief, and freedom, either alone or in community with

others and in public or private, to manifest his religion or belief in teaching, practice, worship and observance.

Article 19. Everyone has the right to freedom of opinion and expression; this right includes freedom to hold opinions without interference and to seek, receive and impart information and ideas through any media and regardless of frontiers.

Article 20. (1) Everyone has the right to freedom of peaceful assembly and association.

(2) No one may be compelled to belong to an association.

Article 21. (1) Everyone has the right to take part in the government of his country, directly or through freely chosen representatives.

(2) Everyone has the right of equal access to public service in his country.

(3) The will of the people shall be the basis of the authority of government; this will shall be expressed in periodic and genuine elections which shall be by universal and equal suffrage and shall be held by secret vote or by equivalent free voting procedures.

Article 22. Everyone, as a member of society, has the right to social security and is entitled to realization, through national effort and international co-operation and in accordance with the organization and resources of each State, of the economic, social and cultural rights indispensable for his dignity and the free development of his personality.

Article 23. (1) Everyone has the right to work, to free choice of employment, to just and favorable conditions of work and to protection against unemployment.

(2) Everyone, without any discrimination, has the right to equal pay for equal work.

(3) Everyone who works has the right to just and favourable remuneration ensuring for himself and his family an existence worthy of human dignity, and supplemented, if necessary, by other means of social protection.

(4) Everyone has the right to form and to join trade unions for the protection of his interests.

Article 24. Everyone has the right to rest and leisure, including reasonable limitation of working hours and periodic holidays with pay.

Article 25. (1) Everyone has the right to a standard of living adequate for the health and well-being of himself and of his family, including food, clothing, housing and medical care and necessary social services, and the right to security

in the event of unemployment, sickness, disability, widowhood, old age or other lack of livelihood in circumstances beyond his control.

(2) Motherhood and childhood are entitled to special care and assistance. All children, whether born in or out of wedlock, shall enjoy the same social protection.

Article 26. (1) Everyone has the right to education. Education shall be free, at least in the elementary and fundamental stages. Elementary education shall be compulsory. Technical and professional education shall be made generally available and higher education shall be equally accessible to all on the basis of merit.

(2) Education shall be directed to the full development of the human personality and to the strengthening of respect for human rights and fundamental freedoms. It shall promote understanding, tolerance and friendship among all nations, racial or religious groups, and shall further the activities of the United Nations for the maintenance of peace.

(3) Parents have a prior right to choose the kind of education that shall be given to their children.

Article 27. (1) Everyone has the right freely to participate in the cultural life of the community, to enjoy the arts and to share in scientific advancement and its benefits.

(2) Everyone has the right to the protection of the moral and material interests resulting from any scientific, literary or artistic production of which he is author.

Article 28. Everyone is entitled to a social and international order in which the rights and freedoms set forth in this Declaration can be fully realized.

Article 29. (1) Everyone has duties to the community in which alone the free and full development of his personality is possible.

(2) In the exercise of his rights and freedoms, everyone shall be subject only to such limitations as are determined by law solely for the purpose of securing due recognition and respect for the rights and freedoms of others and of meeting the just requirements of morality, public order and the general welfare in a democratic society.

(3) These rights and freedoms may in no case be exercised contrary to the purposes and principles of the United Nations.

Article 30. Nothing in this Declaration may be interpreted as implying for any State, group or person any right to engage in any activity or to perform any act aimed at the destruction of any of the rights and freedoms set forth herein.

Thanks a Lot

A Celebration with a Thanksgiving Theme

The concept in this material does not follow the traditional Thanksgiving pattern. Besides expressions of gratitude, devotion, and thanks to God, your group will be doing some thinking about what it means to be good givers. But to be good givers, we also must be good receivers. The receiving side of giving is the aspect we usually overlook or refuse to come to grips with. Your group members will have opportunity during this service to examine their own feelings regarding both giving and receiving and, it is hoped, to come to an understanding of the necessity for them to cultivate an openness to being good receivers. For most people, receiving takes a very special grace.

An actual experience of giving and receiving is provided in this material. It is the ancient custom, or ritual, of foot washing. This ritual has its roots deep in biblical and church custom. If your group decides not to carry out the foot-washing ceremony, use the other parts of this material in a service of thanksgiving. Some groups present a special offering of food, goods, or money for those in need at Thanksgiving. You may consider doing this in place of or in addition to the ceremony.

Preparation

The early church observed the ritual of foot washing. It was in commemoration of the fact that Jesus washed the disciples' feet to show himself to be a servant as well as a king. But Peter felt embarrassed, insecure, or perhaps humble, and he refused at first to allow Jesus to do this act of service and giving for him. Peter refused to be on the receiving end. He was not a good receiver. A few modern-day Christian groups observe the ceremony of foot washing today. And until recently, the custom was viewed with mild humor. But now the observance of foot washing has taken on new significance among some major Christian churches because they see in it the servant role of Christ in vivid ways. There also is another significance to foot washing. We must allow ourselves to be served, ministered to, washed by another person. We must allow someone else to touch us. And for some people this is a difficult, perhaps painful experience. We always have been taught to give—to serve—and in giving there is pride. But we shrink from receiving—from allowing someone else to do something for us.

If your group decides to carry out the foot washing as a part of this worship service, a pitcher, a wash bowl, water, a washcloth, and towel become highly symbolic. These items can be part of a worship center.

Perhaps only one or two people in your group will be doing the foot washing. It would be better to have everyone participate in washing and being washed. Only the members of your group can know if they are willing to participate in this ritual.

The Experience

Hymn: A hymn of thanksgiving.
Scripture: Psalm 65:1, 9-13.
Hymn: "Now Thank We All Our God."
Scripture: Matthew 7:12; Acts 20:35.
Meditation: "The Tin Rule" (Supplement A).
Ritual of Foot Washing: Supplement A.
Closing: Encourage each person in your group to share with each other by shaking hands with every other group member and saying, "Serve, be served, and be thankful."

Thanks a Lot

Meditation: "The Tin Rule"

"Do for others what you want them to do for you. . . ."

This statement of Jesus, as recorded in Matthew 7, is popularly known as the "Golden Rule." Many of us have been taught it or reminded of it since childhood. There is another statement of Jesus, recorded in Acts 20:35, so common in our minds that it may have lost its meaning through familiarity: "It is more blessed to give than to receive" (RSV). Both statements have to do with personal interaction—doing and having done, giving and receiving.

But we always view these classic passages of Scripture from only one perspective—we should do good to others; we should give to those in need.

What of the reverse? What is it like to have good done to us? To receive? This reverse of the Golden Rule and the verse from Acts can be thought of as the "Tin Rule." It is tin because we would rather think about gold. It may be, in fact, painfully hard for us to comprehend, let alone put into practice this "other side of the coin."

There is a joy in giving. Yet the giver sometimes feels pride in giving while the receiver feels humility in receiving. How often have we deprived someone else of the joy of giving because of our own pride—our refusal to admit need or our determination not to take anything from anyone?

Most of us simply are not good receivers. We talk about giving grudgingly. How much more miserly are we when it is our turn to receive?

And why do we always feel the need to repay so that we don't owe?

Let the joy of receiving be ours also. Some things we can never repay. To try to would be an insult to the giver and a robbery of his or her joy in giving. Could we repay mother love? Could we compensate Christ for what he has done for us, except through loyalty and love?

Gladly accept a gift from a child because children are a light which shows us God's kingdom. Their gifts may be homely handcrafted creations or just a hug. Sometimes their gift is simply their desire to be around us. The rule holds regardless of age.

Sometimes there are compliments handed us which we mar through embarrassed reception or even rejection. A compliment is a gift sometimes given with great difficulty. Take it and be glad.

Sometimes we have physical needs—needs so acute that our survival depends on someone else's generosity. Yet people have starved to death rather than ask for help.

There are emotional needs—a burden or problem too great for us to manage alone. Yet we would rather go through life in fear, guilt, or bewilderment rather than ask a trusted friend or counselor to give us his or her time and to listen.

There are people all around us who are looking for the opportunity to do good for us. Let them! Even create the opportunity! Let someone do unto you. Let someone give to you. Give them the joy of giving. We usually get much more than we receive anyway, in one way or another, so enjoy giving and receiving.

In order for us to be good givers, we must also be good receivers. Like good CBers, we must be able to receive as well as transmit.

The Ritual of Foot Washing:

John 13:4-17: So he [Jesus] rose from the table, took off his outer garment, and tied a towel around his waist. Then he poured some water into a washbasin and began to wash the disciples' feet and dry them with the towel around his waist. He came to Simon Peter, who said to him, "Are you going to wash my feet, Lord?"

Jesus answered him, "You do not understand now what I am doing, but you will understand later."

Peter declared, "Never at any time will you wash my feet!"

"If I do not wash your feet," Jesus answered, "you will no longer be my disciple."

Simon Peter answered, "Lord, do not wash only my feet, then! Wash my hands and head, too!"

Jesus said, "Anyone who has taken a bath is completely clean and does not have to wash himself, except for his feet. All of you are clean—all except one." (Jesus already knew who was going to betray him; that is why he said, "All of you, except one, are clean.")

After Jesus had washed their feet, he put his outer garment back on and returned to his place

at the table. "Do you understand what I have just done to you?" he asked. "You call me Teacher and Lord, and it is right that you do so, because that is what I am. I, your Lord and Teacher, have just washed your feet. You, then, should wash one another's feet. I have set an example for you, so that you will do just what I have done for you. I am telling you the truth: no slave is greater than his master, and no messenger is greater than the one who sent him. Now that you know this truth, how happy you will be if you put it into practice!"

VOICE: To show himself both servant and king, Jesus washed the disciples' feet. Peter was not comfortable with this at first but later allowed the Lord to wash him also. The early church observed the ritual of foot washing, and there has been a revival of the custom in modern-day churches. In this act we symbolize our servant role as followers of Christ. But we also illustrate our openness to be good receivers, to allow someone else the opportunity to do something for us. In this act, we both give and receive with thanksgiving. By allowing another person to touch us, we symbolize our willingness to be open to someone else who is reaching out toward us. If we allow touch, which is highly personal, then perhaps we can allow others to be a significant part of our lives. If we can receive the service of another person, then we can better serve.

(Then follows the pouring of water and the ritual of washing, according to how your group has decided to carry this out.)

Thanks a Lot

Meditation: "The Tin Rule"

"Do for others what you want them to do for you. . . ."

This statement of Jesus, as recorded in Matthew 7, is popularly known as the "Golden Rule." Many of us have been taught it or reminded of it since childhood. There is another statement of Jesus, recorded in Acts 20:35, so common in our minds that it may have lost its meaning through familiarity: "It is more blessed to give than to receive" (RSV). Both statements have to do with personal interaction—doing and having done, giving and receiving.

But we always view these classic passages of Scripture from only one perspective—we should do good to others; we should give to those in need.

What of the reverse? What is it like to have good done to us? To receive? This reverse of the Golden Rule and the verse from Acts can be thought of as the "Tin Rule." It is tin because we would rather think about gold. It may be, in fact, painfully hard for us to comprehend, let alone put into practice this "other side of the coin."

There is a joy in giving. Yet the giver sometimes feels pride in giving while the receiver feels humility in receiving. How often have we deprived someone else of the joy of giving because of our own pride—our refusal to admit need or our determination not to take anything from anyone?

Most of us simply are not good receivers. We talk about giving grudgingly. How much more miserly are we when it is our turn to receive?

And why do we always feel the need to repay so that we don't owe?

Let the joy of receiving be ours also. Some things we can never repay. To try to would be an insult to the giver and a robbery of his or her joy in giving. Could we repay mother love? Could we compensate Christ for what he has done for us, except through loyalty and love?

Gladly accept a gift from a child because children are a light which shows us God's kingdom. Their gifts may be homely handcrafted creations or just a hug. Sometimes their gift is simply their desire to be around us. The rule holds regardless of age.

Sometimes there are compliments handed us which we mar through embarrassed reception or even rejection. A compliment is a gift sometimes given with great difficulty. Take it and be glad.

Sometimes we have physical needs—needs so acute that our survival depends on someone else's generosity. Yet people have starved to death rather than ask for help.

There are emotional needs—a burden or problem too great for us to manage alone. Yet we would rather go through life in fear, guilt, or bewilderment rather than ask a trusted friend or counselor to give us his or her time and to listen.

There are people all around us who are looking for the opportunity to do good for us. Let them! Even create the opportunity! Let someone do unto you. Let someone give to you. Give them the joy of giving. We usually get much more than we receive anyway, in one way or another, so enjoy giving and receiving.

In order for us to be good givers, we must also be good receivers. Like good CBers, we must be able to receive as well as transmit.

The Ritual of Foot Washing:

John 13:4-17: So he [Jesus] rose from the table, took off his outer garment, and tied a towel around his waist. Then he poured some water into a washbasin and began to wash the disciples' feet and dry them with the towel around his waist. He came to Simon Peter, who said to him, "Are you going to wash my feet, Lord?"

Jesus answered him, "You do not understand now what I am doing, but you will understand later."

Peter declared, "Never at any time will you wash my feet!"

"If I do not wash your feet," Jesus answered, "you will no longer be my disciple."

Simon Peter answered, "Lord, do not wash only my feet, then! Wash my hands and head, too!"

Jesus said, "Anyone who has taken a bath is completely clean and does not have to wash himself, except for his feet. All of you are clean— all except one." (Jesus already knew who was going to betray him; that is why he said, "All of you, except one, are clean.")

After Jesus had washed their feet, he put his outer garment back on and returned to his place

at the table. "Do you understand what I have just done to you?" he asked. "You call me Teacher and Lord, and it is right that you do so, because that is what I am. I, your Lord and Teacher, have just washed your feet. You, then, should wash one another's feet. I have set an example for you, so that you will do just what I have done for you. I am telling you the truth: no slave is greater than his master, and no messenger is greater than the one who sent him. Now that you know this truth, how happy you will be if you put it into practice!"

VOICE: To show himself both servant and king, Jesus washed the disciples' feet. Peter was not comfortable with this at first but later allowed the Lord to wash him also. The early church observed the ritual of foot washing, and there has been a revival of the custom in modern-day churches. In this act we symbolize our servant role as followers of Christ. But we also illustrate our openness to be good receivers, to allow someone else the opportunity to do something for us. In this act, we both give and receive with thanksgiving. By allowing another person to touch us, we symbolize our willingness to be open to someone else who is reaching out toward us. If we allow touch, which is highly personal, then perhaps we can allow others to be a significant part of our lives. If we can receive the service of another person, then we can better serve.

(Then follows the pouring of water and the ritual of washing, according to how your group has decided to carry this out.)

Thanks a Lot

Meditation: "The Tin Rule"

"Do for others what you want them to do for you. . . ."

This statement of Jesus, as recorded in Matthew 7, is popularly known as the "Golden Rule." Many of us have been taught it or reminded of it since childhood. There is another statement of Jesus, recorded in Acts 20:35, so common in our minds that it may have lost its meaning through familiarity: "It is more blessed to give than to receive" (RSV). Both statements have to do with personal interaction—doing and having done, giving and receiving.

But we always view these classic passages of Scripture from only one perspective—we should do good to others; we should give to those in need.

What of the reverse? What is it like to have good done to us? To receive? This reverse of the Golden Rule and the verse from Acts can be thought of as the "Tin Rule." It is tin because we would rather think about gold. It may be, in fact, painfully hard for us to comprehend, let alone put into practice this "other side of the coin."

There is a joy in giving. Yet the giver sometimes feels pride in giving while the receiver feels humility in receiving. How often have we deprived someone else of the joy of giving because of our own pride—our refusal to admit need or our determination not to take anything from anyone?

Most of us simply are not good receivers. We talk about giving grudgingly. How much more miserly are we when it is our turn to receive?

And why do we always feel the need to repay so that we don't owe?

Let the joy of receiving be ours also. Some things we can never repay. To try to would be an insult to the giver and a robbery of his or her joy in giving. Could we repay mother love? Could we compensate Christ for what he has done for us, except through loyalty and love?

Gladly accept a gift from a child because children are a light which shows us God's kingdom. Their gifts may be homely handcrafted creations or just a hug. Sometimes their gift is simply their desire to be around us. The rule holds regardless of age.

Sometimes there are compliments handed us which we mar through embarrassed reception or even rejection. A compliment is a gift sometimes given with great difficulty. Take it and be glad.

Sometimes we have physical needs—needs so acute that our survival depends on someone else's generosity. Yet people have starved to death rather than ask for help.

There are emotional needs—a burden or problem too great for us to manage alone. Yet we would rather go through life in fear, guilt, or bewilderment rather than ask a trusted friend or counselor to give us his or her time and to listen.

There are people all around us who are looking for the opportunity to do good for us. Let them! Even create the opportunity! Let someone do unto you. Let someone give to you. Give them the joy of giving. We usually get much more than we receive anyway, in one way or another, so enjoy giving and receiving.

In order for us to be good givers, we must also be good receivers. Like good CBers, we must be able to receive as well as transmit.

The Ritual of Foot Washing:

John 13:4-17: So he [Jesus] rose from the table, took off his outer garment, and tied a towel around his waist. Then he poured some water into a washbasin and began to wash the disciples' feet and dry them with the towel around his waist. He came to Simon Peter, who said to him, "Are you going to wash my feet, Lord?"

Jesus answered him, "You do not understand now what I am doing, but you will understand later."

Peter declared, "Never at any time will you wash my feet!"

"If I do not wash your feet," Jesus answered, "you will no longer be my disciple."

Simon Peter answered, "Lord, do not wash only my feet, then! Wash my hands and head, too!"

Jesus said, "Anyone who has taken a bath is completely clean and does not have to wash himself, except for his feet. All of you are clean—all except one." (Jesus already knew who was going to betray him; that is why he said, "All of you, except one, are clean.")

After Jesus had washed their feet, he put his outer garment back on and returned to his place

at the table. "Do you understand what I have just done to you?" he asked. "You call me Teacher and Lord, and it is right that you do so, because that is what I am. I, your Lord and Teacher, have just washed your feet. You, then, should wash one another's feet. I have set an example for you, so that you will do just what I have done for you. I am telling you the truth: no slave is greater than his master, and no messenger is greater than the one who sent him. Now that you know this truth, how happy you will be if you put it into practice!"

Voice: To show himself both servant and king, Jesus washed the disciples' feet. Peter was not comfortable with this at first but later allowed the Lord to wash him also. The early church observed the ritual of foot washing, and there has been a revival of the custom in modern-day churches. In this act we symbolize our servant role as followers of Christ. But we also illustrate our openness to be good receivers, to allow someone else the opportunity to do something for us. In this act, we both give and receive with thanksgiving. By allowing another person to touch us, we symbolize our willingness to be open to someone else who is reaching out toward us. If we allow touch, which is highly personal, then perhaps we can allow others to be a significant part of our lives. If we can receive the service of another person, then we can better serve.

(Then follows the pouring of water and the ritual of washing, according to how your group has decided to carry this out.)

Thanks a Lot

Meditation: "The Tin Rule"

"Do for others what you want them to do for you. . . ."

This statement of Jesus, as recorded in Matthew 7, is popularly known as the "Golden Rule." Many of us have been taught it or reminded of it since childhood. There is another statement of Jesus, recorded in Acts 20:35, so common in our minds that it may have lost its meaning through familiarity: "It is more blessed to give than to receive" (RSV). Both statements have to do with personal interaction—doing and having done, giving and receiving.

But we always view these classic passages of Scripture from only one perspective—we should do good to others; we should give to those in need.

What of the reverse? What is it like to have good done to us? To receive? This reverse of the Golden Rule and the verse from Acts can be thought of as the "Tin Rule." It is tin because we would rather think about gold. It may be, in fact, painfully hard for us to comprehend, let alone put into practice this "other side of the coin."

There is a joy in giving. Yet the giver sometimes feels pride in giving while the receiver feels humility in receiving. How often have we deprived someone else of the joy of giving because of our own pride—our refusal to admit need or our determination not to take anything from anyone?

Most of us simply are not good receivers. We talk about giving grudgingly. How much more miserly are we when it is our turn to receive?

And why do we always feel the need to repay so that we don't owe?

Let the joy of receiving be ours also. Some things we can never repay. To try to would be an insult to the giver and a robbery of his or her joy in giving. Could we repay mother love? Could we compensate Christ for what he has done for us, except through loyalty and love?

Gladly accept a gift from a child because children are a light which shows us God's kingdom. Their gifts may be homely handcrafted creations or just a hug. Sometimes their gift is simply their desire to be around us. The rule holds regardless of age.

Sometimes there are compliments handed us which we mar through embarrassed reception or even rejection. A compliment is a gift sometimes given with great difficulty. Take it and be glad.

Sometimes we have physical needs—needs so acute that our survival depends on someone else's generosity. Yet people have starved to death rather than ask for help.

There are emotional needs—a burden or problem too great for us to manage alone. Yet we would rather go through life in fear, guilt, or bewilderment rather than ask a trusted friend or counselor to give us his or her time and to listen.

There are people all around us who are looking for the opportunity to do good for us. Let them! Even create the opportunity! Let someone do unto you. Let someone give to you. Give them the joy of giving. We usually get much more than we receive anyway, in one way or another, so enjoy giving and receiving.

In order for us to be good givers, we must also be good receivers. Like good CBers, we must be able to receive as well as transmit.

The Ritual of Foot Washing:

John 13:4-17: So he [Jesus] rose from the table, took off his outer garment, and tied a towel around his waist. Then he poured some water into a washbasin and began to wash the disciples' feet and dry them with the towel around his waist. He came to Simon Peter, who said to him, "Are you going to wash my feet, Lord?"

Jesus answered him, "You do not understand now what I am doing, but you will understand later."

Peter declared, "Never at any time will you wash my feet!"

"If I do not wash your feet," Jesus answered, "you will no longer be my disciple."

Simon Peter answered, "Lord, do not wash only my feet, then! Wash my hands and head, too!"

Jesus said, "Anyone who has taken a bath is completely clean and does not have to wash himself, except for his feet. All of you are clean—all except one." (Jesus already knew who was going to betray him; that is why he said, "All of you, except one, are clean.")

After Jesus had washed their feet, he put his outer garment back on and returned to his place

at the table. "Do you understand what I have just done to you?" he asked. "You call me Teacher and Lord, and it is right that you do so, because that is what I am. I, your Lord and Teacher, have just washed your feet. You, then, should wash one another's feet. I have set an example for you, so that you will do just what I have done for you. I am telling you the truth: no slave is greater than his master, and no messenger is greater than the one who sent him. Now that you know this truth, how happy you will be if you put it into practice!"

VOICE: To show himself both servant and king, Jesus washed the disciples' feet. Peter was not comfortable with this at first but later allowed the Lord to wash him also. The early church observed the ritual of foot washing, and there has been a revival of the custom in modern-day churches. In this act we symbolize our servant role as followers of Christ. But we also illustrate our openness to be good receivers, to allow someone else the opportunity to do something for us. In this act, we both give and receive with thanksgiving. By allowing another person to touch us, we symbolize our willingness to be open to someone else who is reaching out toward us. If we allow touch, which is highly personal, then perhaps we can allow others to be a significant part of our lives. If we can receive the service of another person, then we can better serve.

(Then follows the pouring of water and the ritual of washing, according to how your group has decided to carry this out.)

Thanks a Lot

Meditation: "The Tin Rule"

"Do for others what you want them to do for you. . . ."

This statement of Jesus, as recorded in Matthew 7, is popularly known as the "Golden Rule." Many of us have been taught it or reminded of it since childhood. There is another statement of Jesus, recorded in Acts 20:35, so common in our minds that it may have lost its meaning through familiarity: "It is more blessed to give than to receive" (RSV). Both statements have to do with personal interaction—doing and having done, giving and receiving.

But we always view these classic passages of Scripture from only one perspective—we should do good to others; we should give to those in need.

What of the reverse? What is it like to have good done to us? To receive? This reverse of the Golden Rule and the verse from Acts can be thought of as the "Tin Rule." It is tin because we would rather think about gold. It may be, in fact, painfully hard for us to comprehend, let alone put into practice this "other side of the coin."

There is a joy in giving. Yet the giver sometimes feels pride in giving while the receiver feels humility in receiving. How often have we deprived someone else of the joy of giving because of our own pride—our refusal to admit need or our determination not to take anything from anyone?

Most of us simply are not good receivers. We talk about giving grudgingly. How much more miserly are we when it is our turn to receive?

And why do we always feel the need to repay so that we don't owe?

Let the joy of receiving be ours also. Some things we can never repay. To try to would be an insult to the giver and a robbery of his or her joy in giving. Could we repay mother love? Could we compensate Christ for what he has done for us, except through loyalty and love?

Gladly accept a gift from a child because children are a light which shows us God's kingdom. Their gifts may be homely handcrafted creations or just a hug. Sometimes their gift is simply their desire to be around us. The rule holds regardless of age.

Sometimes there are compliments handed us which we mar through embarrassed reception or even rejection. A compliment is a gift sometimes given with great difficulty. Take it and be glad.

Sometimes we have physical needs—needs so acute that our survival depends on someone else's generosity. Yet people have starved to death rather than ask for help.

There are emotional needs—a burden or problem too great for us to manage alone. Yet we would rather go through life in fear, guilt, or bewilderment rather than ask a trusted friend or counselor to give us his or her time and to listen.

There are people all around us who are looking for the opportunity to do good for us. Let them! Even create the opportunity! Let someone do unto you. Let someone give to you. Give them the joy of giving. We usually get much more than we receive anyway, in one way or another, so enjoy giving and receiving.

In order for us to be good givers, we must also be good receivers. Like good CBers, we must be able to receive as well as transmit.

The Ritual of Foot Washing:

John 13:4-17: So he [Jesus] rose from the table, took off his outer garment, and tied a towel around his waist. Then he poured some water into a washbasin and began to wash the disciples' feet and dry them with the towel around his waist. He came to Simon Peter, who said to him, "Are you going to wash my feet, Lord?"

Jesus answered him, "You do not understand now what I am doing, but you will understand later."

Peter declared, "Never at any time will you wash my feet!"

"If I do not wash your feet," Jesus answered, "you will no longer be my disciple."

Simon Peter answered, "Lord, do not wash only my feet, then! Wash my hands and head, too!"

Jesus said, "Anyone who has taken a bath is completely clean and does not have to wash himself, except for his feet. All of you are clean—all except one." (Jesus already knew who was going to betray him; that is why he said, "All of you, except one, are clean.")

After Jesus had washed their feet, he put his outer garment back on and returned to his place

at the table. "Do you understand what I have just done to you?" he asked. "You call me Teacher and Lord, and it is right that you do so, because that is what I am. I, your Lord and Teacher, have just washed your feet. You, then, should wash one another's feet. I have set an example for you, so that you will do just what I have done for you. I am telling you the truth: no slave is greater than his master, and no messenger is greater than the one who sent him. Now that you know this truth, how happy you will be if you put it into practice!"

VOICE: To show himself both servant and king, Jesus washed the disciples' feet. Peter was not comfortable with this at first but later allowed the Lord to wash him also. The early church observed the ritual of foot washing, and there has been a revival of the custom in modern-day churches. In this act we symbolize our servant role as followers of Christ. But we also illustrate our openness to be good receivers, to allow someone else the opportunity to do something for us. In this act, we both give and receive with thanksgiving. By allowing another person to touch us, we symbolize our willingness to be open to someone else who is reaching out toward us. If we allow touch, which is highly personal, then perhaps we can allow others to be a significant part of our lives. If we can receive the service of another person, then we can better serve.

(Then follows the pouring of water and the ritual of washing, according to how your group has decided to carry this out.)

Christmas Cloth

A Celebration for Christmas

This chapter can be used either as a time for intimate worship among members of your group or for a wider church Christmas celebration. It could be part of tree-trimming festivities, the lighting of Christmas candles, the lighting of candles on an Advent wreath, or as a fitting conclusion to group caroling or special Christmas service project.

The chapter is entitled "Christmas Cloth" because your group will be reflecting on some of the garments Jesus wore. The two most significant were the swaddling clothes worn when he was an infant and the grave cloths left after his resurrection.

Contrary to popular belief, Christmas is not the high point of the Christian calendar. Since early times, Lent and Easter have been dominant in Christian liturgy. Christmas is a beginning, but the apex of Christian faith is in the empty tomb. The events of Jesus' life led up to the resurrection.

In this chapter we will be reviewing and remembering Jesus' life as symbolized by the clothes mentioned in Scripture—the infant clothes, the hem of his garment touched by a woman during his ministry, the robe which was gambled away at his death, and the grave cloths, symbol of the living Lord.

Preparation

Make this a time of good fellowship and singing. Use Christmas carols liberally throughout the service. Carols are suggested here, but use other hymns as well, plus solos or special Christmas music. Although we will be considering various aspects of Jesus' life, Christmas music is appropriate. It is fitting at any time of the year!

If you are using this material in a small group, arrange seating in a circle or semicircle around Christmas candles, a small tree, or a display of Christmas art. Spoken parts can be given from within the circle.

If this material is to be used as a part of a wider Christmas celebration in a church sanctuary or meeting hall, consider using two lecterns, one for the Scripture readings and one for voice parts.

The Experience

Carol: "Away in a Manger."
Scripture: Luke 2:1-7 (Supplement A).
Reading: "Baby Clothes" (Supplement A).
Carol: "Angels We Have Heard on High."
Scripture: Matthew 9:20-22 (Supplement A).
Reading: "The Edge of His Cloak" (Supplement A).
Carol: "O Come, O Come, Emmanuel."
Scripture: John 19:23-24 (Supplement A).
Reading: "Gambled Garments" (Supplement A).
Carol: "Hark! The Herald Angels Sing."
Scripture: John 19:38-40; 20:3-8 (Supplement A).
Reading: "The Shroud" (Supplement A).
Prayer: O Lord, we are joyous at the Christmas season because you came in person to bring us redemption, to show us the way to walk in this world, and to give us the hope of life. Amen.
Carol: "Joy to the World" (Or consider using an Easter hymn as a fitting closing to this service).

Christmas Cloth

Scripture: Luke 2:1-7

At that time Emperor Augustus ordered a census to be taken throughout the Roman Empire. When this first census took place, Quirinius was the governor of Syria. Everyone, then, went to register himself, each to his own home town.

Joseph went from the town of Nazareth in Galilee to the town of Bethlehem in Judea, the birthplace of King David. Joseph went there because he was a descendant of David. He went to register with Mary, who was promised in marriage to him. She was pregnant, and while they were in Bethlehem, the time came for her to have her baby. She gave birth to her first son, wrapped him in cloths and laid him in a manger—there was no room for them to stay in the inn.

Reading: "Baby Clothes"

Christmas is a high point in the Christian year. We celebrate the birth of Jesus, God in person, who lived and lives among us. But Christmas is a beginning, a starting point. The manger is linked to the empty tomb. Without the resurrection, Jesus would be only a kind man, a good man, a prophet, an example, a great philosopher along with other great personalities of history. But he was very God—in diapers and baby clothes! He said he came to earth to redeem us and to give us hope for life after life. And as a seal or verification of who he was, his life led to an early and untimely death and to victory over death.

We are contemplating his clothes, the garments that he wore. And he started out in baby clothes or swaddling cloths—simple, loosely fitting garments in which Mary wrapped him.

Billions of babies have been born through the centuries of time. Most were tenderly loved and cared for by their mothers and dressed in infants' apparel. A baby is a helpless person, totally dependent on someone else. Most creatures of our world at least can stand or walk or feed themselves at birth. Not so the human creature. It is usually at least a year before a child can stand, walk, and begin to learn the rudiments of feeding and caring for itself. Total dependency!

And God chose to visit us in person and to become, for a time, totally dependent and trusting in the love and faithfulness of parents. We speak of trust in God! See how he trusted us! He could not even clothe himself. His mother had to do it for him—in baby clothes—in a manger.

Scripture: Matthew 9:20-22

A woman who had suffered severe bleeding for twelve years came up behind Jesus and touched the edge of his cloak. She said to herself, "If only I touch his cloak, I will get well."

Jesus turned around and saw her, and said, "Courage, my daughter! Your faith has made you well." At that very moment the woman became well.

Reading: "The Edge of His Cloak"

And the child grew and developed with the loving nurture given him by Mary and Joseph. Then when he was fully grown, he began doing amazing things, marvelous things, disturbing things, dangerous things, threatening things. He began to spread news—Good News—that God was come to release people from the chains, burdens, and consequences of sin, fear, and guilt. He dared to forgive sins! He dared to cure sickness, even on the sabbath! He dared to promise abundant life in a forsaken, downtrodden, despairing world!

He roamed the countryside with poor people and outcasts, camping out, laughing and celebrating, teaching and reasoning, tending to the sick and disabled. He lived life to its fullest and was weary and exhausted night after night from work and rejoicing and discussions long into the night.

We do not know just what he wore during those brief years—a cloak, a robe, a garment. But on one of his journeys a woman—any woman—felt the need for healing. Not only did she feel the need, she also acted. She did not set up an appointment for counseling or a doctor's examination. She crept up behind Jesus, reached out, and touched his cloak.

There was no magic in the cloth. It was her reaching out and his accepting her act that made the difference. Jesus didn't even take credit for healing, for locked up inside this woman was the cure for her own ills—her faith. Note what he

said to her: "Your faith has made you well."

Lord, how often we are afraid to reach out to another person or to you. We fear rejection or embarrassment. We are too proud to admit need. Give us confidence and courage to reach out to you with assurance that you will stop, pay attention, and help us. Help us to reach out to others as well, and to accept those who reach out for us. Lord God, we would but touch the edge of your cloak this Advent season. Amen.

Scripture: John 19:23-24

After the soldiers had crucified Jesus, they took his clothes and divided them into four parts, one part for each soldier. They also took the robe, which was made of one piece of woven cloth without any seams in it. The soldiers said to one another, "Let's not tear it; let's throw dice to see who will get it." This happened in order to make the scripture come true:

"They divided my clothes among themselves and gambled for my robe."

And this is what the soldiers did.

Reading: "Gambled Garment"

He ended up without a penny. They didn't even allow him the dignity of his last earthly possession— the robe that he wore. As if torture, insult, and death weren't enough, they gambled away his garments.

He ministered to men, and they murdered him. The cycle was complete—the cradle to the grave.

Or was it? Was it all without purpose? God has the strangest ways of turning darkness to day. His birth, his ministry, his death—all had meaning. The baby clothes, the cloak, the gambled robe—all led to a final, finer piece of cloth.

Scripture: John 19:38-40; 20:3-8

After this, Joseph, who was from the town of Arimathea, asked Pilate if he could take Jesus' body. (Joseph was a follower of Jesus, but in secret, because he was afraid of the Jewish authorities.) Pilate told him he could have the body, so Joseph went and took it away. Nicodemus, who at first had gone to see Jesus at night, went with Joseph, taking with him about one hundred pounds of spices, a mixture of myrrh and aloes. The two men took Jesus' body and wrapped it in linen cloths with the spices according to the Jewish custom of preparing a body for burial.

Then Peter and the other disciple went to the tomb. The two of them were running, but the other disciple ran faster than Peter and reached the tomb first. He bent over and saw the linen cloths, but he did not go in. Behind him came Simon Peter, and he went straight into the tomb. He saw the linen cloths lying there and the cloth which had been around Jesus' head. It was not lying with the linen cloths but was rolled up by itself. Then the other disciple, who had reached the tomb first, also went in; he saw and believed.

Reading: "The Shroud"

It all seemed so useless, so tragically useless. A life so worthwhile, so beautiful—snuffed out by one of the most horrible deaths ever contrived.

But it was all over now. No more healing, no more Good News, no more late-night talks, no more bread for the hungry, no more rejoicing. The final chapter had been written to the life of a great person who never really made it. There were such high hopes, such dreams and plans.

It ended something like it began. He was lying down again; this time in a tomb, not a manger; not glowing with life, but stone dead; not dressed in baby clothes, but in a linen sheet and face cloth.

How could the Babe of Bethlehem, the manger child, end up in bloody grave cloths?

Then a spark more potent than a nuclear flash split the dawn. A rumor spread. He had risen from the dead!

Two disciples came running. They entered the tomb. They found nothing. Absolutely nothing! Nothing except a linen shroud and a face cloth that once covered a dead man.

He is risen! The Lord is risen indeed! This is not only the message of Easter, but also of Christmas. Christmas is the joyous celebration of baby clothes and a folded burial shroud. He came to bring hope, Good News, and the promise of life!

Christmas Cloth

Scripture: Luke 2:1-7

At that time Emperor Augustus ordered a census to be taken throughout the Roman Empire. When this first census took place, Quirinius was the governor of Syria. Everyone, then, went to register himself, each to his own home town.

Joseph went from the town of Nazareth in Galilee to the town of Bethlehem in Judea, the birthplace of King David. Joseph went there because he was a descendant of David. He went to register with Mary, who was promised in marriage to him. She was pregnant, and while they were in Bethlehem, the time came for her to have her baby. She gave birth to her first son, wrapped him in cloths and laid him in a manger—there was no room for them to stay in the inn.

Reading: "Baby Clothes"

Christmas is a high point in the Christian year. We celebrate the birth of Jesus, God in person, who lived and lives among us. But Christmas is a beginning, a starting point. The manger is linked to the empty tomb. Without the resurrection, Jesus would be only a kind man, a good man, a prophet, an example, a great philosopher along with other great personalities of history. But he was very God—in diapers and baby clothes! He said he came to earth to redeem us and to give us hope for life after life. And as a seal or verification of who he was, his life led to an early and untimely death and to victory over death.

We are contemplating his clothes, the garments that he wore. And he started out in baby clothes or swaddling cloths—simple, loosely fitting garments in which Mary wrapped him.

Billions of babies have been born through the centuries of time. Most were tenderly loved and cared for by their mothers and dressed in infants' apparel. A baby is a helpless person, totally dependent on someone else. Most creatures of our world at least can stand or walk or feed themselves at birth. Not so the human creature. It is usually at least a year before a child can stand, walk, and begin to learn the rudiments of feeding and caring for itself. Total dependency!

And God chose to visit us in person and to become, for a time, totally dependent and trusting in the love and faithfulness of parents. We speak of trust in God! See how he trusted us! He could not even clothe himself. His mother had to do it for him—in baby clothes—in a manger.

Scripture: Matthew 9:20-22

A woman who had suffered severe bleeding for twelve years came up behind Jesus and touched the edge of his cloak. She said to herself, "If only I touch his cloak, I will get well."

Jesus turned around and saw her, and said, "Courage, my daughter! Your faith has made you well." At that very moment the woman became well.

Reading: "The Edge of His Cloak"

And the child grew and developed with the loving nurture given him by Mary and Joseph. Then when he was fully grown, he began doing amazing things, marvelous things, disturbing things, dangerous things, threatening things. He began to spread news—Good News—that God was come to release people from the chains, burdens, and consequences of sin, fear, and guilt. He dared to forgive sins! He dared to cure sickness, even on the sabbath! He dared to promise abundant life in a forsaken, downtrodden, despairing world!

He roamed the countryside with poor people and outcasts, camping out, laughing and celebrating, teaching and reasoning, tending to the sick and disabled. He lived life to its fullest and was weary and exhausted night after night from work and rejoicing and discussions long into the night.

We do not know just what he wore during those brief years—a cloak, a robe, a garment. But on one of his journeys a woman—any woman—felt the need for healing. Not only did she feel the need, she also acted. She did not set up an appointment for counseling or a doctor's examination. She crept up behind Jesus, reached out, and touched his cloak.

There was no magic in the cloth. It was her reaching out and his accepting her act that made the difference. Jesus didn't even take credit for healing, for locked up inside this woman was the cure for her own ills—her faith. Note what he

said to her: "Your faith has made you well."

Lord, how often we are afraid to reach out to another person or to you. We fear rejection or embarrassment. We are too proud to admit need. Give us confidence and courage to reach out to you with assurance that you will stop, pay attention, and help us. Help us to reach out to others as well, and to accept those who reach out for us. Lord God, we would but touch the edge of your cloak this Advent season. Amen.

Scripture: John 19:23-24

After the soldiers had crucified Jesus, they took his clothes and divided them into four parts, one part for each soldier. They also took the robe, which was made of one piece of woven cloth without any seams in it. The soldiers said to one another, "Let's not tear it; let's throw dice to see who will get it." This happened in order to make the scripture come true:

"They divided my clothes among themselves and gambled for my robe."

And this is what the soldiers did.

Reading: "Gambled Garment"

He ended up without a penny. They didn't even allow him the dignity of his last earthly possession— the robe that he wore. As if torture, insult, and death weren't enough, they gambled away his garments.

He ministered to men, and they murdered him. The cycle was complete—the cradle to the grave.

Or was it? Was it all without purpose? God has the strangest ways of turning darkness to day. His birth, his ministry, his death—all had meaning. The baby clothes, the cloak, the gambled robe—all led to a final, finer piece of cloth.

Scripture: John 19:38-40; 20:3-8

After this, Joseph, who was from the town of Arimathea, asked Pilate if he could take Jesus' body. (Joseph was a follower of Jesus, but in secret, because he was afraid of the Jewish authorities.) Pilate told him he could have the body, so Joseph went and took it away. Nicodemus, who at first had gone to see Jesus at night, went with Joseph, taking with him about one hundred pounds of spices, a mixture of myrrh and aloes. The two men took Jesus' body and wrapped it in linen cloths with the spices according to the Jewish custom of preparing a body for burial.

Then Peter and the other disciple went to the tomb. The two of them were running, but the other disciple ran faster than Peter and reached the tomb first. He bent over and saw the linen cloths, but he did not go in. Behind him came Simon Peter, and he went straight into the tomb. He saw the linen cloths lying there and the cloth which had been around Jesus' head. It was not lying with the linen cloths but was rolled up by itself. Then the other disciple, who had reached the tomb first, also went in; he saw and believed.

Reading: "The Shroud"

It all seemed so useless, so tragically useless. A life so worthwhile, so beautiful—snuffed out by one of the most horrible deaths ever contrived.

But it was all over now. No more healing, no more Good News, no more late-night talks, no more bread for the hungry, no more rejoicing. The final chapter had been written to the life of a great person who never really made it. There were such high hopes, such dreams and plans.

It ended something like it began. He was lying down again; this time in a tomb, not a manger; not glowing with life, but stone dead; not dressed in baby clothes, but in a linen sheet and face cloth.

How could the Babe of Bethlehem, the manger child, end up in bloody grave cloths?

Then a spark more potent than a nuclear flash split the dawn. A rumor spread. He had risen from the dead!

Two disciples came running. They entered the tomb. They found nothing. Absolutely nothing! Nothing except a linen shroud and a face cloth that once covered a dead man.

He is risen! The Lord is risen indeed! This is not only the message of Easter, but also of Christmas. Christmas is the joyous celebration of baby clothes and a folded burial shroud. He came to bring hope, Good News, and the promise of life!

Christmas Cloth

Scripture: Luke 2:1-7

At that time Emperor Augustus ordered a census to be taken throughout the Roman Empire. When this first census took place, Quirinius was the governor of Syria. Everyone, then, went to register himself, each to his own home town.

Joseph went from the town of Nazareth in Galilee to the town of Bethlehem in Judea, the birthplace of King David. Joseph went there because he was a descendant of David. He went to register with Mary, who was promised in marriage to him. She was pregnant, and while they were in Bethlehem, the time came for her to have her baby. She gave birth to her first son, wrapped him in cloths and laid him in a manger—there was no room for them to stay in the inn.

Reading: "Baby Clothes"

Christmas is a high point in the Christian year. We celebrate the birth of Jesus, God in person, who lived and lives among us. But Christmas is a beginning, a starting point. The manger is linked to the empty tomb. Without the resurrection, Jesus would be only a kind man, a good man, a prophet, an example, a great philosopher along with other great personalities of history. But he was very God—in diapers and baby clothes! He said he came to earth to redeem us and to give us hope for life after life. And as a seal or verification of who he was, his life led to an early and untimely death and to victory over death.

We are contemplating his clothes, the garments that he wore. And he started out in baby clothes or swaddling cloths—simple, loosely fitting garments in which Mary wrapped him.

Billions of babies have been born through the centuries of time. Most were tenderly loved and cared for by their mothers and dressed in infants' apparel. A baby is a helpless person, totally dependent on someone else. Most creatures of our world at least can stand or walk or feed themselves at birth. Not so the human creature. It is usually at least a year before a child can stand, walk, and begin to learn the rudiments of feeding and caring for itself. Total dependency!

And God chose to visit us in person and to become, for a time, totally dependent and trusting in the love and faithfulness of parents. We speak of trust in God! See how he trusted us! He could not even clothe himself. His mother had to do it for him—in baby clothes—in a manger.

Scripture: Matthew 9:20-22

A woman who had suffered severe bleeding for twelve years came up behind Jesus and touched the edge of his cloak. She said to herself, "If only I touch his cloak, I will get well."

Jesus turned around and saw her, and said, "Courage, my daughter! Your faith has made you well." At that very moment the woman became well.

Reading: "The Edge of His Cloak"

And the child grew and developed with the loving nurture given him by Mary and Joseph. Then when he was fully grown, he began doing amazing things, marvelous things, disturbing things, dangerous things, threatening things. He began to spread news—Good News—that God was come to release people from the chains, burdens, and consequences of sin, fear, and guilt. He dared to forgive sins! He dared to cure sickness, even on the sabbath! He dared to promise abundant life in a forsaken, downtrodden, despairing world!

He roamed the countryside with poor people and outcasts, camping out, laughing and celebrating, teaching and reasoning, tending to the sick and disabled. He lived life to its fullest and was weary and exhausted night after night from work and rejoicing and discussions long into the night.

We do not know just what he wore during those brief years—a cloak, a robe, a garment. But on one of his journeys a woman—any woman—felt the need for healing. Not only did she feel the need, she also acted. She did not set up an appointment for counseling or a doctor's examination. She crept up behind Jesus, reached out, and touched his cloak.

There was no magic in the cloth. It was her reaching out and his accepting her act that made the difference. Jesus didn't even take credit for healing, for locked up inside this woman was the cure for her own ills—her faith. Note what he

said to her: "Your faith has made you well."

Lord, how often we are afraid to reach out to another person or to you. We fear rejection or embarrassment. We are too proud to admit need. Give us confidence and courage to reach out to you with assurance that you will stop, pay attention, and help us. Help us to reach out to others as well, and to accept those who reach out for us. Lord God, we would but touch the edge of your cloak this Advent season. Amen.

Scripture: John 19:23-24

After the soldiers had crucified Jesus, they took his clothes and divided them into four parts, one part for each soldier. They also took the robe, which was made of one piece of woven cloth without any seams in it. The soldiers said to one another, "Let's not tear it; let's throw dice to see who will get it." This happened in order to make the scripture come true:

"They divided my clothes among themselves
and gambled for my robe."

And this is what the soldiers did.

Reading: "Gambled Garment"

He ended up without a penny. They didn't even allow him the dignity of his last earthly possession— the robe that he wore. As if torture, insult, and death weren't enough, they gambled away his garments.

He ministered to men, and they murdered him. The cycle was complete—the cradle to the grave.

Or was it? Was it all without purpose? God has the strangest ways of turning darkness to day. His birth, his ministry, his death—all had meaning. The baby clothes, the cloak, the gambled robe—all led to a final, finer piece of cloth.

Scripture: John 19:38-40; 20:3-8

After this, Joseph, who was from the town of Arimathea, asked Pilate if he could take Jesus' body. (Joseph was a follower of Jesus, but in secret, because he was afraid of the Jewish authorities.) Pilate told him he could have the body, so Joseph went and took it away. Nicodemus, who at first had gone to see Jesus at night, went with Joseph, taking with him about one hundred pounds of spices, a mixture of myrrh and aloes. The two men took Jesus' body and wrapped it in linen cloths with the spices according to the Jewish custom of preparing a body for burial.

Then Peter and the other disciple went to the tomb. The two of them were running, but the other disciple ran faster than Peter and reached the tomb first. He bent over and saw the linen cloths, but he did not go in. Behind him came Simon Peter, and he went straight into the tomb. He saw the linen cloths lying there and the cloth which had been around Jesus' head. It was not lying with the linen cloths but was rolled up by itself. Then the other disciple, who had reached the tomb first, also went in; he saw and believed.

Reading: "The Shroud"

It all seemed so useless, so tragically useless. A life so worthwhile, so beautiful—snuffed out by one of the most horrible deaths ever contrived.

But it was all over now. No more healing, no more Good News, no more late-night talks, no more bread for the hungry, no more rejoicing. The final chapter had been written to the life of a great person who never really made it. There were such high hopes, such dreams and plans.

It ended something like it began. He was lying down again; this time in a tomb, not a manger; not glowing with life, but stone dead; not dressed in baby clothes, but in a linen sheet and face cloth.

How could the Babe of Bethlehem, the manger child, end up in bloody grave cloths?

Then a spark more potent than a nuclear flash split the dawn. A rumor spread. He had risen from the dead!

Two disciples came running. They entered the tomb. They found nothing. Absolutely nothing! Nothing except a linen shroud and a face cloth that once covered a dead man.

He is risen! The Lord is risen indeed! This is not only the message of Easter, but also of Christmas. Christmas is the joyous celebration of baby clothes and a folded burial shroud. He came to bring hope, Good News, and the promise of life!

Christmas Cloth

Scripture: Luke 2:1-7

At that time Emperor Augustus ordered a census to be taken throughout the Roman Empire. When this first census took place, Quirinius was the governor of Syria. Everyone, then, went to register himself, each to his own home town.

Joseph went from the town of Nazareth in Galilee to the town of Bethlehem in Judea, the birthplace of King David. Joseph went there because he was a descendant of David. He went to register with Mary, who was promised in marriage to him. She was pregnant, and while they were in Bethlehem, the time came for her to have her baby. She gave birth to her first son, wrapped him in cloths and laid him in a manger—there was no room for them to stay in the inn.

Reading: "Baby Clothes"

Christmas is a high point in the Christian year. We celebrate the birth of Jesus, God in person, who lived and lives among us. But Christmas is a beginning, a starting point. The manger is linked to the empty tomb. Without the resurrection, Jesus would be only a kind man, a good man, a prophet, an example, a great philosopher along with other great personalities of history. But he was very God—in diapers and baby clothes! He said he came to earth to redeem us and to give us hope for life after life. And as a seal or verification of who he was, his life led to an early and untimely death and to victory over death.

We are contemplating his clothes, the garments that he wore. And he started out in baby clothes or swaddling cloths—simple, loosely fitting garments in which Mary wrapped him.

Billions of babies have been born through the centuries of time. Most were tenderly loved and cared for by their mothers and dressed in infants' apparel. A baby is a helpless person, totally dependent on someone else. Most creatures of our world at least can stand or walk or feed themselves at birth. Not so the human creature. It is usually at least a year before a child can stand, walk, and begin to learn the rudiments of feeding and caring for itself. Total dependency!

And God chose to visit us in person and to become, for a time, totally dependent and trusting in the love and faithfulness of parents. We speak of trust in God! See how he trusted us! He could not even clothe himself. His mother had to do it for him—in baby clothes—in a manger.

Scripture: Matthew 9:20-22

A woman who had suffered severe bleeding for twelve years came up behind Jesus and touched the edge of his cloak. She said to herself, "If only I touch his cloak, I will get well."

Jesus turned around and saw her, and said, "Courage, my daughter! Your faith has made you well." At that very moment the woman became well.

Reading: "The Edge of His Cloak"

And the child grew and developed with the loving nurture given him by Mary and Joseph. Then when he was fully grown, he began doing amazing things, marvelous things, disturbing things, dangerous things, threatening things. He began to spread news—Good News—that God was come to release people from the chains, burdens, and consequences of sin, fear, and guilt. He dared to forgive sins! He dared to cure sickness, even on the sabbath! He dared to promise abundant life in a forsaken, downtrodden, despairing world!

He roamed the countryside with poor people and outcasts, camping out, laughing and celebrating, teaching and reasoning, tending to the sick and disabled. He lived life to its fullest and was weary and exhausted night after night from work and rejoicing and discussions long into the night.

We do not know just what he wore during those brief years—a cloak, a robe, a garment. But on one of his journeys a woman—any woman—felt the need for healing. Not only did she feel the need, she also acted. She did not set up an appointment for counseling or a doctor's examination. She crept up behind Jesus, reached out, and touched his cloak.

There was no magic in the cloth. It was her reaching out and his accepting her act that made the difference. Jesus didn't even take credit for healing, for locked up inside this woman was the cure for her own ills—her faith. Note what he

said to her: "Your faith has made you well."

Lord, how often we are afraid to reach out to another person or to you. We fear rejection or embarrassment. We are too proud to admit need. Give us confidence and courage to reach out to you with assurance that you will stop, pay attention, and help us. Help us to reach out to others as well, and to accept those who reach out for us. Lord God, we would but touch the edge of your cloak this Advent season. Amen.

Scripture: John 19:23-24

After the soldiers had crucified Jesus, they took his clothes and divided them into four parts, one part for each soldier. They also took the robe, which was made of one piece of woven cloth without any seams in it. The soldiers said to one another, "Let's not tear it; let's throw dice to see who will get it." This happened in order to make the scripture come true:

> "They divided my clothes among themselves
> and gambled for my robe."

And this is what the soldiers did.

Reading: "Gambled Garment"

He ended up without a penny. They didn't even allow him the dignity of his last earthly possession— the robe that he wore. As if torture, insult, and death weren't enough, they gambled away his garments.

He ministered to men, and they murdered him. The cycle was complete—the cradle to the grave.

Or was it? Was it all without purpose? God has the strangest ways of turning darkness to day. His birth, his ministry, his death—all had meaning. The baby clothes, the cloak, the gambled robe—all led to a final, finer piece of cloth.

Scripture: John 19:38-40; 20:3-8

After this, Joseph, who was from the town of Arimathea, asked Pilate if he could take Jesus' body. (Joseph was a follower of Jesus, but in secret, because he was afraid of the Jewish authorities.) Pilate told him he could have the body, so Joseph went and took it away. Nicodemus, who at first had gone to see Jesus at night, went with Joseph, taking with him about one hundred pounds of spices, a mixture of myrrh and aloes. The two men took Jesus' body and wrapped it in linen cloths with the spices according to the Jewish custom of preparing a body for burial.

Then Peter and the other disciple went to the tomb. The two of them were running, but the other disciple ran faster than Peter and reached the tomb first. He bent over and saw the linen cloths, but he did not go in. Behind him came Simon Peter, and he went straight into the tomb. He saw the linen cloths lying there and the cloth which had been around Jesus' head. It was not lying with the linen cloths but was rolled up by itself. Then the other disciple, who had reached the tomb first, also went in; he saw and believed.

Reading: "The Shroud"

It all seemed so useless, so tragically useless. A life so worthwhile, so beautiful—snuffed out by one of the most horrible deaths ever contrived.

But it was all over now. No more healing, no more Good News, no more late-night talks, no more bread for the hungry, no more rejoicing. The final chapter had been written to the life of a great person who never really made it. There were such high hopes, such dreams and plans.

It ended something like it began. He was lying down again; this time in a tomb, not a manger; not glowing with life, but stone dead; not dressed in baby clothes, but in a linen sheet and face cloth.

How could the Babe of Bethlehem, the manger child, end up in bloody grave cloths?

Then a spark more potent than a nuclear flash split the dawn. A rumor spread. He had risen from the dead!

Two disciples came running. They entered the tomb. They found nothing. Absolutely nothing! Nothing except a linen shroud and a face cloth that once covered a dead man.

He is risen! The Lord is risen indeed! This is not only the message of Easter, but also of Christmas. Christmas is the joyous celebration of baby clothes and a folded burial shroud. He came to bring hope, Good News, and the promise of life!

Christmas Cloth

Scripture: Luke 2:1-7

At that time Emperor Augustus ordered a census to be taken throughout the Roman Empire. When this first census took place, Quirinius was the governor of Syria. Everyone, then, went to register himself, each to his own home town.

Joseph went from the town of Nazareth in Galilee to the town of Bethlehem in Judea, the birthplace of King David. Joseph went there because he was a descendant of David. He went to register with Mary, who was promised in marriage to him. She was pregnant, and while they were in Bethlehem, the time came for her to have her baby. She gave birth to her first son, wrapped him in cloths and laid him in a manger—there was no room for them to stay in the inn.

Reading: "Baby Clothes"

Christmas is a high point in the Christian year. We celebrate the birth of Jesus, God in person, who lived and lives among us. But Christmas is a beginning, a starting point. The manger is linked to the empty tomb. Without the resurrection, Jesus would be only a kind man, a good man, a prophet, an example, a great philosopher along with other great personalities of history. But he was very God—in diapers and baby clothes! He said he came to earth to redeem us and to give us hope for life after life. And as a seal or verification of who he was, his life led to an early and untimely death and to victory over death.

We are contemplating his clothes, the garments that he wore. And he started out in baby clothes or swaddling cloths—simple, loosely fitting garments in which Mary wrapped him.

Billions of babies have been born through the centuries of time. Most were tenderly loved and cared for by their mothers and dressed in infants' apparel. A baby is a helpless person, totally dependent on someone else. Most creatures of our world at least can stand or walk or feed themselves at birth. Not so the human creature. It is usually at least a year before a child can stand, walk, and begin to learn the rudiments of feeding and caring for itself. Total dependency!

And God chose to visit us in person and to become, for a time, totally dependent and trusting in the love and faithfulness of parents. We speak of trust in God! See how he trusted us! He could not even clothe himself. His mother had to do it for him—in baby clothes—in a manger.

Scripture: Matthew 9:20-22

A woman who had suffered severe bleeding for twelve years came up behind Jesus and touched the edge of his cloak. She said to herself, "If only I touch his cloak, I will get well."

Jesus turned around and saw her, and said, "Courage, my daughter! Your faith has made you well." At that very moment the woman became well.

Reading: "The Edge of His Cloak"

And the child grew and developed with the loving nurture given him by Mary and Joseph. Then when he was fully grown, he began doing amazing things, marvelous things, disturbing things, dangerous things, threatening things. He began to spread news—Good News—that God was come to release people from the chains, burdens, and consequences of sin, fear, and guilt. He dared to forgive sins! He dared to cure sickness, even on the sabbath! He dared to promise abundant life in a forsaken, downtrodden, despairing world!

He roamed the countryside with poor people and outcasts, camping out, laughing and celebrating, teaching and reasoning, tending to the sick and disabled. He lived life to its fullest and was weary and exhausted night after night from work and rejoicing and discussions long into the night.

We do not know just what he wore during those brief years—a cloak, a robe, a garment. But on one of his journeys a woman—any woman—felt the need for healing. Not only did she feel the need, she also acted. She did not set up an appointment for counseling or a doctor's examination. She crept up behind Jesus, reached out, and touched his cloak.

There was no magic in the cloth. It was her reaching out and his accepting her act that made the difference. Jesus didn't even take credit for healing, for locked up inside this woman was the cure for her own ills—her faith. Note what he

said to her: "Your faith has made you well."

Lord, how often we are afraid to reach out to another person or to you. We fear rejection or embarrassment. We are too proud to admit need. Give us confidence and courage to reach out to you with assurance that you will stop, pay attention, and help us. Help us to reach out to others as well, and to accept those who reach out for us. Lord God, we would but touch the edge of your cloak this Advent season. Amen.

Scripture: John 19:23-24

After the soldiers had crucified Jesus, they took his clothes and divided them into four parts, one part for each soldier. They also took the robe, which was made of one piece of woven cloth without any seams in it. The soldiers said to one another, "Let's not tear it; let's throw dice to see who will get it." This happened in order to make the scripture come true:

"They divided my clothes among themselves
and gambled for my robe."

And this is what the soldiers did.

Reading: "Gambled Garment"

He ended up without a penny. They didn't even allow him the dignity of his last earthly possession— the robe that he wore. As if torture, insult, and death weren't enough, they gambled away his garments.

He ministered to men, and they murdered him. The cycle was complete—the cradle to the grave.

Or was it? Was it all without purpose? God has the strangest ways of turning darkness to day. His birth, his ministry, his death—all had meaning. The baby clothes, the cloak, the gambled robe—all led to a final, finer piece of cloth.

Scripture: John 19:38-40; 20:3-8

After this, Joseph, who was from the town of Arimathea, asked Pilate if he could take Jesus' body. (Joseph was a follower of Jesus, but in secret, because he was afraid of the Jewish authorities.) Pilate told him he could have the body, so Joseph went and took it away. Nicodemus, who at first had gone to see Jesus at night, went with Joseph, taking with him about one hundred pounds of spices, a mixture of myrrh and aloes. The two men took Jesus' body and wrapped it in linen cloths with the spices according to the Jewish custom of preparing a body for burial.

Then Peter and the other disciple went to the tomb. The two of them were running, but the other disciple ran faster than Peter and reached the tomb first. He bent over and saw the linen cloths, but he did not go in. Behind him came Simon Peter, and he went straight into the tomb. He saw the linen cloths lying there and the cloth which had been around Jesus' head. It was not lying with the linen cloths but was rolled up by itself. Then the other disciple, who had reached the tomb first, also went in; he saw and believed.

Reading: "The Shroud"

It all seemed so useless, so tragically useless. A life so worthwhile, so beautiful—snuffed out by one of the most horrible deaths ever contrived.

But it was all over now. No more healing, no more Good News, no more late-night talks, no more bread for the hungry, no more rejoicing. The final chapter had been written to the life of a great person who never really made it. There were such high hopes, such dreams and plans.

It ended something like it began. He was lying down again; this time in a tomb, not a manger; not glowing with life, but stone dead; not dressed in baby clothes, but in a linen sheet and face cloth.

How could the Babe of Bethlehem, the manger child, end up in bloody grave cloths?

Then a spark more potent than a nuclear flash split the dawn. A rumor spread. He had risen from the dead!

Two disciples came running. They entered the tomb. They found nothing. Absolutely nothing! Nothing except a linen shroud and a face cloth that once covered a dead man.

He is risen! The Lord is risen indeed! This is not only the message of Easter, but also of Christmas. Christmas is the joyous celebration of baby clothes and a folded burial shroud. He came to bring hope, Good News, and the promise of life!

Celebrating Christmas Personalities

A Celebration for Advent

This worship experience concentrates on many of the major personalities who were part of the Christmas story. These include Mary, Joseph, Caesar Augustus, Herod, the kings, the shepherds, the heavenly messengers, and Jesus. What were the dynamics of their lives as their paths crossed and intermingled in the greatest drama of human history? Your group will explore these dynamics as they worship together this Christmas.

You may be planning a Christmas party or get-together. Let worship be a part of this festive event. You may be looking for a service of dignity and meaning which your group could sponsor for your entire congregation at a special Christmas Eve service. Consider using this chapter in dramatic form, together with carols and special Christmas music.

Preparation

Christmas carols and special songs are not suggested in this material, as any hymnal will offer you a wide selection. Use special solos and instrumentals as well throughout this service. The word "music" appears in this text, and you will need to make your own choices in this regard. If no special Christmas music can be offered by members of your group, the playing of records will help make this service more meaningful.

This service is designed to be presented in the form of a simple vignette drama. As each personality of Christmas is presented, there will be a Scripture selection and a voice-reading part. The vignette drama is not intended to be a traditional church "bathrobe" drama with speaking parts and movements. The idea is to create an image or a mood, to stylize an idea, and to present a brief concept of a personality.

The simplest form of vignette drama is to have group members dressed in costume which you feel is appropriate to the personality being depicted. Have that person stand in a central location away from readers and use a spotlight. If no spotlight is available, simply have the personality stand in some prominent location in the meeting room or on the church platform.

A striking effect can be achieved by the use of a thin curtain, sheet, or cloth hung between the vignette person and the congregation. Place a spotlight or lamp behind the person so that his or her reflection or shadow appears in silhouette form on the curtain. Costuming will be less elaborate using this method, and the effect will be greater. You will need to experiment with this idea to get the right amount of light and determine proper distances from the curtain, and other such considerations.

Use special Christmas music or carols throughout the service wherever "music" is indicated. Have one person do all of the readings, or have various group members share in this leadership.

An idea which is becoming popular is the "living tableau." This is done outdoors, and times of presentations (there usually are more than one) are announced to the community in advance. A life-size manger (usually a simple, three-sided structure) is built outside of a church or in a public park, and the drama of Christmas is reenacted with real people. Some youth groups have even used real animals as part of the scenery. If you undertake this project, use the material in this chapter with the Christmas personalities appearing in appropriate costume. Because this service ends with the idea of celebrating Jesus' birthday, you might even have helium-filled balloons. Release them at the end of the service, and let them rise to the sky in celebration.

The Experience

Use the material in Supplements A and B. There are four copies of each supplement, an original and three duplicates. Since there are four characters in each case, you will need to use all copies, including the original.

Begin with a Christmas carol, and end with "Joy to the World."

SUPPLEMENT A

Celebrating Christmas Personalities

Music

Joseph: (Read Matthew 1:18-24 aloud.)

VOICE: Joseph showed himself to be a man among men: a man of virtue, dignity, composure, and compassion. He was engaged to Mary, and people were talking because, though unmarried, she was going to have a child.

In trust and love he believed her and what she told him about the message God had given her. And he had enough confidence in himself to believe that he had seen an angel vision and not pictures played by his imagination. Can there be a higher expression of human love—love between male and female—than his devotion and trust?

He did not become outraged or filled with hurt and self-pity. He did not break the engagement. With the heart of faith, he believed both Mary and God, and because of the sensitive person he was he became known as Jesus' father.

One could wish that more had been written about Joseph. We could have learned a lot about dealing with life's complexities from him. But perhaps a brief notation is all we really need: Joseph the carpenter. He had life all together. He loved with compassion. He understood what he could of the mysteries of God, and he trusted in spite of all circumstances.

Music

Caesar Augustus: (Read Luke 2:1-7 aloud.)

VOICE: The decree went out that all the world should be enrolled in a census for the purpose of taxation. The Roman Empire was large and powerful, but it only covered a relatively small part of the world's geography and population. How proud and provincial Caesar was! There were people in China, India, Africa, Japan, Australia, North and South America, and elsewhere whom he never knew existed. Yet, according to an older biblical translation, all the world was to be taxed! Caesar's world. He never realized that his world was God's world.

Death and taxes. Perhaps people way back then said the same thing as we do today: The only certainty in this world is death and taxes.

Let Caesar have his gold and goods. Our world is God's world. When some people asked Jesus if they should pay taxes to Caesar, he asked them whose image was on the currency. It was Caesar's image, and Jesus said to give to Caesar what was Caesar's and to give to God what is God's. Our world is God's world. Yet we are not exempt from paying tribute. Even Mary and Joseph had to be signed up on the tax rolls, and she was heavy with child. That is why Jesus was born in a stable instead of in the comforts and dignity of home—because they had to meet that "April 15 deadline."

Hail, Caesar! Your gold and your glory are past history and your empire is broken bits in museums. God lives! Our world is his world.

Music

Herod: (Read Matthew 2:1-3 aloud.)

VOICE: Herod was upset, troubled, shook because of the rumor that a king was born. He was a one-horse governor in a forsaken province, fearful, threatened, determined to hang on to his territory and position regardless of the cost. He was so notorious that when he became upset, the whole countryside shook with him because people knew what he was capable of doing.

They were not disappointed. He acted in cruelty and murdered many mothers' sons. There was weeping, grief, death, terror, hysteria—all for one man's claim to fame and power.

Herod interpreted the coming of Christ as bad news. His demonic ploy for power was felt by many. Such things always are. We do not act alone. What we do affects others in one way or another. Others suffer for our sins of selfishness.

And Herod's bad news was meant to be Good News—Christ came to bring release from the dungeon of self-will and the slavery of sin.

If only Herod had come as the shepherds and the wise men did. If only, if only, if only.

Music

The Shepherds: (Read Luke 2:8-20 aloud.)

VOICE: The life of shepherds in Israel probably was not an exciting one. They worked hard and felt fortunate just to make a living or to survive. That night was just like every other night—they were trying to keep warm, to keep awake, to keep the wolves away.

Then their humdrum existence was jolted by a blinding light which few people saw or have ever seen. The heavenly messengers, who have access to the presence of God himself, material-

ized before these shepherds' eyes.

The shepherds became incoherent with fear. Anyone would when confronted with a vision so vibrant. But the mission of the angel was not one of bringing terror, harm, or condemnation.

God's news was Good News! Glory to God in the highest and on earth, peace, good will!

Hallelujah! Christ is born!

One would have thought that governors, dignitaries, and princes would have been privileged with such a visitation. But no, it was the humble folk of the world who were among the first to see and adore God's gift to humanity—himself made human.

Celebrating Christmas Personalities

Music

Joseph: (Read Matthew 1:18-24 aloud.)

VOICE: Joseph showed himself to be a man among men: a man of virtue, dignity, composure, and compassion. He was engaged to Mary, and people were talking because, though unmarried, she was going to have a child.

In trust and love he believed her and what she told him about the message God had given her. And he had enough confidence in himself to believe that he had seen an angel vision and not pictures played by his imagination. Can there be a higher expression of human love—love between male and female—than his devotion and trust?

He did not become outraged or filled with hurt and self-pity. He did not break the engagement. With the heart of faith, he believed both Mary and God, and because of the sensitive person he was he became known as Jesus' father.

One could wish that more had been written about Joseph. We could have learned a lot about dealing with life's complexities from him. But perhaps a brief notation is all we really need: Joseph the carpenter. He had life all together. He loved with compassion. He understood what he could of the mysteries of God, and he trusted in spite of all circumstances.

Music

Caesar Augustus: (Read Luke 2:1-7 aloud.)

VOICE: The decree went out that all the world should be enrolled in a census for the purpose of taxation. The Roman Empire was large and powerful, but it only covered a relatively small part of the world's geography and population. How proud and provincial Caesar was! There were people in China, India, Africa, Japan, Australia, North and South America, and elsewhere whom he never knew existed. Yet, according to an older biblical translation, all the world was to be taxed! Caesar's world. He never realized that his world was God's world.

Death and taxes. Perhaps people way back then said the same thing as we do today: The only certainty in this world is death and taxes.

Let Caesar have his gold and goods. Our world is God's world. When some people asked Jesus if they should pay taxes to Caesar, he asked

them whose image was on the currency. It was Caesar's image, and Jesus said to give to Caesar what was Caesar's and to give to God what is God's. Our world is God's world. Yet we are not exempt from paying tribute. Even Mary and Joseph had to be signed up on the tax rolls, and she was heavy with child. That is why Jesus was born in a stable instead of in the comforts and dignity of home—because they had to meet that "April 15 deadline."

Hail, Caesar! Your gold and your glory are past history and your empire is broken bits in museums. God lives! Our world is his world.

Music

Herod: (Read Matthew 2:1-3 aloud.)

VOICE: Herod was upset, troubled, shook because of the rumor that a king was born. He was a one-horse governor in a forsaken province, fearful, threatened, determined to hang on to his territory and position regardless of the cost. He was so notorious that when he became upset, the whole countryside shook with him because people knew what he was capable of doing.

They were not disappointed. He acted in cruelty and murdered many mothers' sons. There was weeping, grief, death, terror, hysteria—all for one man's claim to fame and power.

Herod interpreted the coming of Christ as bad news. His demonic ploy for power was felt by many. Such things always are. We do not act alone. What we do affects others in one way or another. Others suffer for our sins of selfishness.

And Herod's bad news was meant to be Good News—Christ came to bring release from the dungeon of self-will and the slavery of sin.

If only Herod had come as the shepherds and the wise men did. If only, if only, if only.

Music

The Shepherds: (Read Luke 2:8-20 aloud.)

VOICE: The life of shepherds in Israel probably was not an exciting one. They worked hard and felt fortunate just to make a living or to survive. That night was just like every other night—they were trying to keep warm, to keep awake, to keep the wolves away.

Then their humdrum existence was jolted by a blinding light which few people saw or have ever seen. The heavenly messengers, who have access to the presence of God himself, material-

ized before these shepherds' eyes.

The shepherds became incoherent with fear. Anyone would when confronted with a vision so vibrant. But the mission of the angel was not one of bringing terror, harm, or condemnation.

God's news was Good News! Glory to God in the highest and on earth, peace, good will!

Hallelujah! Christ is born!

One would have thought that governors, dignitaries, and princes would have been privileged with such a visitation. But no, it was the humble folk of the world who were among the first to see and adore God's gift to humanity—himself made human.

Celebrating Christmas Personalities

Music

Joseph: (Read Matthew 1:18-24 aloud.)

VOICE: Joseph showed himself to be a man among men: a man of virtue, dignity, composure, and compassion. He was engaged to Mary, and people were talking because, though unmarried, she was going to have a child.

In trust and love he believed her and what she told him about the message God had given her. And he had enough confidence in himself to believe that he had seen an angel vision and not pictures played by his imagination. Can there be a higher expression of human love—love between male and female—than his devotion and trust?

He did not become outraged or filled with hurt and self-pity. He did not break the engagement. With the heart of faith, he believed both Mary and God, and because of the sensitive person he was he became known as Jesus' father.

One could wish that more had been written about Joseph. We could have learned a lot about dealing with life's complexities from him. But perhaps a brief notation is all we really need: Joseph the carpenter. He had life all together. He loved with compassion. He understood what he could of the mysteries of God, and he trusted in spite of all circumstances.

Music

Caesar Augustus: (Read Luke 2:1-7 aloud.)

VOICE: The decree went out that all the world should be enrolled in a census for the purpose of taxation. The Roman Empire was large and powerful, but it only covered a relatively small part of the world's geography and population. How proud and provincial Caesar was! There were people in China, India, Africa, Japan, Australia, North and South America, and elsewhere whom he never knew existed. Yet, according to an older biblical translation, all the world was to be taxed! Caesar's world. He never realized that his world was God's world.

Death and taxes. Perhaps people way back then said the same thing as we do today: The only certainty in this world is death and taxes.

Let Caesar have his gold and goods. Our world is God's world. When some people asked Jesus if they should pay taxes to Caesar, he asked them whose image was on the currency. It was Caesar's image, and Jesus said to give to Caesar what was Caesar's and to give to God what is God's. Our world is God's world. Yet we are not exempt from paying tribute. Even Mary and Joseph had to be signed up on the tax rolls, and she was heavy with child. That is why Jesus was born in a stable instead of in the comforts and dignity of home—because they had to meet that "April 15 deadline."

Hail, Caesar! Your gold and your glory are past history and your empire is broken bits in museums. God lives! Our world is his world.

Music

Herod: (Read Matthew 2:1-3 aloud.)

VOICE: Herod was upset, troubled, shook because of the rumor that a king was born. He was a one-horse governor in a forsaken province, fearful, threatened, determined to hang on to his territory and position regardless of the cost. He was so notorious that when he became upset, the whole countryside shook with him because people knew what he was capable of doing.

They were not disappointed. He acted in cruelty and murdered many mothers' sons. There was weeping, grief, death, terror, hysteria—all for one man's claim to fame and power.

Herod interpreted the coming of Christ as bad news. His demonic ploy for power was felt by many. Such things always are. We do not act alone. What we do affects others in one way or another. Others suffer for our sins of selfishness.

And Herod's bad news was meant to be Good News—Christ came to bring release from the dungeon of self-will and the slavery of sin.

If only Herod had come as the shepherds and the wise men did. If only, if only, if only.

Music

The Shepherds: (Read Luke 2:8-20 aloud.)

VOICE: The life of shepherds in Israel probably was not an exciting one. They worked hard and felt fortunate just to make a living or to survive. That night was just like every other night—they were trying to keep warm, to keep awake, to keep the wolves away.

Then their humdrum existence was jolted by a blinding light which few people saw or have ever seen. The heavenly messengers, who have access to the presence of God himself, material-

ized before these shepherds' eyes.

The shepherds became incoherent with fear. Anyone would when confronted with a vision so vibrant. But the mission of the angel was not one of bringing terror, harm, or condemnation.

God's news was Good News! Glory to God in the highest and on earth, peace, good will!

Hallelujah! Christ is born!

One would have thought that governors, dignitaries, and princes would have been privileged with such a visitation. But no, it was the humble folk of the world who were among the first to see and adore God's gift to humanity—himself made human.

Celebrating Christmas Personalities

Music
Joseph: (Read Matthew 1:18-24 aloud.)

VOICE: Joseph showed himself to be a man among men: a man of virtue, dignity, composure, and compassion. He was engaged to Mary, and people were talking because, though unmarried, she was going to have a child.

In trust and love he believed her and what she told him about the message God had given her. And he had enough confidence in himself to believe that he had seen an angel vision and not pictures played by his imagination. Can there be a higher expression of human love—love between male and female—than his devotion and trust?

He did not become outraged or filled with hurt and self-pity. He did not break the engagement. With the heart of faith, he believed both Mary and God, and because of the sensitive person he was he became known as Jesus' father.

One could wish that more had been written about Joseph. We could have learned a lot about dealing with life's complexities from him. But perhaps a brief notation is all we really need: Joseph the carpenter. He had life all together. He loved with compassion. He understood what he could of the mysteries of God, and he trusted in spite of all circumstances.

Music
Caesar Augustus: (Read Luke 2:1-7 aloud.)

VOICE: The decree went out that all the world should be enrolled in a census for the purpose of taxation. The Roman Empire was large and powerful, but it only covered a relatively small part of the world's geography and population. How proud and provincial Caesar was! There were people in China, India, Africa, Japan, Australia, North and South America, and elsewhere whom he never knew existed. Yet, according to an older biblical translation, all the world was to be taxed! Caesar's world. He never realized that his world was God's world.

Death and taxes. Perhaps people way back then said the same thing as we do today: The only certainty in this world is death and taxes.

Let Caesar have his gold and goods. Our world is God's world. When some people asked Jesus if they should pay taxes to Caesar, he asked them whose image was on the currency. It was Caesar's image, and Jesus said to give to Caesar what was Caesar's and to give to God what is God's. Our world is God's world. Yet we are not exempt from paying tribute. Even Mary and Joseph had to be signed up on the tax rolls, and she was heavy with child. That is why Jesus was born in a stable instead of in the comforts and dignity of home—because they had to meet that "April 15 deadline."

Hail, Caesar! Your gold and your glory are past history and your empire is broken bits in museums. God lives! Our world is his world.

Music
Herod: (Read Matthew 2:1-3 aloud.)

VOICE: Herod was upset, troubled, shook because of the rumor that a king was born. He was a one-horse governor in a forsaken province, fearful, threatened, determined to hang on to his territory and position regardless of the cost. He was so notorious that when he became upset, the whole countryside shook with him because people knew what he was capable of doing.

They were not disappointed. He acted in cruelty and murdered many mothers' sons. There was weeping, grief, death, terror, hysteria—all for one man's claim to fame and power.

Herod interpreted the coming of Christ as bad news. His demonic ploy for power was felt by many. Such things always are. We do not act alone. What we do affects others in one way or another. Others suffer for our sins of selfishness.

And Herod's bad news was meant to be Good News—Christ came to bring release from the dungeon of self-will and the slavery of sin.

If only Herod had come as the shepherds and the wise men did. If only, if only, if only.

Music
The Shepherds: (Read Luke 2:8-20 aloud.)

VOICE: The life of shepherds in Israel probably was not an exciting one. They worked hard and felt fortunate just to make a living or to survive. That night was just like every other night—they were trying to keep warm, to keep awake, to keep the wolves away.

Then their humdrum existence was jolted by a blinding light which few people saw or have ever seen. The heavenly messengers, who have access to the presence of God himself, material-

ized before these shepherds' eyes.

The shepherds became incoherent with fear. Anyone would when confronted with a vision so vibrant. But the mission of the angel was not one of bringing terror, harm, or condemnation.

God's news was Good News! Glory to God in the highest and on earth, peace, good will! Hallelujah! Christ is born!

One would have thought that governors, dignitaries, and princes would have been privileged with such a visitation. But no, it was the humble folk of the world who were among the first to see and adore God's gift to humanity—himself made human.

Celebrating Christmas Personalities

Music

The Angels: (Read Luke 2:13, 14 aloud.)

VOICE: These heavenly messengers had witnessed the unfolding of the drama of human history since its beginning. They knew the sinfulness of humankind and the horror of which it was capable. They had seen wars, murder, deceit, and sin all along. They had seen that which was contrary to God's very nature enacted in the lives of people.

They knew that God was completely reliable. They also knew he was totally unpredictable, unconventional.

What on earth was God doing? Why should the Most High humble himself? And yet they knew that somehow, for some reason, God loved the world so much that he was willing to give of himself so that people—shepherds and kings, rich and poor, you and I—could claim the status of his children.

Music

The Wise Men: (Read Matthew 2:1-2, 9-11 aloud.)

VOICE: We don't know who these men were or where they came from. Perhaps they came from Africa or from different places. We don't know their philosophies. We don't even know that there were three of them, only that they brought three kinds of gifts: gold, frankincense, and myrrh. We only know their motivation.

One of the major sciences in ancient times was astronomy—the study of the stars. The wise men knew the heavens because they watched the movements of the stars and could chart every position, every formation. Nothing particularly new had happened in the heavens in their lifetimes or for aeons before. Then they detected something different—a new star appeared, and this, for them, was startling, exciting, sensational.

Were they the only ones who saw it? Surely others throughout the world noticed. But perhaps not. Perhaps they were a small minority who saw, took notice, and acted. They needed no sophisticated observatory. Their telescope was the eyes of faith.

Did they believe in daily horoscopes? Were they convinced that the stars controlled their lives? Perhaps not. Yet they knew that without the sun, life on earth would not exist. If the sun had such profound powers of life and death, could it be that this new sun had greater powers?

They decided to risk the journey, to the ends of the earth if necessary, to find its meaning. Were they disappointed at journey's end when they found only a baby? By no means! They came and worshiped. They were intelligent men, knowledgeable men, smart men. And through the eyes of faith, they saw the potential God had placed in a child.

Music

Mary: (Read Luke 1:26-38 aloud.)

VOICE: Mary was a woman so special, so unique, that the Most High God selected her for a key role in the greatest event in human history. She could not comprehend the significance of her child or of the message the angel had given her. She only knew in her heart that she was God's special servant, chosen to become the mother of the person who would be called the Son of the Most High God!

Like any mother, she was proud of her Son and gently nurtured him through infancy and childhood. One cannot help wondering what she thought as Jesus began proclaiming the Good News. How did she feel when he selected fishermen and common folk—even prostitutes and sinners—as his followers? What did she wonder when she realized that his message was not traditional? That it was dangerous? Did she shudder at the far-out concepts Jesus taught about himself, the world, and God? Was she glad when he healed the sick and fed the hungry? Did she wonder who he was? Was he a teacher? A doctor? A prophet? A rebel? A revolutionary? A troublemaker? All of these? Some of them? None of them?

Was she disappointed when people in power began criticizing her Son?

Were her highest hopes smashed to bits when he hung on the cross?

Or was the heavenly message given her before the birth of Jesus grace enough to see her through? Did she ponder that message, and did it give her strength to live through Calvary to Easter morning?

Surely Mary's role in the drama of redemption elevated womanhood to its highest level.

Hail, Mary! Peace be with you! The Lord is with you and has greatly blessed you!

Music

Jesus: (Read John 1:1-5, 14 aloud.)

Voice: Have we forgotten anyone? We have taken a look at the personalities who surrounded the coming of our King. Did we leave anyone out?

I fear so. We sometimes leave him out of Christmas, Christmas festivities and celebrations, and out of life itself. May we never forget the Christ of Christmas. It is his birthday we celebrate and him we worship and serve. Let's celebrate his coming!

Celebrating Christmas Personalities

Music

The Angels: (Read Luke 2:13, 14 aloud.)

VOICE: These heavenly messengers had witnessed the unfolding of the drama of human history since its beginning. They knew the sinfulness of humankind and the horror of which it was capable. They had seen wars, murder, deceit, and sin all along. They had seen that which was contrary to God's very nature enacted in the lives of people.

They knew that God was completely reliable. They also knew he was totally unpredictable, unconventional.

What on earth was God doing? Why should the Most High humble himself? And yet they knew that somehow, for some reason, God loved the world so much that he was willing to give of himself so that people—shepherds and kings, rich and poor, you and I—could claim the status of his children.

Music

The Wise Men: (Read Matthew 2:1-2, 9-11 aloud.)

VOICE: We don't know who these men were or where they came from. Perhaps they came from Africa or from different places. We don't know their philosophies. We don't even know that there were three of them, only that they brought three kinds of gifts: gold, frankincense, and myrrh. We only know their motivation.

One of the major sciences in ancient times was astronomy—the study of the stars. The wise men knew the heavens because they watched the movements of the stars and could chart every position, every formation. Nothing particularly new had happened in the heavens in their lifetimes or for aeons before. Then they detected something different—a new star appeared, and this, for them, was startling, exciting, sensational.

Were they the only ones who saw it? Surely others throughout the world noticed. But perhaps not. Perhaps they were a small minority who saw, took notice, and acted. They needed no sophisticated observatory. Their telescope was the eyes of faith.

Did they believe in daily horoscopes? Were they convinced that the stars controlled their lives? Perhaps not. Yet they knew that without the sun, life on earth would not exist. If the sun had such profound powers of life and death, could it be that this new sun had greater powers?

They decided to risk the journey, to the ends of the earth if necessary, to find its meaning. Were they disappointed at journey's end when they found only a baby? By no means! They came and worshiped. They were intelligent men, knowledgeable men, smart men. And through the eyes of faith, they saw the potential God had placed in a child.

Music

Mary: (Read Luke 1:26-38 aloud.)

VOICE: Mary was a woman so special, so unique, that the Most High God selected her for a key role in the greatest event in human history. She could not comprehend the significance of her child or of the message the angel had given her. She only knew in her heart that she was God's special servant, chosen to become the mother of the person who would be called the Son of the Most High God!

Like any mother, she was proud of her Son and gently nurtured him through infancy and childhood. One cannot help wondering what she thought as Jesus began proclaiming the Good News. How did she feel when he selected fishermen and common folk—even prostitutes and sinners—as his followers? What did she wonder when she realized that his message was not traditional? That it was dangerous? Did she shudder at the far-out concepts Jesus taught about himself, the world, and God? Was she glad when he healed the sick and fed the hungry? Did she wonder who he was? Was he a teacher? A doctor? A prophet? A rebel? A revolutionary? A troublemaker? All of these? Some of them? None of them?

Was she disappointed when people in power began criticizing her Son?

Were her highest hopes smashed to bits when he hung on the cross?

Or was the heavenly message given her before the birth of Jesus grace enough to see her through? Did she ponder that message, and did it give her strength to live through Calvary to Easter morning?

Surely Mary's role in the drama of redemption elevated womanhood to its highest level.

Hail, Mary! Peace be with you! The Lord is with you and has greatly blessed you!

Music

Jesus: (Read John 1:1-5, 14 aloud.)

VOICE: Have we forgotten anyone? We have taken a look at the personalities who surrounded the coming of our King. Did we leave anyone out?

I fear so. We sometimes leave him out of Christmas, Christmas festivities and celebrations, and out of life itself. May we never forget the Christ of Christmas. It is his birthday we celebrate and him we worship and serve. Let's celebrate his coming!

Celebrating Christmas Personalities

Music

The Angels: (Read Luke 2:13, 14 aloud.)

VOICE: These heavenly messengers had witnessed the unfolding of the drama of human history since its beginning. They knew the sinfulness of humankind and the horror of which it was capable. They had seen wars, murder, deceit, and sin all along. They had seen that which was contrary to God's very nature enacted in the lives of people.

They knew that God was completely reliable. They also knew he was totally unpredictable, unconventional.

What on earth was God doing? Why should the Most High humble himself? And yet they knew that somehow, for some reason, God loved the world so much that he was willing to give of himself so that people—shepherds and kings, rich and poor, you and I—could claim the status of his children.

Music

The Wise Men: (Read Matthew 2:1-2, 9-11 aloud.)

VOICE: We don't know who these men were or where they came from. Perhaps they came from Africa or from different places. We don't know their philosophies. We don't even know that there were three of them, only that they brought three kinds of gifts: gold, frankincense, and myrrh. We only know their motivation.

One of the major sciences in ancient times was astronomy—the study of the stars. The wise men knew the heavens because they watched the movements of the stars and could chart every position, every formation. Nothing particularly new had happened in the heavens in their lifetimes or for aeons before. Then they detected something different—a new star appeared, and this, for them, was startling, exciting, sensational.

Were they the only ones who saw it? Surely others throughout the world noticed. But perhaps not. Perhaps they were a small minority who saw, took notice, and acted. They needed no sophisticated observatory. Their telescope was the eyes of faith.

Did they believe in daily horoscopes? Were they convinced that the stars controlled their lives? Perhaps not. Yet they knew that without the sun, life on earth would not exist. If the sun had such profound powers of life and death, could it be that this new sun had greater powers?

They decided to risk the journey, to the ends of the earth if necessary, to find its meaning. Were they disappointed at journey's end when they found only a baby? By no means! They came and worshiped. They were intelligent men, knowledgeable men, smart men. And through the eyes of faith, they saw the potential God had placed in a child.

Music

Mary: (Read Luke 1:26-38 aloud.)

VOICE: Mary was a woman so special, so unique, that the Most High God selected her for a key role in the greatest event in human history. She could not comprehend the significance of her child or of the message the angel had given her. She only knew in her heart that she was God's special servant, chosen to become the mother of the person who would be called the Son of the Most High God!

Like any mother, she was proud of her Son and gently nurtured him through infancy and childhood. One cannot help wondering what she thought as Jesus began proclaiming the Good News. How did she feel when he selected fishermen and common folk—even prostitutes and sinners—as his followers? What did she wonder when she realized that his message was not traditional? That it was dangerous? Did she shudder at the far-out concepts Jesus taught about himself, the world, and God? Was she glad when he healed the sick and fed the hungry? Did she wonder who he was? Was he a teacher? A doctor? A prophet? A rebel? A revolutionary? A troublemaker? All of these? Some of them? None of them?

Was she disappointed when people in power began criticizing her Son?

Were her highest hopes smashed to bits when he hung on the cross?

Or was the heavenly message given her before the birth of Jesus grace enough to see her through? Did she ponder that message, and did it give her strength to live through Calvary to Easter morning?

Surely Mary's role in the drama of redemption elevated womanhood to its highest level.

Hail, Mary! Peace be with you! The Lord is with you and has greatly blessed you!

Music

Jesus: (Read John 1:1-5, 14 aloud.)

Voice: Have we forgotten anyone? We have taken a look at the personalities who surrounded the coming of our King. Did we leave anyone out?

I fear so. We sometimes leave him out of Christmas, Christmas festivities and celebrations, and out of life itself. May we never forget the Christ of Christmas. It is his birthday we celebrate and him we worship and serve. Let's celebrate his coming!

Celebrating Christmas Personalities

Music

The Angels: (Read Luke 2:13, 14 aloud.)

VOICE: These heavenly messengers had witnessed the unfolding of the drama of human history since its beginning. They knew the sinfulness of humankind and the horror of which it was capable. They had seen wars, murder, deceit, and sin all along. They had seen that which was contrary to God's very nature enacted in the lives of people.

They knew that God was completely reliable. They also knew he was totally unpredictable, unconventional.

What on earth was God doing? Why should the Most High humble himself? And yet they knew that somehow, for some reason, God loved the world so much that he was willing to give of himself so that people—shepherds and kings, rich and poor, you and I—could claim the status of his children.

Music

The Wise Men: (Read Matthew 2:1-2, 9-11 aloud.)

VOICE: We don't know who these men were or where they came from. Perhaps they came from Africa or from different places. We don't know their philosophies. We don't even know that there were three of them, only that they brought three kinds of gifts: gold, frankincense, and myrrh. We only know their motivation.

One of the major sciences in ancient times was astronomy—the study of the stars. The wise men knew the heavens because they watched the movements of the stars and could chart every position, every formation. Nothing particularly new had happened in the heavens in their lifetimes or for aeons before. Then they detected something different—a new star appeared, and this, for them, was startling, exciting, sensational.

Were they the only ones who saw it? Surely others throughout the world noticed. But perhaps not. Perhaps they were a small minority who saw, took notice, and acted. They needed no sophisticated observatory. Their telescope was the eyes of faith.

Did they believe in daily horoscopes? Were they convinced that the stars controlled their lives? Perhaps not. Yet they knew that without the sun, life on earth would not exist. If the sun had such profound powers of life and death, could it be that this new sun had greater powers?

They decided to risk the journey, to the ends of the earth if necessary, to find its meaning. Were they disappointed at journey's end when they found only a baby? By no means! They came and worshiped. They were intelligent men, knowledgeable men, smart men. And through the eyes of faith, they saw the potential God had placed in a child.

Music

Mary: (Read Luke 1:26-38 aloud.)

VOICE: Mary was a woman so special, so unique, that the Most High God selected her for a key role in the greatest event in human history. She could not comprehend the significance of her child or of the message the angel had given her. She only knew in her heart that she was God's special servant, chosen to become the mother of the person who would be called the Son of the Most High God!

Like any mother, she was proud of her Son and gently nurtured him through infancy and childhood. One cannot help wondering what she thought as Jesus began proclaiming the Good News. How did she feel when he selected fishermen and common folk—even prostitutes and sinners—as his followers? What did she wonder when she realized that his message was not traditional? That it was dangerous? Did she shudder at the far-out concepts Jesus taught about himself, the world, and God? Was she glad when he healed the sick and fed the hungry? Did she wonder who he was? Was he a teacher? A doctor? A prophet? A rebel? A revolutionary? A troublemaker? All of these? Some of them? None of them?

Was she disappointed when people in power began criticizing her Son?

Were her highest hopes smashed to bits when he hung on the cross?

Or was the heavenly message given her before the birth of Jesus grace enough to see her through? Did she ponder that message, and did it give her strength to live through Calvary to Easter morning?

Surely Mary's role in the drama of redemption elevated womanhood to its highest level.

Hail, Mary! Peace be with you! The Lord is with you and has greatly blessed you!

Music

Jesus: (Read John 1:1-5, 14 aloud.)

VOICE: Have we forgotten anyone? We have taken a look at the personalities who surrounded the coming of our King. Did we leave anyone out?

I fear so. We sometimes leave him out of Christmas, Christmas festivities and celebrations, and out of life itself. May we never forget the Christ of Christmas. It is his birthday we celebrate and him we worship and serve. Let's celebrate his coming!